Letters from Elmer Keith

Letters from Elmer Keith

A Half Century of Advice on Guns, Ammo, Handloading, Hunting, and Other Pursuits

Timothy J. Mullin

PALADIN PRESS • BOULDER, COLORADO

Letters from Elmer Keith:
A Half Century of Advice on Guns, Ammo, Handloading,
Hunting, and Other Pursuits
by Timothy J. Mullin

Copyright © 2008 by Timothy J. Mullin

ISBN 13: 978-1-58160-653-9
Printed in the United States of America

Published by Paladin Press, a division of
Paladin Enterprises, Inc.
Gunbarrel Tech Center
7077 Winchester Circle
Boulder, Colorado 80301, USA
+1.303.443.7250

Direct inquiries and/or orders to the above address.

PALADIN, PALADIN PRESS, and the "horse head" design
are trademarks belonging to Paladin Enterprises and
registered in United States Patent and Trademark Office.

All rights reserved. Except for use in a review, no portion of this book may
be reproduced, stored in or introduced into a retrieval system, or transmitted
in any form without the express written permission of the publisher. The
scanning, uploading and distribution of this book by the Internet or any other
means without the permission of the publisher is illegal and punishable by
law. Please respect the author's rights and do not participate in the any form
of electronic piracy of copyrighted material.

Neither the author nor the publisher assumes any responsibility
for the use or misuse of information contained in this book.

Visit our website at www.paladin-press.com

Contents

Introduction 1

A Guide to the Letters 3

Letters 20

Photographs 197

Conclusion 215

To Eleanor, a better wife and mother could not be desired, and Catherine, our daughter and her father's joy.

Introduction

ELMER MEFFIELD KEITH WAS BORN ON MARCH 8, 1899, in Hardin, Missouri (Ray County), and died on February 14, 1983, in Boise, Idaho. He left Missouri at 5 years of age and lived in Montana, Oregon, and finally Idaho. His writing career stretched from 1926, when his first material was published in *American Rifleman*. Interestingly enough, this was in the form of a private letter written to the leading gun writer of the period, Chauncey Thomas. This letter was so interesting (and useful) that Thomas thought it was worth printing for general consumption, although Keith modestly thought it not sufficient for "real" publication. From that time until a disabling stroke felled him in 1981, Keith wrote articles for a wide variety of publications, including *American Rifleman, Outdoor Life, Western Sportsman, Western Horseman, Guns,* and *Guns & Ammo,* among others.

Keith was unlike most, if not all, of the current crop of gun writers in that he wrote about a wide variety of topics. Today we have writers who specialize in certain subjects: Massad Ayoob writes about police issues; Leroy Thompson about counterterrorism and executive protection; Craig Bodington of big-game hunting, and so forth. Keith covered a wide variety of subjects: waterfowl hunting, big-game hunting, load development, and self-defense issues. He wrote about shotguns, rifles, and handguns. Although he covered muzzleloaders to the latest cartridges, throughout his emphasis was on practical tips and use of the weapons.

It might seem logical to assume that Keith was a rich man with ample leisure time and money to explore his firearms interests, but this was not the case. Instead, he had limited formal education and was originally a cowboy and small ranch operator. He guided during the seasons and was in the field all the time. He wrote of his experiences both to share his knowledge and also to supplement the family income. It is hard today for some to even visualize the Keith's lifestyle, living and working on small, isolated, high-country ranches where running water and electricity did not exist. Keith lived in a time when black powder shooting and casting bullets were not merely hobbies but rather practical ways to save money and get reliable performance from one's firearms in the field.

At the same time Keith was writing articles for various magazines and writing books for a variety of publishers, he also answered hundreds of letters from people from all over the world. In his tribute to Keith in 1984, John Taffin noted that Keith personally answered, without any secretarial help, 300–500 letters per month. Sometimes answering letters from readers was a condition of employment, as it was when he was a staff writer for *American Rifleman*, but mostly he replied because people had taken the time and effort to write him of their problems and experiences, and he felt like he owed them a response. These letters from Keith were clearly cherished by the recipients. They kept them safely put away because they knew the letters were an important piece of Americana. Keith was the real deal, and it was apparent to anyone he corresponded with.

The letters from Keith were not filtered by some editor who might be concerned with space constraints or advertising considerations. While all of Keith's material was clearly good, we know from Keith's autobiography (and some of the letters in this book) that editors did sometimes change, delete, or augment some of his material, and it drove him wild, as you might expect. In the letters that follow, we are free from such third-party alterations. This material is unfiltered Elmer Keith. It is not just 100 proof; it is 200 proof!

Elmer Keith was a gunman par excellence, but remember he typed these letters himself on a manual typewriter up in the hills, frequently by lantern light in the early letters. He wanted to get the letters out; he was not worried about getting a good grade in typing or grammar class. I have chosen to reproduce the letters just the way the original recipients of the letters would have seen them. Some of these letters needed a little additional information to explain what the historical context was at the time the letter was sent, so I added commentary to help set the stage for the reader. By no means are my comments meant to do anything more. I certainly am not attempting to correct Keith's positions on any subject, as he knew and understood more on the matters he conversed about than I will ever know. Some folks may be upset at some of the political comments made by Keith. For those individuals, I can only urge you to grow out of your political correctness mode. I would also have to say in retrospect he was more correct in his opinions and judgments than more-famous political commentators of the same period.

I got the idea to do this project when my good friend Kent Lomont allowed me to read the letters he had saved from Keith over the years. Reading them was rather like finding a new, previously unpublished Keith book. For those of you who do not know him, Kent Lomont is about as close to Elmer Keith as we are likely to get in the 21st century. I am honored to be able to say I knew Elmer Keith slightly and that I know Kent Lomont very well.

Obviously, I needed more Keith letters than the ones Lomont had, so I spread the word within the firearms community that I was looking for letters. I ran advertisements in *Shotgun News* and placed a large sign at the Elmer Keith Museum in Salmon, Idaho, seeking letters. Soon, I started hearing from Elmer Keith fans. As Lomont and I had done with our Keith letters, people who had received them had held them dear, but being real "gun people" they were more than willing to share them with other like-minded individuals.

I got letters from as early as 1924 up to when he suffered his stroke in 1981. Naturally, some of the letters were short and others long. Some dealt with hunting issues, others strictly guns. Most were a mixed bag of subjects. Some letters were better than others, in the sense of involving gun matters of a more general interest to readers. From each of them, however, the reader can get a sense of who Elmer Keith was, as a firearms and hunting authority and as a man. He set a high standard for both.

For this compilation, I sorted through these letters and now present you with the results. Sit back and enjoy opening your mail over a 60-year period from possibly the finest firearms and hunting authority I know. I trust you will find, as I did, that you can almost smell sagebrush and old campfires or see the reflected light of an oil lamp as you read the advice from Keith on hunting, shooting, loading ammo, and other topics that were of inerest to him. If the grip of a well-worn Colt Single Action is like the handshake of an old friend, reading these letters will leave you feeling like you have had an extended visit with a remarkable companion.

A Guide to the Letters

Date	Recipient	Subject
1924, February 29	Capt. George Shank Fort Sumter, NY	About some Sharps rifles and barrels Keith has for sale. References Chauncey Thomas to verify his honesty.
1924, April 9	Capt. George Shank Fort Sumter, NY	Confirms order for three Sharps rifles and one barrel fore-end. Notes taking horse team into Winston, Montana, to ship the stuff to Shank.
1924, May 25	Capt. George Shank Fort Sumter, NY	More about the Sharps rifles Keith sold to Shank. Keith is interested in buying a Springfield from Shank.
1926	Chauncey Thomas French, ID	This letter to Chauncey Thomas, noted gun writer of period, was reprinted as an article, at the insistence of Thomas. This is the first article appearing in print by Elmer Keith. Discusses sighting techniques in 1,000-yard matches; mentions first pistols he ever owned.
1935, January 18	Mr. McDaniels	Recommends Frank Packmayr as source of good gunsmithing work. This was written shortly after all the experiments with the single-action Colt.
1944, July 10	Maj. Gen. George V. Strong Washington, D.C.	Keith describes the shooting death of General Strong's brother in 1919 on a hunt where Keith was present. Keith has described the event on numerous occasions, including in an earlier article in *American Rifleman*. Keith also describes his wartime ordnance work.
1948, July 8	James Hedgecoke Amarillo, TX	Inquires whether the men who rebore his .303 British rifle at Hedgecoke's Hoffman plant were still around. He also expresses his desire to hunt buffalo with Sharps rifle.

4 LETTERS FROM ELMER KEITH

Date	Recipient	Subject
1956, April	Bob Albrecht New Brunswick, NJ	Notes that .38-caliber loads give excellent sectional density, which is especially valuable at long range.
1956, April 13	Bob Albrecht New Brunswick, NJ	Complains about the mistakes the publisher introduced into his captions in his book *Sixguns*. Also offers advice on what ammunition to use for various animals.
1956, July 8	Orin H. Council Miami, FL	Offers advice on ammunition and modifications for his .44-40 revolver. Notes preferences for .44 Special over .44-40 Ashley Haines like .44/40, also notes preference for solids over shot for snakes.
1956, August 5	C.E. Vest Phoenix, AZ	Notes his preference for the newly released .44 Magnum cartridge for big game hunting and self-defense. Prefers it to old .44 Special or .45 Colt loadings.
1956, November 6	Orin H. Council Miami, FL	Discusses new .44 Magnum cartridges, loads, and results.
1957, October 5	Orin H. Council Miami, FL	Notes leaving *American Rifleman* for *Guns* magazine and long-range shooting experience with Harold Croft in 1920s.
1960, January 16	Bob Albrecht	Laments the death of a young cop in New York as the result of police departments' equipping officers with the wrong guns. Recommends .44/.45 for police, with .38 for backup duty only.
1960, October 11	Kent Lomont Fort Wayne, IN	Clears up an error that appeared as to the distances you get with various grains. Discusses converting Lomont's Springfield.
1961, August 26	Allen C. Lomont Fort Wayne, IN	Criticizes .22 Jet and notes preferences for .44. Describes technique for iron sights on a revolver.
1961, November 20	George B. Bredsten Sacramento, CA	Notes preference for .44 Special over .45 Colt. Thinks a single-action cylinder is too small and even if put .45 Colt in .44 Ruger single action, Keith thinks a .44 Magnum would be better.
1962, June 26	George B. Bredsten Sacramento, CA	Notes killing deer with .44 Magnum revolver at 250–300 yards with 4-inch M29 and shorter ranges with S&W 6 1/2 inch and Ruger in 4 5/8 and 7 1/2 lengths.

A GUIDE TO THE LETTERS

Date	Recipient	Subject
1962, November 22	George B. Bredsten Sacramento, CA	Advises against using .44 Magnum handgun on elephants.
1964, January 16	Kent Lomont Fort Wayne, IN	Discusses the accuracy of 8-inch S&W .44 Magnums. Offers other shooting advice.
1964, September 8	George B. Bredsten Sacramento, CA	Commiserates with Bredsten over the problems of shooting with 4-inch and 4 1/2-inch S&Ws and tells how he fixed that problem. Offers loading suggestions for .340 Weatherby.
1965, January 15	[Name not given]	Notes how the .41 Magnum is close but not up to the .44 Magnum. Adds that he worked with Douglas Wesson developing the .357 Magnum and still has the pistol that Wesson gave him and that Phil Sharpe claimed credit for .357 Magnum. Repeats his preference for solids over shot for snakes.
1965, February 9	[Name not given]	Reiterates his preference for .41 or .44 caliber. Talks about crimping .38 Special and .357 Magnum cases.
1965, March 20	Kent Lomont Fort Wayne, IN	Says rear sight notch in hammer spur on single action revolvers often doesn't line up with front sight. Advises Lomont about hunting license requirements in Idaho.
1965, June 22	Chris Holman San Jose, CA	Refers to transaction with Captain Shank in 1924, in which Keith sold Shank three Sharps rifles (see letters on pages 21–26) and discusses elk shooting with Springfield.
1965, August 12	Kent Lomont Fort Wayne, IN	Talks about killing sharks with .44 Magnum—he hit a flying fish actually. An article in *Gun World* also discussed point shooting and eye focus on target while shooting from the draw.
1966, April 22	Capt. D.B. Wheeler Jr. Claude, TX	Relates that Keith-designed knives were used as subscription inducement by *Guns & Ammo*.
1966, October 31	Kent Lomont Fort Wayne, IN	Criticizes long shooting periods and notes that he frequently doesn't shoot for a week but carries all the time. Likes gold inserts on front sights, but red plastic shows up better in some lighting.

LETTERS FROM ELMER KEITH

Date	Recipient	Subject
1967, January 4	Jack R. Tishue Ferndale, MD	Offers to autograph a copy of his book if Tishue will send it to him. Offers the names of a couple of businesses to purchase ammo and components from.
1967, January 22	Kent Lomont Fort Wayne, IN	Discusses Kent Lomont's accident involving the .450 Alaskan and shares his thoughts about various firearms and ammo.
1967, February 21	Jack R. Tishue Ferndale, MD	Makes an interesting comment (and so true) about how so many of his critics later come around to his way of thinking!
1967, April 11	Kent Lomont Fort Wayne, IN	Talks about how his new Champlin and Haskins rifle, which he helped design, will perform with 500-grain gas check bullets.
1967, April 16	Kent Lomont Fort Wayne, IN	Bemoans the problem that "thin, lousy brass" causes in double rifles. Talks about a point mold for soft lead tip cast into a hard lead .44-caliber bullet body.
1967, May 24	Kent Lomont Fort Wayne, IN	Discusses putting 500 rounds through M27/M42 S&W 38/44—500 rounds and got M1950 Target 4-inch for the effort by S&W. His hands were sore and could only shoot 50 rounds at a time.
1967, July 12	Kent Lomont Fort Wayne, IN	Notes that Chief Special, if properly held, is accurate at long range and difficult for many to believe. Praises the new Champlin and Haskins. Tells how Les Bowman, after he heard of Keith's design partnership with Champlin and Haskins, rushed to the gunmaker to get his own rifle.
1967, September 14	J.P. Tishue Jr. Ferndale, MD	Observes how much there still is to learn about ammunition even by those who have made a habit of learning everything they can about it for years, and yet there are writers who appear from nowhere to tell people in print how to do everything. Mentions the number of columns he has written that have never been published, in order to print the work of others with no apparent knowledge of their subject. Suggests rifles for women.
1967, October 1	J.P. Tishue Jr. Ferndale, MD	Advises against using anything less than 250-grain or .33 caliber for elk hunting, and recommends a .338 Winchester Magnum with 250- and 300-grain rounds, or .375 H&H with with 300-grain ammo.

A GUIDE TO THE LETTERS 7

Date	Recipient	Subject
1967, November 11	George Bredsten Honolulu, HI	Notes that single-action pistol frame for police work was fast to put into action and five shots were plenty. States that he himself carries an M29 but acknowledges that the only benefits are six rounds and faster reloading. Opines that M29 in 4- or 5-inch is the best police weapon, and the M57 or Ruger in 4- to 4 5/8 inches in .41 is next best. Remarks that he has been an officer "a good part of my life."
1967, November 12	Kent Lomont Fort Wayne, IN	Pronounces the .44 best in accuracy, with .41 second, and .357 third. He notes that the .41 is a flatter shooter than .44, however. Talks about over-boring in a 10 gauge.
1967, December 13	Jack Tishue Jr. Ferndale, MD	Notes killing deer at 600 yards, as well as 200–225 yards in front of witnesses.
1967, December 14	Kent Lomont Fort Wayne, IN	Comments on the "good, fast, and very tough" wingshooting he had just done in Europe, and that he was recovering from a coronary.
1968, January 18	Jack Tishue Jr. Ferndale, MD	Lambasted the copy editors on one of his books for making errors in the captions, inserting photos he did not authorize, and deleting some he thought essential. Especially galled by the notation in the front of the book that the book had been edited and "rewritten" by John Lachuck.
1968, January 24	Kent Lomont Fort Wayne, IN	Describes the use of a .22 Jet on a bull and tells how the bullet blew up in brain. Considers the 250-grain Keith .44 Magnum much better.
1968, January 30	Jack Tishue Jr. Ferndale, MD	Reveals his contempt for P.O. Ackley, which dates back to their days during World War II at Ogden Arsenal.
1968, February 20	Jack Tishue Jr. Ferndale, MD	States that he thinks the .340 Weatherby is good at long distances.
1968, March 1	Jack Tishue Jr. Ferndale, MD	Feels that the Churchill is a fine gun and acknowledges that he has owned a couple of them himself. Also states that he has had unsatisfactory accuracy from the Ferlach over-unders and much prefers side by sides.

8 LETTERS FROM ELMER KEITH

Date	Recipient	Subject
1968, March 2	Jack Tishue Jr. Ferndale, MD	Gives permission for Winslow to use the same pattern of checkering on Tishue's rifle as on Keith's. Again praises the Champlin and Haskins Keith-grade firearm.
1968, July 8	Jack Tishue Jr. Ferndale, MD	Observes that he and four "Alaskan Sourdoughs" designed the Model 70 rifle years ago and that it is still an excellent rifle. States his preference for not using muzzle brakes because they "ruin your ears."
1968, August 2	Kent Lomont Fort Wayne, IN	Requests Lomont to take photos of rifles and game heads for Keith's upcoming book on African hunting.
1968, August 16	Kent Lomont Fort Wayne, IN	Thanks Lomont for the photographs he took and asks for a few more.
1968, August 16	C.K. Carroll, Columbus, OH	Discusses holster restraining strap design by Hardy to allow carrying six rounds, hammer firing pin sticking through hole in safety strap. Prefers double-action revolver for defense to auto; thinks double action is only better than single action because of reloading speed.
1968, August 16	[Name not given]	Argues against using small calibers to hunt big game.
1968, August 22	Kent Lomont Fort Wayne, IN	Discusses his ideas about the antigun proposals that are circulating.
1968, September 19	Kent Lomont Fort Wayne, IN	Encourages Lomont to read Keith's article in the October 1968 issue of *Guns & Ammo* and let the editor know what he thinks, good or bad.
1968, October 9	Jack Tishue Jr. Ferndale, MD	Notes working as booking agent since 1957 for White Hunters Ltd., Africa, on a 10 percent basis.
1968, December 13	Postmaster, Baltimore, MD	Apparently, selling gun books was a steady source of income for Keith. Here he writes about a missing book and recalls selling hundreds of them over the years.
1968, December 18	Jack Tishue Jr. Ferndale, MD	Inquiring whether the *Sixgun* book ordered by Tishue's wife had ever arrived. Believes it was stolen by a postal employee.
1969, January 8	Jack Tishue Jr. Ferndale, MD	Comments about Les Bowman and Jack O'Connor not measuring up to his standards.

A GUIDE TO THE LETTERS

Date	Recipient	Subject
1969, January 25	[Name not given]	Remarks that he never saw any man who could place his shots in the field 100 percent of the time, the reason he likes big bores.
1969, February 7	[No name given]	Criticizes Ackley, Bowman, and O'Connor for small-bore advocacy and lack of weapon development over the years; they weren't up to his standard as men.
1969, February 11	Kent Lomont Fort Wayne, IN	Thinks Ruger will handle longer period heavy loads than S&W, although H.P. White said Ruger blew up first—the difference between durability and ability to withstand peak pressure.
1969, March 6	[Name not given]	Again he writes, "I have been a peace officer a good part of my life."
1969, March 18	Jack R. Tishue Jr. Ferndale, MD	States his preference for 2400 gunpowder over 4227. Confirms he will be at the NRA convention.
1969, April 14	Kent Lomont Fort Wayne, IN	Calls the 5-inch .44 a good revolver—close to 6 1/2 for game work and, while not quite as good as 4-inch for police work, it is acceptable. Writes that he got a 5-inch from H.H. Harris for his son and is looking to get another for himself from the factory. Plans to go to Africa with Truman Fowler for elephant hunt—at age 70!
1969, May 17	[Name not given]	Expresses his disdain for any bullet lighter than 250 grains in any of the .338s.
1969, May 22	Jack R. Tishue Jr. Ferndale, MD	Offers his advice for cast bullets for the .375 H&H.
1969, May 26	Kent Lomont Fort Wayne, IN	Observes the lack of firearms training in the army and remarks that if you don't know how to shoot before you go in, you will not learn (how true!). Labels those who advocate gun control as communists and wishes that the government would spend money teaching citizens to shoot rather than spending it on space travel—also true.
1969, June 12	Jack R. Tishue Jr. Ferndale, MD	Interesting information about duplex loadings.
1969, June 22	Jack R. Tishue Jr. Ferndale, MD	Offers recommendations about axes and other camping equipment for hunting expeditions.

Date	Recipient	Subject
1969, October 17	George Bredsten Fairbanks, AL	Just back from six weeks in Africa hunting elephant with Truman Fowler using .500 Boswell Double Rifle. Notes that a .41/44 Magnum, if placed correctly at close range, will take any game in North America.
1969, October 17	Jack R. Tishue Jr. Ferndale, MD	States preference for .338 over .375 due to sectional density and also for elk in preference to .30'06, as one cannot depend on perfect placement while hunting.
1969, October 27	Kent Lomont Fort Wayne, IN	Relates that he broke ribs falling in a boat in Africa on the way home. Recounts his African trip and observes that a 5-inch M29 is a good weapon overall.
1969, December 1	Jack R. Tishue Jr. Ferndale, MD	Recommends someone in Missoula, Montana, to make the .333 OKH (a wildcat cartridge developed by Charles O'Neill, Elmer Keith, and Don Hopkins).
1969, December 19	Etter	Discusses long-range shooting and Askins' *Gun World* article criticizing and doubting Keith's shooting.
1970, January 22	John T. Stuart Milwaukee, WI	Observes that often handheld groups are better than machine rests for accuracy testing. Also states his preference for short-barrel revolvers. Remarks on the odd fact surrounding some loads that, while they are more powerful, faster loads exit the barrel at lower angle of barrel flip than lighter, slower loads, and thus can be zeroed in identical fashion. He notes that he answers a lot of letters: he received 33 the day before this letter went out. That was a big job for a 70-year-old man with no secretary, in my opinion.
1970, March 2	Jack R. Tishue Jr. Ferndale, MD	Notes that the problem of getting cases for fine old British double rifles was resolved by suppliers, but it was a critical problem at one time.
1970, March 30	Jack R. Tishue Jr. Ferndale, MD	Comments that John Taylor was a knowledgeable person and the best book on African shooting discusses Taylor's World War II record a bit.
1970, April 9	George Bredsten Fairbanks, AL	Remarks that he hasn't had the chance to try the new .44 auto Magnum yet, but thinks it should be good fun to hunt with for those who like autos.

A GUIDE TO THE LETTERS

Date	Recipient	Subject
1970, April 28	Jack R. Tishue Jr. Ferndale, MD	No fiberglass/Kevlar stocks for Elmer Keith! Walnut was his choice for stocks.
1970, May 27	Jim Leatherwood Stephenville, TX	States preference for 1.5 x 4.5 variable scope for hunting (not pest shooting). Comments on shooting coyotes for a living with target rifle of 14 pounds lugging his shoulder while on horseback.
1971, February 22	Jack R. Tishue Jr. Ferndale, MD	Tells about his engraved and inlaid .338-378 Champlin and Haskins, which is valued at $5,000.
1971, March 15	Jack R. Tishue Jr. Ferndale, MD	Accuses Jack O'Connor of plagiarizing his material. Keith points out that he shoots better with rifle/shot gun/handgun than O'Connor, and insists that he never did anything to O'Connor, which means that O'Connor must be jealous. Figures that O'Connor is to be pitied, as O'Connor does not measure up to Keith's standards as a man.
1971, August 4	[Name not given]	Discusses O'Connor's proposing .270 for Elk and why that is a bad idea, as well as the effectiveness of .375 H&H.
1971, October 6	George Bredsten Fairbanks, AK	Praises .444 Marlin. Insists that consistent bullet weight and caliber, not velocity, are critical for game shooting, while velocity is changing all the time. Notes preference for .44 Magnum with Keith loads over .45 Colt, as Askins' penetration on game. Notes that long barrels have more velocity but not more accuracy.
1971, October 12	George Bredsten Fairbanks, AK	Restates preference for weight and caliber over velocity, and observes that if a person shoots game with both small and big cartridges, he will typically choose the big cartridge option. Thinks .33-caliber 250-grain minimum bullet is best for 1,850- to 2,000-pound game.
1971, November 5	George Bredsten Fairbanks, AK	Notes that he does not hunt with less than .338 currently.

Date	Recipient	Subject
1971, November 7	Kent Lomont Fort Wayne, IN	Says Gold Cup with stronger recoil spring and pin through rear sight will hold up to abuse, despite Jeff Cooper's comment. But Keith prefers double-action S&W revolvers or even Ruger single action. Also notes his preference for 22-grain 2400, 24,000 psi and 1,400 fps velocity, according to HP White Lab, less than 3,000 psi variation, unlike factory loads with 11,000 psi variation.
1971, November 26	[Name not given]	Notes his .338 Browning with 1:12 twist stabilizes 275-grain bullets very well, but not 300 grain. States that he guided for 30 years, hunted big game since age 12, and that he was 70 when he wrote letters and never saw the man who could always hit his game right and anyone who has hunted much has lost game—but few admit it. Noted that there is seldom a perfect shot on game in field. He also discusses leading in sixguns.
1971, December 17	Jack R. Tishue Jr. Ferndale, MD	Notes he paid out $4,000 for African trips, and the actual hunting was given to him.
1972, January 5	[Name not given]	Disagrees with the statement made by the vice president of a magazine that the 6.5mm bullet is good on medium-sized game out to 1,500 yards.
1972, January 11	Jack R. Tishue Jr. Ferndale, MD	Decries lack of royalty payments on books; comments on declining situation in Africa regarding hunting and politics; comments about poor performance of 7mm Magnum/300 Magnum on anything except pests.
1972, January 24	Jack R. Tishue Jr. Ferndale, MD	Doesn't want 7mm for African game. Again comments on book sales and small vs. medium calibers for hunting, also long, heavy bullets.
1972, April 4	Kent Lomont Fort Wayne, IN	Notes that the Colt New Frontier is the best single-action Colt ever made, and he has an original Flat Top. States that he does not mind the recoil of .44 Magnum, but notes that some "lilly-fingered gents" do almost cry when they shoot it.
1972, September 13	[Name not given]	Writes that he is typing his autobiography and that he nominated Charlie Askins for the first Handgunner award.

Date	Recipient	Subject
1973, January 3	Jack R. Tishue Jr. Ferndale, MD	Points out that he never asked for any free hunts, unlike O'Connor.
1973, January 3	Jerry L. Nelsen Ranchester, WY	Considers the double-action S&W and Ruger/Colt SA best revolvers and imported copies junk.
1973, January 5	Jerry L. Nelsen Ranchester, WY	Refers to going to Handgunner Award show in Indiana, and it is clear that he does not think he has won.
1973, February 23	[Name not given]	Blames biologists for lack of game. Comments that he does not like handgun with barrel over 7 1/2 inches and that the 7 1/2-inch model is only for horseback. He prefers 4-inch M29 and packs it all the time.
1973, February 26	Jack R. Tishue Jr. Ferndale, MD	Concedes that he will probably not hunt any more in Africa.
1973, March 5	[Name not given]	Acknowledges he got the Handgunner award and notes that more shooters are moving to large, heavy bullets.
1973, March 8	Jack R. Tishue Jr. Ferndale, MD	Lists some of his favorite shotguns.
1973, March 28	George	Mentions that he has been sick, and his weight is down to 146 pounds.
1973, April 24	George	Expresses concern for friend Don Martin, whose cancer has returned.
1973, May 2	George	On double rifle ribs are separating and it doesn't group. He will use the stock and action to build a 20-bore shotgun.
1973, July 3	[Name not given]	Reveals that he was in car accident June 9 and that he broke a bone but refused to go to the hospital.
1973, August 31	[Name not given]	Discusses his relationship with Jack O'Connor. States he, Keith, is not a writer but only reporter of facts, and that he writes what he sees and knows to be true from experience.
1973, October 16	[Name not given]	Discusses .358 Winchester and .350 Rem. Mag cartridges on elk, also loss of sheep and goats to eagles and coyotes. Notes that a 19-page article he sent to *Guns & Ammo* was lost.

Date	Recipient	Subject
1973, December 1	George Bredsten Fairbanks, AK	Reflects that he considers the Cape buffalo the toughest game animal and notes that he killed only three. He also explains that the best shot will break the buffalo's shoulder/spine, or the animal will run away. Praises the .45-70 over the .375 up to 150 yards.
1973, December 4	[Name not given]	Criticizes Guns & Ammo for the way his articles are used.
1974, January 15	[Name not given]	Recounts trials with Guns & Ammo losing his material and retells of O'Connor pointing a shotgun at him and letting the bolt go forward into battery, hoping Keith thought it would go off and shoot him.
1974, March 12	[Name not given]	Rails against the state game department and biologists.
1974, May 25	[Name not given]	Comments on the declining health of Don Martin. Reveals that he is getting $1,200 per month from Guns & Ammo as executive editor.
1974, October 16	[Name not given]	Notes the death of Don Martin.
1975, February 3	[Name not given]	Remarks on the receipt of old S&W M1917 from Don Martin's estate, which he used to kill jackrabbits in haystack story.
1975, February 19	[Name not given]	Says that he thought highly of Bill Jordan and Skeeter Skelton.
1975, February 28	George Bredsten Fairbanks, AK	Comments that he loads 20.0-grain 2400 in Colt single action NF with no problems in .45 Colt sized to .451 and cast hard. Notes failures with expanding SuperVel .357 Magnum loads. Also tells of use of .41 Magnum on caribou while hunting polar bear in Alaska; he killed five.
1975, March 6	George Bredsten Fairbanks, AK	Notes actual need for penetration on game animal and discusses his switch to .44 Special over .45 Colt in early 1920s as more powerful load 17.0 grain 2,400 and 250-grain bullet in .44 Special close to .44 Magnum.
1975, March 9	George Bredsten Fairbanks, AK	Displeased that Winchester changed his autobiography photo caption and used bragging style he did not use or like.

Date	Recipient	Subject
1975, March 9	[Name not given]	In a letter to Lawrence Holster Company about holster it sent him, Keith mentions that he has been using Lawrence rigs and recommending them for a long time.
1975, April 10	[Name not given]	Links the development of .44 Magnum in 1953 to Remington's concern about heavy loads for .44 Special in Triplelocks. Reveals his regard for M1950 Target models in .44 Special/.45 Colt.
1975, April 28	George Bredsten Fairbanks, AK	Discusses killing African lion with Keith load .44 Magnum as acceptable if within 50 yards, but he declines to go on safari because it is costly and he is 76 years old at the time.
1975, June 3	[Name not given]	Prefers heavy bullets in sixguns because of the need for penetration on game. Likes .45 Auto for man work much better than 9mm or .38 Super; for jackrabbits to mule deer, though, he thinks the .41/44 Magnum is much better.
1975, June 10	[Name not given]	Discusses the new 250-grain Sierra bullet for elk and bear. Complains about the management of wildlife by the game department and ecologists.
1975, June 19	[Name not given]	Another letter discussing heavy .44 Special hand loads, cautioning his correspondent to use his favorite loads only in weapons with good modern steel.
1975, June 30	[Name not given]	Notes penetration needed; prefers bullet to exit game animal to produce a good blood trail.
1975, July 14	[Name not given]	This letter was sent to a man going to gunsmithing school who wrote about a class project involving making a .444 Marlin or .45-70 single action revolver. Obviously Keith did not think too much of such big monsters. He always preferred practical packing pieces. I imagine he would not be a fan of the new big .500 S&W revolvers, but John Linebaugh's conversions to .475 or .500 might well get his enthusiastic approval, as might the 5-inch John Ross model for the .500 S&W Magnum.
1975, August 10	[Name not given]	Discusses .38 S&W, .38 Special, and .357 Magnum loads.

16 LETTERS FROM ELMER KEITH

Date	Recipient	Subject
1975, August 10	[Name not given]	Talks about heavy .338-caliber bullets.
1975, October 27	George	States his preference for bullet weight and caliber for anchoring man or beast; rejects computer man tests popular at the time. Says he packs M29 4-inch all the time with 22.0-grain 2400/250 SWC. Commends Harlon Carter and Bill Ruger for fighting gun control.
1975, December 9	George Bredsten Fairbanks, AK	Discusses that penetration is critical for game shooting and notes that he always gets complete penetration on deer with his .44 Magnum load. Recounts killing salmon under 4 feet of water with 18.5-grain 2400 .44 Special loads and sharks with .44 Magnum. Mentions his shot on a buck at 600 yards with .44 Magnum.
1976, January 7	[Name not given]	A response from Keith to some early questions about loads for the then-new Marlin 1895 reintroduction and about a T-lock .45 conversion from .455 using Keith loads. Discusses .45/70 loads and rechambering .455 S&W Triplelocks to .45 Colt with good results. Discusses issues of bullet diameter in .45 Colt pistols, always a problem, and concern only overcome by slugging barrels, one of reasons for Keith to ultimately go to .44 Special as his load of choice. Chauncey Thomas also noted the same problem in getting good loads for .45 Colt. The book Keith mentions is *Sixguns*, the 1961 bonanza edition, with the inscription shown on the flyleaf.
1976, February 19	George Bredsten Fairbanks, AK	He discusses the Krag on elk, and big bore single-shot rifles.
1976, February 29	George Bredsten Fairbanks, AK	He dislikes the blast from Magnaported guns. Mentions a load for the .45-70.
1976, March 6	George Bredsten Fairbanks, AK	Complains about the government.
1976, May 12	William Powell	Thank-you note for a knife given as gift by noted firearms authority William Powell of Texas. Discusses preferred loading for .44 Special.
1976, June 9	William Powell	Notes story obtained from Douglas Wesson about last pair of Triplelocks leaving factory in 1930s for $75 each with shipment to South America. Also discusses .45 Colt loads and bullet size issues.

A GUIDE TO THE LETTERS 17

Date	Recipient	Subject
1976, July 8	[Name not given]	Makes note of his 50th wedding anniversary. Explains that if the first shot is not right, then one has to hit the spine or brain or bleed them out, and that takes time. Thinks .45 Colt in Ruger loaded 250-grain bullet, 22-grain 2400 more effective under 50 yards than .44 Magnum over 50 yards; sectional density of .44 Magnum better and more so at long range. Notes he sights rifles 3 inches higher and 1/2 inch left at 100 yards for long-range work.
1976, September 9	[Name not given]	Discusses testing .45/70 handguns.
1976, September 16	[Name not given]	Notes that big game in Idaho "damn well shot out."
1976, October 5	George Bredsten Fairbanks, AK	Discusses .45/70 revolver and notes it would be good in shoulder holster for bear hunt guide.
1976, October 23	George Bredsten Fairbanks, AK	Notes he believes that a properly loaded handgun is better on game than .30/30, 170-grain. Recounts hitting flying fish with M29; observes that they need twice as much lead as ducks. Expresses his preference for Reagan in election and views Carter with disdain and alarm.
1977, February 16	[Name not given]	Use of slower-burning powders, wads, and lube in .338 rifles.
1978, January 5	[Name not given]	Recounts penetration tests with .44 Magnum.
1978, February 4	[Name not given]	Notes that Keith .44 Magnum load penetrates better than factory .44 Magnum ammo and expanding rifle ammo, and that penetration is critical in game hunting, as one often has to take shots that are not perfect. Observes that all American big game is killed with .44 Magnum. Gives his opinion of gun control.
1978, July 7	[Name not given]	Notes his preference for .38 Special loadings, which, based on my experience, are certainly heavy but also accurate and clean shooting. The source of the Border Patrol photos in *Sixguns* is revealed also.
1978, November 11	[Name not given]	Keith was well known for his .44 Special and .44 Magnum loads. Here he clearly sets forth his exact loading that served him so well.

Date	Recipient	Subject
1979, April 24	[Name not given]	Mule deer hunting with his single-shot rifle in .338-74 Keith.
1979, July 25	Ed Doherty Charlton Publications, Derby, CN	Letter from prospective publisher wherein Keith declines an offer of employment, noting that he writes many daily letters to "gun cranks." This interesting, polite letter from best-known gun writer declining an offer to write for obscure publication illustrates the manner of Keith as a man, I believe.
1979, August 8	[Name not given]	Notes excellent results with .338 275-grain bullets on everything from deer to polar bear.
1979, December 15	[Name not given]	Remarks on problems with book sales/royalties and mistreatment by publishers (except Petersen and Little Brown).
1979, December 28	[Name not given]	Comments on deciding not to attend the Outdoorsman of the Year Awards.
1980, January 17	[Name not given]	Notes use of Colt single-action revolver in .44/.45 modified for S&W rear sights and used for 50 years or more.
1981, February 4	[Name not given]	Keith always liked the Sharps big-bore rifles but knew they were for black powder only. For pure shooting with smokeless, he preferred the Ruger single shot, but certainly it was not in the same class as a black powder Sharp's rifle (or current copy).
1981, March 20	[Name not given]	Notes his longest shot at mule deer 600 yards; he hit two or three shots but no bullet expansion. Also killed mule deer at same range with .44 Magnum.
1981, April 15	[Name not given]	Calls the Colt New Frontier single action in .44/.45 the best single-action Colt made and prefers old flattop style to standard fixed-sight weapon.
1981, October 18	T.J. Mullin St. Louis, MO	Acknowledges getting a copy of *Training the Gunfighter* and calls it one of the best books ever on subject. Designates the .45 ACP Colt as the best army sidearm.

Date	Recipient	Subject
1984, February 23		A copy of the article which appeared in Keith's hometown newspaper reporting on his funeral. It was a nice ceremony, which I am certain Keith would have approved of.

Winston, Montana
Feb 29 – 1924

Captain George T. Shaw,
18th. Infantry.
Fort Slocum, N.Y.

Dear Sir:

I advertised four of my ten sharps. Have sold two of the four advertised. Both were calibre 45-120. One weighed 14#, other 10#. Both octagon.

The best of the two I have left is a 44-77-470 original Christian sharp. 30" octagon, double set trigger, weight 11# outside fine shape, inside good but light pits throughout. very accurate however. Have killed coyotes at 300 yds. with it. A few pits does not affect the accuracy of these big bore rifles. Have over 200 shells for this rifle. Some loaded. 44-470 gr. patch mould.

Also have an extra barrel & found. Sharps. calibre 45-70. 30" oct. fine shape – nearly new. have made 1½" ten shot groups at 100 yds. This barrel has an 8 power cummins scope mounted on it. also has (Old Reliable) stepdown barrel. Have 44 everlasting shells for it also some commercial shells. Can furnish all the bullets you would want.

Will take $40. F.O.B. Winston for both rifle & barrel or $25. for the 44 outfit and 15 over for the extra barrel, scope & shells.

Have a 50-70 Sharps military type snipers rifle. peep sight. 30" round, long forend, sling swivels, single trigger. in good cond inside & out. very accurate. Have original Sharps 50-473 gr. pitch mould. (only one I know of) about 3000 wax lubricators and extra wads & few shells & patches. Also a makeshift capper. $20 outfit.

I also have a Caliber 45-90 Sharps that I loaned a friend in Helena, in pretty good shape when I let him have it. Have about 200 new primed shells for it $25 outfit.

If you just want a good specimen of C. Sharps. Oct. barrel for collection only, in serviceable cond. I can fix you up for about $15. subject to your approval of course. Shells are worth nearly as much as rifles now and very hard to find in good cond. Would not care for the mauser. I'm no dealer just a crank and collector. Also there are quite a few Sharps around here. Let me hear from you if these interest you. For reference write Chauncey Thomas of Denver, Colo. Sincerely Elmer W. Keith

Winston, Montana
April 9 - 1924

Capt. George T. Shank.
Dear Sir:

Have been packing up your things since receiving your letter last eve.

Will ship the first of next week. Will be going to Winston with team then. Will ship you three rifles and one barrel & one end. Cal. 45-70-420, one 44-77 Barrel a 40-90 B.N. and a 50-70 str.

Have all the shells etc. packed. There is a raft of 44 & 45 cal shells. This 44 cal mould is oversize and makes a fine accurate patch mould for the 45-70. Moulded you some 45-420 gr. patch bullets. Moulds for 40 & 50 cal also and about 60 loads 44's wad cutters. In fact a whole lot of sharps stuff you will use sooner or later.

I believe the three sharps etc are worth a little more than the $60. But you are sending 200 rounds natl. match - and when you look these over (if they are worth it) would like to have some of that 180 gr. Western International match. I quoted you I think the three at $85 with scope. Have traded off the scope before you wrote for a trade.

Valued it at $10. Hence 44 & 45 outfit $30. 40-90 B.N. $25 — 50-70 &c.

So if they are worth anymore to you then please send it in Western 180 g. Lubaloy 96's. Hope you like these rifles. Only reason for letting them go was I had to move and am going to move this summer.

Am keeping 4 on a ya: 45-100 — 18 lb. 44-405 — 9 lb. 40-90 B.N. 16 lb. and 16 to 18 lb. 45-120 that Omeara is fitting to the stock and action off of 44-77.

The 45-70 was better gun so robbed the 44's action and let you have the 45 as it was.

Very truly yours
Elmer Keith.

P.S. Have a 4x75 power John W. Sidle scope fine cond. Stevens micrometer mounts. $20 or trade for 30-06 Ammunition. Let me know E.K.

Winston, Mont. May 15

Cpt. J. T. Shank.

Dear Sir.

Your letter here tonight, via cow pony last seven miles. Have put the 45-70 barrel on the Sharps action. I kept one stock & action for my Bannerman barrel. This 45-70 barrel is in very good cond. inside & out. Have 44 everlasting hand made shells and a raft of commercial empties. The 46 barrel is in better shape than the 44 inside. I will run you a batch of 45-420 gr. patch bullets. I will have to pack these shells also 200 44-77 shells some loaded and moulds. etc in one box and the 45-70 rifle extra 44-77 barrel & forend and whichever of the other sharps you want in another box.

Please let me know which of the others you want and I'll pack them up and ship to you

This 45-70 has (Old Reliable) stpt. on barrel. 30" oct. double set triggers stock which was on 44-77. Very dark grain walnut. good figure. Have made 1½" groups with it at 100 yds. but takes lots of patience and old maid fussing.

Of the other Sharps I'd suggest you take either the 50-70 military with peep sight or the 40-90 B.N. Both have moulds. 40-90 has (Old reliable) on barrel 30" oct double. set fine inside. — new stock — found badly worn. 50-70 has 30" round bbl. sling swivels. 50-473 gr. Sharps brass mould. peepsight. single trig 8 lb.

I've shot the .50 is accurate never fired the 40-90. have 40 shells for it tho. empty.

Let me know which one you want also how you want them shipped. And I'll get them off soon as I can. Live on cow ranch here pretty busy now.

3

Now in regards that Spfld. your description suits me fine however if you have to buy the stock new, would like to have one of the new sporting 1922 stocks without any cut for the Service bbl. sight. no bbl. sight Or if either you have the P.G. Service stock now. Then I'd like to have the regular service rear sight as well as the 48.

Can they change off and use the 48 for hunting and turkey matches and the military for range work. where 48 is not allowed.

Please let me know. If the 1922 stock to fit service rifle with rear sight stud removed costs more than military P.G. then I'll stand the additional cost. But if you already have military P.G. stock then fit rear military sight & Lyman 48 and send.

Sincerely Elmer M Keith

Bullet Experience on Big Game

By Elmer Keith

A stranger rides into camp. This is Elmer Keith's first attempt in public print. He is a typical young rancher and cowman, about 24 years old, born and raised in the Rockies, the way I was thirty years before his time. I have known Keith for about five years, and know that what he says is accurate. His experience ad knowledge is more of the Outdoors than of books. He is one of the best shots in the Hills today, and was on the Camp Perry team from Montana last year. He has won several championships for broncho busting, and is as good a rider as he is a shot with both rifle and six-gun, especially with the rifle. I have been trying to get him to allow me to publish some of his letters to me; but through lack of confidence, and the modesty and silence which seems natural to Hill men, even to bashfulness, he has held back. But I finally have his consent to venture at least one of these letters. This is only one of the, which in itself reveals actual hunting experience more than 99 x 100 city hunters can ever hope to have. The details he gives can be depended on.

Chauncey Thomas

Dear C. T.:   French, Idaho

Received your letters all O. K. Am back on the ranch again this time with the cattle. Keeps me busy now between cooking my own meals and riding herd on these critters, also playing nurse for a lot of them. Good weather for calves now though, except a bit windy and cold. Got letter and bullets at French too. Address me at French now.

Thanks for editing and starting that letter along. You must have had quite a bit of work on it. I know less than nothing about such things or writing either. Wish I were able to make a little money writing but believe it would take me another 50 years. However, if any time I write you a letter that contains anything you think worth printing, why O. K. with me, and will be glad to pay you for trouble editing it, busted now. Sold a Sharps .40-90 B. N., 16 pounds, for $50.00 last month, new condition. The one I sent you 50 yard target from.

Have absorbed what you wrote about changing sights after two shots. It shows up even more at 1,000 yards. One never knows which part of his normal group those two shots are. On the military target where one has never more than two sights and at Perry in most matches none at all. I've gotten the habit of just correcting for half the distance I am out from center on first sighter. Thus, if I had a 4 at 3 o'clock, I just move sights over half the distance to center, so if that shot happens to be on the right edge of my normal group than the next one will probably be in black.

I sometimes think it better to use both one's sighters without a change, then correct. but then tow even not enough to tell position of one's group. And unless you get centered, even a fine group the size of bull or smaller won't get you anywhere in a match. You know how it goes. Lieutenant Siler, I think it was, wrote a fine article on this very thing about a year ago in THE AMERICAN RIFLEMAN. By the way Siler told me to tell you he hoped to meet you some day.

Have seen it at long range, at Perry especially when conditions appear normal, no wind and scope shows no mirage and yet you need one to three points windage. Maybe light or some atmospheric condition it worked out the same all along the firing line so not due to canting by one individual.

Thanks for dope on group. I never thought of groups as saucer of cinch ring but it is all right and makes it easier to understand and to correct for. No wonder one misses coyotes sometimes. Missed a big eagle 150 yards the other day. Don't know yet what was wrong, held dead center in middle of breast, never ruffled a feather. Would have sworn I could have hit his head. Have shot rabbits through head that far with this free rifle and green wing teal only one inch out of water at 200 yards.

Have a set Belding & Mull .30-06 calibrated mounts for Winchester scope. Like the rear mount but not the way it is arranged to keep scope from rotating. My brother is on his way to Montana. Will soon have my .30 loading tools here. Had letter from Omeara, has been about half sick with grippe. Got a .40-90 str. 3-inch everlasting shell Sharps rifle 11 to 12 pounds, 30 inch round barrel, fine shape but shells stick tight, as if glued after firing. Accurate, too fancy, but can't get shells in and out gun very easy. Maybe chambered too straight or shells being thick and after being fired many times are so strong they won't spring or give any. May swap off or get Omeara to put on a heavy .45 barrel.

Have been shooting a .44 cap and ball Navy Colt—really .45. Loaded with 40 grains black, a felt was saturated with tallow and let harden. wad out of an old hat and round ball on top. It shoots about the same as any big six gun, very accurate, and cheap too.

My first six gun was a Colt Police Positive target .32. It was wonderfully accurate little gun but no killing power. Would not kill pine squirrels unless hit in heart or shoulders, or head. Next I tackled one of the old Derringer stock .38 Colt's lighting double actions. Was a better gun than the .32 but not as accurate. Then when I was 14 or 15 years old bought a new. 32-20 S. A. Army 7 1/2 inch for $15.50. (sic) out of gun store. this gun did the trick. I killed an awful lot of small game with it. For three years I kept record of grouse. I got 129 birds with this gun alone. Also many rabbits, hawks, and eagle and several coyotes off horse.

One day I had chance to try it on venison at about 40 yards, 2 year old blacktail doe. Shout out of back seat of Ford top down. Gun in both hands. Landed first shot in right shoulder, breaking it. Was using .32 Winchester soft nose, low velocity. Next three shots all landed in 4 inch of first one, on or behind shoulder as deer staggered around first on one side of road then on other. The deer got started up hill at a poor gait. Fifth shot hit a limb and missed, sixth one broke back, loaded up and shot through head.

Killed my next deer a very big old blacktail at about 50 yards, running around steep hill above me with same gun and load. First shot struck belly about where I split open afterwards and angled upward through paunch. Deer humped up and turned hill past me about 40 yards. Held under nose and next shot broke neck. Both bullets went clear through and out the deer.

Afterwards killed a yearling blacktail at around 100 yards with same gun. First shot struck a lodge pole pine and did not hit deer. Could just see part of deer through trees. Next one went through paunch and lung cavity. Trailed deer about one mile and found it dead. This is still a fine accurate six gun although badly scarred from many years in mountains and on broncs. Have since fitted it with 5 1/2 inch barrel. I always use both hand on six gun when after meat unless shooting off horse or running a coyote. Have gotten fine results with this gun with a 113 grain (about) Ideal pointed bullet, and 3 1/2 grains bull's-eye, although this load too heavy for anything but a S. A. Colt, or maybe modern heat treated S. & W. Have used as much as 4 grains in this gun but swelled shells badly and pierced primers. Finally had heads blown off shells so went back to 3 1/2 grain ball.

One thing I never understood was why this gun with Winchester soft nose would expand or mushroom bullets perfectly in a deer, jackets bust and split, and when fired in hard dry pine the soft point would smear off leaving jacket part of bullet in almost original condition.

I once killed a mountain goat when still a small kid with .45 Colt S. A. Army, 5 1/2 and Remington black powder loads, 38 grains black and 250 grains lead. Got first shot at 40 paces as goat was going around side hill. Made a near center hit on goat's west end as he was going east. Bullet traveled full length of body broke left shoulder and lodged under hide on neck, point battered a little. The old Billy turned up the hill in high gear, next shot hit a granite boulder that got between the goat and me just as I squeezed trigger. Third shot hit back of shoulders and penetrated both lungs, going clear through the goat and out of side. Goat went over a little hill out of sight.

I ran to top of long ridge that ended in cliffs nearly three miles away. Ran along the top of this ridge with the goat going parallel below me. This country was all burned over, and could see my bullets kick up dust or ashes on off side of goat. I missed next two shots at about 150 yards running, then goat stopped and I hit him last shot, knocking him down for the first time. He got up and over the hill while I was loading up. Ran him about a mile before I got another chance. This time about 300 yards down hill as he was crossing a little hollow. First shot fell way low. Held up about half of front sight over his back and heard next bullet plunk. It knocked him over. Knocked him over once more out of this gun full of shells. Was sitting with back against tree and gun between knees. Was puffing from the run until I could not hold any other way. Loaded up and ran goat nearly to cliff before I had another chance. Then was within 30 yards of him. Sat down and took my time and tried to break his neck. I hit neck all right but missed the bone. Knocked him over but he was up and going in an instant. Ran a little more and put two more bullets lengthwise clear through him. Both came out chest. These stopped him. I worked around to side and tried to hit heart. About 60 yards missed clean, so ran up to about 30 yards, and put last two through him. I think both hit heart, as there were two holes through it broadside. both knocked him down but each time he got up and after my last shot he went down hill about 150 yards and laid down behind a burned snag. I knocked him on back of head with little Marble's belt axe and finished the job.

After examining him I found a hole through outside half of right hind foot, so hit 10 of the 18 shots I fired at him, one through foot, three lengthwise through him, one through neck, two broadside through heart and three through lungs broadside.

The bullets did not tear, just punched a 40 to 50 caliber hole. And only first one stopped in him as I could see ashes and dust raise from the others. I see Major Whelen credits the goat as being one of our toughest game animals. Believe he is right unless the coyote. But the coyote is too small to be compared with the goat.

And old bull elk nearly ended my hunting in Montana in 1919. Shot him through neck broadside with Springfield and 220 grain soft nose, missed bone and bullet lodged under skin on off side. The old fellow dropped like he was dead and kicked and rolled down the mountain about 50 yards into a hole where a big spruce had uprooted. When I went up to him, I could not see his eyes as his head was doubled back under him and deep down ground. So being younger and a little more foolish then than now, I prodded him in top of shoulders with muzzle of rifle to see if he were dead. I got results instantly. The brow points caught me somewhere near pit of stomach and I landed about 15 or 20 yards down the hill, on my back and half covered with snow. Lost track of the Springfield for time being. My .38-40 S. A. Army was up under my right arm pit, belt around my chest. Got hold of gun and bull was jumping up and down with his feet bunched where I had been much like a sheep killing a snake. Believe he was still dazed and could not see me. When I cocked the six gun, however, he whirled around and faced me. I tried to hit his forehead, but landed a little high between base of horns, as I afterwards found out. The .38-40 Remington soft nose low velocity spread to the size of a quarter on the skull without even denting bone. The elk just shook his head and came for me. I shot again when he hit the snow. This time with black powder, lead bullet. It struck almost between eyes and too low for brain but went clear through to jaws. Bull dropped about same as a beef when shot in brain. I got up and supposed the old fellow was dead, reloaded my six gun, and got the Springfield, cleaned snow out of action and was walking around the old bull looking him over and thinking what a nice head I had and how lucky I was to stop him. I thought I'd make sure he was dead before looking at his teeth. His head was under snow, so poked him in rump with my foot. He lashed out with his hind legs and knocked me over and jumped up and started to run off. I dropped the rifle when I fell, so grabbed the six gun and started shooting as fast as I could bring sights on him and work the gun. First shot hit left beam (Remington soft nose). Went half way through and expanded. Next two landed in hams and fourth one broke his back about half way between hips and shoulders. That let his hind quarters down. Then he started dragging himself towards me with his fore feet making a sort of clicking noise (with his teeth I think). His hair all turned on end and on back of his neck like a dog's. I took my time and broke his neck last shot I fired. I spent nearly a quarter of an hour throwing snow and sticks at the old fellow, then before I had nerve enough to venture up again.

Had my partner, Capt. W. R. Strong of 363rd Infantry, killed in front of me for an elk the next day, October 19,1919, while we were cutting trail out from this bull or the pack horses.

I once shot an old cow elk at about 60 yards, facing me with a 250 Savage lever action, 87 grain soft nose. Hit her square in neck and bullet went to pieces, part of it going into lung cavity and breaking two ribs the rest coming back out brisket. Blew up before it ever got near neck bone. Should have broken neck. Anyway it dropped her but she got up instantly. I next shot her broadside through neck, cutting both jugular veins, although I did not know it at the time. She went down again and likewise got up again. I leaned the rifle against a big spruce and taking the .32-20 S. A. Colt in both hands shot her in forehead, killing instantly. I had walked up each time she went down form Savage so was only 35 or 40 yards when I shot her with six gun. No one can convince me that the .250 Savage with 87 grain bullet is big enough for elk. I killed three blacktail deer with this same rifle and load. All three taking two shots each. Sometimes it will go through an animal sometimes go to pieces soon as it penetrates the hide.

The S. A. Colt may be a bit heavy to carry especially wen also carrying a rifle, but for my part I will always feel better if I have it along. If I had left that .38-40 Colt in camp in 1919 I would not now be here and its doubtful if my friends would ever have found my carcass after the elk had finished tramping me to pieces.

Have two fine .45 S. A. Armys, one 4 3/4 inches one 5 1/2 inches and believe them the best six guns one can pack for the hills. Have no use for modern smokeless squibb loads in the peace maker. The old .45-40 black 255 or 260 grain load suits me best for all around use. It will not tear a grouse or rabbit bad and will give better penetration on heavy game than any six gun load I've ever tried. Write when you have time. Am tired writing for one time. Sincerely,

ELMER KEITH.

ELMER KEITH
NORTH FORK, IDAHO

Jan 18th.

Dear Mr Mc Daniels :

Write to Frank Pachmayr of 1232 SO. Grand Ave Los Angeles Calif. for prices on this work, He can do a nice job in all particulars, fit a S & W rear target sight and re-case harden frame also front sights and all the act on work you have listed. He has been doing this work for me for some t time. His prices are very reasonable and the workmanship the best I have seen. Tell him I recommended him and he will do your job I know.

He alo fits a skeletonized Bisley type hammer to S. A. Colts and you could have your gun remodeled or have him furnish a new one. Tell him to make sure cylinder and barrel align correctly.

In haste but with best wishes,

Sincerely,

Elmer Keith

North Fork, Idaho
July 10th, 1944.

Major General George V. Strong,
U.S.Army,
G-2
Washington, D.C.

Dear Gen. Strong:

At long last have an opportunity to give you the full and complete details of your brother's death. Ordnance has kept me very busy since writing you last fall. Have been in charge final inspection and proof firing as well as functional firing small arms at Ogden Arsenal. Then was ordered back to Frankford Arsenal for five weeks on interior ballistics calibre 50, and gave them some 200 feet more velocity with same standard pressures. Home now for a months furlough to settle up my fathers estate.

Will was as you probably know in civilian life State Accountant of Montana. H.L.Hart was state treasurer and Hans DeYoung was chief clerk Will wrote me several times from France and wanted to go elk hunting with me on his return, so I arranged a trip with him, my father and a Mr. Stewart. However after his return Hart and DeYoung insisted he go with them instead. Will would not do so however unless I was included in the party. Had left my pack horses at Ovando after the summers work with the Forst Service, intending using them for elk hunt. Plans were for Will, DeYoung and Hart to foot all expenses and I to furnish the pack stock and necessary guideing. Will and I were constant shooting and hunting companions for several years before he went to the Army. Though I was but a kid then he developed a likeing for me and was my constant coach and we were about as close friends as men ever get to be.
Arriving at Ovando, Mont. Hart proposed that he keep record of expendi-ures and books of the trips expenses. We packed in to Sullivans cabin on the head of the So. Fork of the Flathead and thence up a side creek 15 miles whose name have now forgotten. I killed a buck deer and Hart and Deyoung a spike bull elk the second day. Then Hart proposed that he would hunt up the left fork, while Will, Deyoung and I hunted the main fork of Babcock creek. We were to travel up the trail and then one of us drop off and a mile further another and one to head the creek. The first day went off as to schedule from our main camp on Babcock. But Will dropped off first and I went on up the creek with DeYoung, but for some unknown reason I had a strong presentiment of impending trajedy and was suspicious of DeYoung, but for the life of me could not tell anyone why. So , when I dropped off I cautiously watched Deyoung around the bend of the trail out of sight, then turned back down the trail and I did not leave it until I was close to where Will left it. I did not find him during the day in the heavy spruce timber though we ate lunch not over 100 yds apart as I learned from Will next day. Late that evening I killed an enormous bull elk and nearly got killed myself as I went up to him with his head under snow and he jumped up and threw me down the mountian with his brow points and came for me, but I downed him again with a sixgun and arrived in camp long after dark with his heart after dressing him out.

Next morning, Hart again said he would hunt the left fork while the three of us went up main Babcock.

Page two Gen Strong.

Hart again cautioned us that if anything went wrong and we needed help to fire three shots and repeat after about a five minute interval. He had thus cautioned us the first day also.

Again we three trudged up the creek and Will and I dropped off together intending to hunt up to my bull and skin out the fine head and quarter him up and hang on spiked ready for packing out, then we would go on around the side of the mountain and try and get Will a shot if time permitted. We sighted nothing before reaching my elk and proceeded to skin out and quarter the beast and hang the meat. Will took some photos of the elk and I and I then wanted to go down the mountain to our right and circle and try and get him an elk that day, but he said would be best to cut a trail out from my elk to the main trail and find a way for the horses to get up as it looked like a snow storm was brewing, then we could get him an elk next day. All that day we each had a strong presentiment of impending trouble and both Will and I spoke of the feeling to each other and he said he felt as though he had gone off half cocked on this trip and there was something he should have done before leaving but only thing he could think of was failing to pay premium on his army insurance and said he wished he had done that. Once a big black turkey buzzard sailed over us very low, and I started to shoot it but Will remonstrated saying it was bad luck to kill it so I did not shoot. We each had such a presentiment of bad luck that we were neither very cheerful.

We struck out straight down the mountain from my kill, I blazing trees and cutting over small ones to leave a well marked trail some four or five feet above ground incacse of a big snow, and heading for the main trail which petered out about a mile below the head of the creek into which we were heading. Arriving down in the dense timbered spruce bottom with its muskeg wet floor, Will broke a Hershey bar in half and handed me half of it. I was blazing trees and anyone could have heard that belt axe. Will stepped past me a couple paces and stopped and half turned toward me saying " I believe I can help most by picking out a way a horse can get through these down logs while you blaze the trail. Just then I heard the sharp ping of a spitzer as it went between me and a huge spruce with not a foot clearance. It struck Will in the back jsut over center of right lung. he gasped and doubled up and fell backwards. I dived on my nosebehind the spruce. Then I yelled to quit shooting, no answer after repeated yelling, so drew my heavy sixgun and fired three times in the air and yelled some more still no answer, then I saw red, and taking the Springfield off my back I turned the safety over and started a big circle on my belly in the dense snow brush being careful to not move any brush and worked around in behind of where that shot had come from. I knew who-ever fired it could not have been over sixty yards away on account of visibility. Then I spotted the brush moving and drew a bead on it intending to kill whoever emerged from said brush. DeYoung came out and I held my fired but yelled at him again and then when he saw me with rifle on him, he stopped and I told him he had shot Bill. He said no" and I walked up as he was in motion of shooting himself. Then he dropped the rifle and I made him go back with me only to find Will doubled up in the log jam. I did everything possible but he was barely alive then just gasping and eyes set. De Young did not seem to want to touch him so I gave him what first aid I could and tried to stop external hemorrhage. I asked DeYoung to go to camp and get Will's medicine kit, some food, blankets and a bottle of whiskey and bring Hart back with him and also an axe. Told him we could not dare move Will and would have to establish a camp over him right there. By this time it started raining and DeYoung said he could not go, so asked him to hold Will's head up level and do what he could for him and I would go.

I ran that three miles, first one without any trail, by running along a fallen log until I fell off in the swamp and thence on another log until I reached upper end of main trail. All the time I fired three shots at five minute intervals as near as I could tell from the sixgun.

When I arrived at Camp, Hart was calmly cooking supper and I asked him if he had not heard all my shots. He said yes but supposed you had all killed your elk and were celebrating. This made me mad and I told him plainly I never wasted ammunition especially in game country. Then I told him DeYoung had shot Will and even then it did not seem to me he showed much surprise. I grabbed medicine kit, whisket and blankets and an Axe and asked Hart to grab some food and more bedding and follow me. He said he couldnt make it back up there in the dark, so I left without him and ran the three miles back until I was certain I was close to where I had left Will and DeYoung. Then I shot the sixgun and Deyoung answered with his rifle. I soon found him then in the dark where he had built a big fire. When I asked how Will was, he answered he only lived a minute after you left, then I asked why he did not get his rifle and call me back and he did not answer. I asked him to help me get Will's body out of that log jam so I could wrap him up in the blankets but he said he could'nt. About an hour later Hart showed up with a flashlight, and I got him to hold the flashlight while I dragged Will's body out of the logs to a clear spot, removed his watch, rings, glasses and contents of pockets and straightened him out and wrapped him carefully in the blankets I had brought back.

His little belongings I tied up in my old silk neckerchief and later gave to Erma. Then Hart said we had just as well go back to camp as we could do nothing more for Will, and again I saw red and informed them both that no man left there that night alive, so they sat with me around the fire by Will's body. Hart either had mighty good control of himself or something as he did not seem shocked or surprised to me.

The rain turned to snow and we had over a foot by morning, so I covered Will as best I could and blazed a trail out from his body to the main trail and we went to camp and ate a big mulligan that Will had started the morning before he was killed. Dont think he ever had a chance after that shot as the 150 grain umbrella point and went square through right lung and hemmorrhage had done the rest. After breakfast I started hunting horses and finally found them ten miles below camp, working out on our back trail. Arrived back at Camp at 2 P.M. and Hart immediately said I will take the saddle horse and go down to Sullivans Cabin where there is a phone and also the McKinnon party should be out there by now and get help, then I will come back in morning. He left alright but never came back, simply telling the McKinnon party and asking them to help and then with the McKinnons he headed on for Ovando, a two day trip. McKinnons packer Earl Watts came back up the second day after Hart left bringing a little Doctor from Gt. Falls. and arrived after dark. The Day Hart left I took DeYoung back up the trail that evening after working all day packing elk to camp and we slept out in the snow

rage four Gen Strong.
with Will's body, and again the next night. Then Earl Watts and I
worked the biggest tallest pack animal we had in either string in
to where Will lay by cutting logs and jumping the horse over what
we could and managed to wrap Will's body in all the manties we had
and pack him out. It took about all the heart out of me. Watts
promised to take Wills body and extra horses and go straight through
to Ovando, while I gathered up all our camp and elk and moved down
to Sullivans Cabin, then joined up with Bailey the other McKinnon guide
and their cooknadn helped bring out both outfits. It snowed steadily
and we had over 30 head of horses to get over the divide before we
were snowed in and I broke snow in the trail right up to my belt
buckle. Took us three days to get out after getting everything moved
down to Sullivans cabin.

Hart went straight on to Helena from our camp fast as he could make it
and put piece in paper that Will was accidently shot, saying that
Will's rifle projected up over his back and he wore a buckskin shirt
and was mistaken for a bull elk. Will wore a buckskin shirt but his
model ' 95 Winchester carbine hung on his back by the sling with the
muzzle below the level of his shoulders. The Coroners inquest examined
DeYoung and I at Ovando and pronounced it an accident. I was another
week breaking trail over Priest Pass with my pack string long after all
traffic had stopped account the deep snow.

Before Hart left our main camp, I proposed that on getting home we
figure up total expenses of the trip and each pay one third of them
and say nothing to Erma of any expense whatever. They both agreed.
Soon as I got my pack string home tonthe ranch at Winston, I shaved
and cleaned up and saddled a fresh bronc and rode the 20 miles to
Helena to see Irma. Will had been buried some time by then and she
showed me a bill from H.L.Hart for Will's share of the expenses of
the trip. He had already sent me a bill and my Dad gave me a check
at Winston which I mailed to him that covered as near as I could
figure about half of the trip, but I paid it. Hart had even itemized
the bill and included $ 20. to Earl Watts for packing Will's body out.
As I remember her bill was around $ 80, and mine around $ 60. I told
her not to pay it, and I went to see DeYoung andtold him I would pay
half of bill sent Irma if he would pay other half and he agreed, but
the next time I came to Helena, Irma showed me a cancelled check she
had given Hart. Neither of them kept their word, so I took the matter
to the Masonic Lodge King Solomon, # 9 of which I was a member.

Next election Hart ran again for state treasurer but received but one
or two votes I was informed. You of course know Irma's baby was born
at seven months premature from the shock and was a tinly little
wreck until its death in a short time. I sold as many of Will's guns
for her as I could whenver I could find a buyer who would pay full
value

The trips and its trajedy are one of the blackest pages in my life
and had I known at the time what was to follow, am afraid I and Will's
body would have been all that would ever have come out of the So. Fork
that fall. Though I may be wrong, have never been able to reconcile mysel
on the accident angle, especially after what followed. I went to
Irma and offered to pay half of the bill Hart had sent her and told her
DeYoung had agreed to pay other half. She would not accept it from me
, saying you have already done more than your part. But DeYoung never
went near her nor paid as he agreed.

Page five General Strong.

Am Afriad General, this is a pretty gruesome tale, but it is the truth and as near exact as I now remember it over the years. I thought the world of Irma and Will and also your mother and many nights I stayed with your mother while Irma and Will went to some social function as she was afraid of being alone.

Years ago, I believe between 1927 and 1928 I wrote an article for the American Rifleman titled Look Before You Shoot and told the details of Wills death therin, when still fresh in my memory. Heard Hart and DeYoung at Helena branded me as a liar after it came out. You can look it up in back fiels of the American Rifleman.

Please pardon such a long winded epistle and the bum typeing, but have been away from my machine for 20 months an am very rusty on typeing. Should you ever get out this way would like very much to haveyou visit me if you can stand primitive ranch life. Best wishes believe me,

                                              Sincerely,
                                              Elmer Keith.

P.S. Am enclosing a snapshot of Will taken down at Presidio I think before he went to France. Have another he gave me so thought you might like this one. E.K.

OutDoorsMan
the Informative Magazine for Active Outdoorsmen

919 NORTH MICHIGAN AVENUE
CHICAGO

North Fork, Idaho
July 8th.

Mr. James Hedgecoke,
Amarillo, Texas.

Dear Jim:
Has been a long time since I was down there with Geo. Turner and you then owned the old Hoffman plant. A friend of mine had a double 303 British rifle rebored at your plant to take the 35 W.C.F and it came out wonderfully well. I would like to know if the men who did that job are still there, Polly or Dubiel whoever it was re-bored it as a friend has another that he wants recut to 35 W.C.F.

Incidentally, did you see the article on buffalo killing in the June Rifleman. It surely was a disgrace to the old timers as hat man Hunt surely gave them no credit either as to their ability as riflemen or their fine old long range Sharps rifles. From my own experience on all lesser game I still place the 45-120-550 Sharps in first place as a killer of all American made sporting ammunition and would someday like to try my 16 pound 45-120 on a goodbull buffalo. If you still have your herd and still have any old surplus bulls to be killed off each year or so, then I would very much like to some day drive down there and kill one with the old sharps with a clean lung shot. Like to do it in the winter when robe and head would be in best shape for a mount and a robe.

Someone told me you had sold the Hoffman plant and I have not seen anything in the way of adds since the war, but if you do ever open it up again or go into custom gun making, let me know and will do my best to help you put it over through answering the hundreds of magazine inquiries each month that I receive as Arms & Ammo ed. All best wishes belive me and be glad to hear from you when you have the time. Also let me know what has become of Geo. Turner, have not heard from him since he went into partnership with Ackley. I know Acklet, Too Well as I worked with him at Ogden Arsenal during the war.

Sincerely,
Elmer Keith.

Sixguns by Keith

Bob - Duplex loading seems to add nothing to the 33 calibers because they are not large enough except to give a softer and longer sustained recoil.

I have long used 60 grains 4350 behind the 250, 275 and 300 grain bullets in our three 333 O.K.H. rifles on the 06 case but the Belted version of the 333 O.K.H. will handle a few grains more powder. (63)

For the 334 O.K.H. I used 75 grains 4350 with 250 grain, 73 grains with 275 grain and 67 grains with the 300 grain.

Velocities with the 250 grain in the 333 O.K.H. run around 2600 to 2700 depending on barrel life, with 275 grain around 2500 and with 300 grain around 2400. Pressures must be around 43.000 to 50,000 pounds.

Velocities for the 334 O.K.H. made from the magnum case left full length run around 2350 for the 250 grain 2700 to 2750 for the 275 grain and around 2600 fet the 300 grain. All of them too high and too fast except for long range work as bullets tend to blow to atoms on impact. Nosler is supposed to bring us out a 250 grain and 300 grain this year and that would solve the blow up problem. Pressures are not over 43,000

These long heavy high scetional density slugs far outrange even the 375 magnum even though they do not start out so fast they lose velocity at a very slow rate and they have now killed about all species American game and most species of African game as well with solid and soft point bullets.

C.M.Oneil, Alberton, Montana makes the rifles and good ones though he does not go in for fancy work at all. The 333 O.K.H. dropped big Alaskan browies for us quicker than anything I have seen used except the 404 and 400 Jeffery.

Sincerely
Keith.

April 1956

NATIONAL RIFLE ASSOCIATION OF AMERICA
Publishers of THE AMERICAN RIFLEMAN

1600 Rhode Island Avenue, N. W. • Washington 6, D. C. • DIstrict 7-3412

April 13th -56

Mr. Bob Albrecht,
88 Welton St.,
New Brunswick, N.J.

Dear Bob:

→ Home at last from the Wash meetings and trying to catch up with letters that were piled high. Glad you like the * book and have to clean all the publishers mistakes out of the captions for next edition ere long as they say they will have to reprint this year as only printed 7500 copies that will be another chore as they surely messed up the captions and I sent them clean copy.

Your 9.3X 74 is a darn good rifle barrel for any game on this continent from deer to moose and grizzly and is but little short of the 375 magnum in killing power. Its a whale of a fine load and about the best rimcartridge we have short of the big Cordite loads.

I would be careful not to over Load the little 270 Mannlicher as they dont handle escaping gas worth a whoop but have the finest magazine in the world and are a swell little hunting rifle.

For deer, antelope and pests I would use different bullets the 100 and 130 grain for the vermin coyotes eagles chucks etc and the 150 grain for all meat aniamls or larger game shooting. I consider it a very good rifle for all the lighter big game up to and including the small barren ground caribou but do not think it near large enough for elk and the larger species and this from actual experience as lost four bull elk one fall for men I was guideing with broken shoulders and the little slug had broken up and never went on into chest on broadside shots.

For the 100 grain use 52 grains 4064 or 52 grains 4320. For the 130 grain use 47 grains 4064 or 50 grains 4320 and for the 150 grain for game shooting use 50 grains 4350. Hope to see you next year if I am still with the N.R.A.

Sincerely
Keith.

* "SIXGUNS"
by E. Keith

This service is one of the benefits of NRA membership. It is one more reason why every gun owner should belong to the NRA. Have you signed up a new member recently?

THE American Rifleman

1600 RHODE ISLAND AVENUE — WASHINGTON 6, D.C.

ELMER KEITH
Salmon, Idaho

July 5th

Dear Mr. Council:

The 44-40 cylinder is much thinner than the 44 Spl. as the 44-40 is a bottle neck case and is usually chambered excessively long in the body of the case so that the fired cases have very little neck left on them. This in turn means still further weakening of the cylinder. The best load I know of for the 44-40 revolver is around 18 grains Hercules 2400 powder with the 200 grain factory soft point bullet. My bullets in 44 caliber are designed for the 44 Spl and to seat and crimp right in it and as it is a much better revolver load than the 44-40 I never did try to redesign the slug for the latter. However your gun being in good shape I would say use 18 grains 2400 and the factory soft point bullet and you will have a very powerful accurate big load that will kill deer nicely if placed right.

You could fit a 44 Spl cylinder providing you barrel groove diamter is from .4265" to .4285" as most Colts go and make a 44 Spl out of it and use my heavy 44 Spl loads with Keith 250 or 235 grain hollow point or hollow base bullets and 18.5 grains Hercules 2400 powder. I would no advise trying to have the barrel and cylinder rebored to 45. The cylinder ould cbe rechambered for the 45 alright but the barrel I hardly think could be ever rebored as is too near the 45 caliber and you would have to fit a new 45 caliber barrel. Those shot cartridges are so short ranged I would no advise them in a sixgun, better to stick to slugs in my opinion and have shot many a big rattler with a sixgun and some of them from the hip and very fast as in one case I stepped on a big one all coiled up and scared the devil out of me in fact shot down through him as was at the heighth of my jump upwards an again as I landed on the ground and was not even conscious of having drawn the damn gun.

The shot loads would develop far less pressures than the factory bullet loads but the charge is so small and scatters so badly I would not recommend it. You can try it anyway by loading about 9 grains shotgun and a card wad or two and a charge of fine shot to the mouth of case leaving just room enough for another card wad and a good crimp, but results will be only at a very few feet range and you are better off with bullets.

Charley Ren once emptied Doc DuCombs K-22 into a big 8 foot diamond back that was coiled under our breakfast table down in Sonorra and only made him mad then grabbed my 357 S&W Mag and blew his head clean off with one of my 160 grain hollow points.

Sincerely
Keith.

PLEASE ADDRESS ALL QUESTIONS TO "DOPE BAG" NATIONAL RIFLE ASSOCIATION, 1600 RHODE ISLAND AVENUE N.W. WASHINGTON 6, D.C.
PUBLISHED MONTHLY BY THE NATIONAL RIFLE ASSOCIATION OF AMERICA

NATIONAL RIFLE ASSOCIATION OF AMERICA

Publishers of THE AMERICAN RIFLEMAN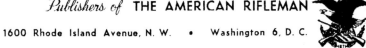

1600 Rhode Island Avenue, N. W. • Washington 6, D. C. DIstrict 7-3412

Aug 5th-56

Mr. C.E.Vest,
3025 E. Pinchot Ave.,
Phoenix, Ariz.

Dear Mr. Vest:

First, glad ypu like the Sixgun book and appreciate your opinion on it and you are not alone if I may judge from the hundreds of letters I have received already and from the way Stackpole tells me it has outsold all other gun books.

Col. Whelen always claimed Big Game Hunting was the best ever published on the subject and understand Outdoor Life Book Club is distributing or has done so 15,000 copies. They must have seen it the same as Whelen.

Just for jack shooring and target, not much use to change over to 44 magnum as the 357 and heav 38 Special loads will take care of all the john bunnies you want to shoot, but on a cougar or for deer or serious self defence work when the chips are down, then the 44 magnum if the feinest gun and load in existance and even better than my old heavy 44 Spl loads that were tops for over 25 years.

It despnds somewhat also on your temperament, if you like the big gun and can handle it as well or better. Ishoot better with the 44s than with the 38s , but can shoot any sixgun if it is accurate. I consider the Smith & Wesson 44 magnum in aclass by itself, the finest sixgun ever made and considerthe 44 magnum load in the same way. However this powerful load is not needed for any but long range, or game shooting of some big game or defense. You can of course get very fine accuracy from the 44 Specials in the 44 magnum. but they require a different sighting and shoot high and right in my gun when it is sighted for the big loads. I have the first one S & W made and friends have now bought two more in this little town and all are equally fine guns in every way. We tested one of the first of the heavy frame Rugers in 6½" barrel 44 mag about a month ago and returned it and I co sider it the finest single action yet produced by anyone and far ahead of any Colt. Trigger pull still needed improvement but the gun is a peach otherwise. Likewise I wanted Bosley hammer spur and wide trigger and may get them someday. From what I see of pressures of the fac ory 44 mag load I would not recommend rechambering any 44 Special to 44 magnum, as pressures must be around 40,000 to 42,000 from all indications. Great Western do chamber their S.A. For 44 mag withbtheir fine modern steels, but cylinder to short for reloads with my bullet.

Sincerely,
Keith

NATIONAL RIFLE ASSOCIATION OF AMERICA

Publishers of THE AMERICAN RIFLEMAN

1600 Rhode Island Avenue, N.W. • Washington 6, D.C. DIstrict 7-3412

Nov 6th-56

Mr. Ken H. Council,
7930 S.W. 36th St.,
Miami, Fla.

Dear Mr. Council:

A revolver bullet should upset to fill the chamber tjroats before entering the barrel throat. A gas check is to my notion all wrong in arevolver as it cannot be large enough to seal off the gas in cylinder without being so large as to distort the case when loaded. Many copies and changes have been engineered in my bullets awith no improvemnt and none sost as well as a hell of a lot of experiement went into my design. I want a plain cast bullet long enough for long bearing on rifling with wide enough bandsto hol rifling and that front b andout in front of the case full groove diamter to true up the cartridge in cylinder and cut downjukp to rifling and n o man or factory has ever produced anything more accurate than my design nor will they. The Remington factory bullet is not a gas check as advertised at all but apart jacket as itcovers whole base band and first grease groove andis very thin an deasily upsets to fill chamberthroats andoes a nice job and is only way so soft a bullet can shoot accurately at that velocity.

Hank Jenson and I have been shooting our 6½" 44 mags in S & W make for some timeon target and we fin dthem he finest target revolvers ever made and superior in accuracy t o any 38 Spl belive it or not.

Best bullets are my 250 grain solid or 235 grain hollow base or hollow point cast oneto 16 tin and lead and we size em .429 groove diater of our guns andload 5 grains Bullseye for a light load and 8.5 grains Unique for a medium o tdoor 50 yard load and 22 grains 2400 for a heavy load. the heavy load is still at least 5,000 pounds under the factory load and also slower in velocity but is a darn good load.

You can try my hollow base 235 grain or hollow point 235 grain to cut down weight but the long length and that wide forward band infront of case are mandatory for finest accuracy and the Thompson andothergas checks will never equal it. We get many one hole groups with 5 grains Bullsye at Hanks 45 ffot range off hand. Hank is an N.R.A. Director an our best small bore man in this country. I had a fight with Lyman to keep hert from changing front band on my bullet and making is smaller in diamter. Well I wantedit full groove diater to take the thrust of rifling whenn t hits the lands and that is why I designed it with those two forwardbands where most of stripping occurs in any revolver. Seven grains of No 6 is also a very accurate load for target. I dont agree with Lyman on a small front band at all.

Sincerely, Keith

Dope Bag — This service is one of the benefits of NRA membership. It is one more reason why every gun owner should belong to the NRA. Have you signed up a new member recently?

Guns

8150 NORTH CENTRAL PARK BOULEVARD • SKOKIE, ILLINOIS • ORCHARD 5-5(

RADIO & CABLE ADDRESS "VON ROSEN" CHICAGO

ELMER KEITH
Salmon, Idaho

Oct 5th-57.

Mr. Orin H. Council,
7930 S.W. 36th St.,
Miami, Fla.

Dear Mr. Council:

    I also found my bullet the most accurate of all in both 44 Spl and 44 mag. and the good Lord knows I done enough work to get the 44 mag or it would never have come into being but a lot of lads tried their best to discredit me but the truth will come put in time. Have had many reports on finest of all revolver accuracy from the 44 mag S & W even one hole 25 yard ten shot machine rest groups with my load of 250 grain Keith and 22 grains 2400. It beats anything I have shot as a target gun with same bullet and lighter powder load like 5 grains Bullseye or 8.5 grains Unique.

    Am sorry but can give you no dope at all on Hodgdons powder H-240 as never saw or used any of it, so you will have to write him for loads as I know nothing of its characteristics and tick to 2400 for all my heavy loads. Bullseye makes cheap loads alsomin 5 grain charges but of course is only a light gallery load with my 250 grain slug. I should think Hodgdons powder would work nicely at 2100 1200 feet but you would have to get pressures and loads from him.

    I hit that old board 4' X 8' target at 700 yards woth about all heavy sixguns and shot at it daily for some years HaroldCroft of Philly was out to Durkee Oregon and spent a full month with me shooting and witnessed it with 38/40 44/40. 45 colt and 44 Spl but the best work was done with the 44 Spl anz My ideal 429421 bullet and 12 grains No 80 all the heavy load powder we had at that time 1927 or 1928 as I remember. Think I also wrote this up in my big book Sixguns, that the Lyamn Ideal Hand Book on page 136 now credits to one Elmer Smith whoever he is.

    I found last fall that the 44 mag was more effective at beyond 600 yards on mu e deer than a 300 mag whose bullets would not openbat that range. The 44 mag is most accurate lon range sixgun I have ever used. See my article on reloading it in the Oct. issue of GUNS. Id rather havea good 44 mag than a dozen 30 carbines for any serious work and are also more accurate.

    44 Associates now defunct as an organization, Some friends in East started it ad several died during the war and have heard npthing more for years.

    Am now no longer with Rifle an and am Shooting Editor for this mag.

TARGET • HISTORIC
MILITARY • WESTERN
POLICE • HUNTING

8150 NORTH CENTRAL PARK BOULEVARD • SKOKIE, ILLINOIS • ORCHARD 5-5600

RADIO & CABLE ADDRESS "VON ROSEN" CHICAGO

Jan 16th-60

ELMER KEITH
Salmon, Idaho

Mr. Bob Albrecht,
88 Welton St.,
New Brunswick, N.J.

Dear Bob:

    Thanks for the clipping and dope on that killing in N.Y. A damn shame that good young cop was not carrying a 4" 44 mag S & W, and his killing is directly due to so many police Depts arming their men with inadequate toys when it comes to stopping a man who has went berserk.

    As you well know I have recommended 44 and 45 caliber gun for all police and peace officers for a great many years with the 357 Magnum the very minimum for the main armament and the little 38 Spls only for second hide out guns for emergency.

    I had another case brought to my attention from Roseburg Oregon where a lad put a 357 Western factory in a mans chest at 15 feet and stopped but did not knock him down then gave him one in stomach and he slowly went down, then the lad put the other four from the 357 Ruger into chest and stomach and not one single slug mushroomed or was deformed or went through the man and at this close range, factory loading.

    Unless this magazine sends me back wont see you at the N.R.A. Show and have had nothing on it so far. Best,

Sincerely,
Keith.

Oct 11th-60

ELMER KEITH
Salmon, Idaho

Mr. Kent Lomont,
4421 So. Wayne Ave.,
F rt Wayne, Ind.

Dear Mr. Lomont:
As I stated when I wrote up that 338-30 caliber those loads sounded fantastic to me and so they proved and I was quited in error as to any 3500 feet with 200 grain. Chronographed records prove you an get 300 to 33 0 with 150 grain and around 3150 to 3200 with 180 grain and 2950 to 3000 feet with 200 grain and around 2800 with 220 grain and that is it.

Your Spfld should be O.K. to convert. The dies are made by R.C.B.S Co. Oroville, Calif and you can resize and neck down fired cases in one stroke from 338 to 338-30 caliber. The faster you send any bullet the faster the barrel wears out and I would expect bot over 2000 rounds fine accuracy life from any load over 3000 feet and it may not go that. Have seen a 220 Swift well washed in throat with 700 rounds and Weathwrby 300 mags aboyt gone with 500 roubds in the throat. I= much prefer the original 338 to any necked downn30 caliber from that brass. You will have to write tha co in Prescott I l sted for prices in case they have changed. Marquart & forget the other name. I cannot supply loads as have no time to load my own most of the time.

Sincerely,
Keith.

Salmon, Idaho
Aug 26th-61.

Mr. Allen C. Lomont,
4421 So. Wayne Ave.,
Fort Wayne, Ind.

Dear Mr. Lomont:
        You can find exactly what you want in the Pahsimeroi valley and could camp up along the road through double springs pass.You may have to buy some kind of license to shoot in Idaho and they used to have a pest license but so many abused it they cut it out, but you can shoot all the jacks you want at long range in that country.

        Its some 50 to 75 miles above here and high and dry and open. You can shoot anything you want up there.

        I doubt if you ever get any load in the 357 and 44 Spl and Magnum that will beat my bullets properly loaded, not softer than one to 16 tin and lead as I put in a hell of a lot of work on them many years ago and they still have not been improved. Norma just sen me the best factory 357 load I have seen to date and they also make a darn good 44 mag load but my 250 grain cast hard and 22 grains 2400 beats em all on heavy game for penetration.

        B & L mounts with an aluminum tube scope not so hot nd you are getting thebusual. I would prefer Werver top Mounts or Buehler or Tilden or even Reffiled. The Williams however is a good sturdy mount and should take it indefinitely.Never shot the 200 grain 338 for trajectory and dont care for it too short and light. With the 300 grain and 69 grains 4831 sighted for 200 yards I got nine inch drop at 300 same as 180 gain 30-06 but their new 300 grain factory load is better bullet and s oud do better. I sighted one of my 338s with 275 grain Speer and 74 grains 4831. Had it three inc es high at 100 yards and was still four inches high at 200 and about on at 300.Think the new 300 grain Powr Point Winchester and 70 grains 4831 will be better load even than the factory load as they cliam but 2450 and you get 2669 with 75 grains 4831 and 275 grain Speer so think the 300 grain can easily give 2500 from 70 grains 4831.

        Tjis Jet most overrated ctg have used and dont like it. The gun S & W is a fine job but that damn tapered case sets back and ties p gun with every load. Fades out at long range and I can do better shooting any day with my 44 mags at any range. Half jackets no good for long range but Spert has a full jacket out just soft tip in front of case that shoots pretty good. I hold front sight up above top level of rea sigt and perch target on top front sight for long range. Have no use for either scope or peep on a sixgun.The Gun Reblue Co. Biltmore No. Car last ones to make my front sight, Tr them, Sincerely,eith

MAGAZINE 5959 HOLLYWOOD BOULEVARD, LOS ANGELES 28, CALIFORNIA • HOLLYWOOD 6-2111

ELMER KEITH
SHOOTING EDITOR

Salmon, Idaho
Nov 20th-61.

Mr. George B. Bredsten,
Draper Hall, Room 240B
6010 Jay St.,
Sacramento 19, Calif.

Dear Mr. Bredsten:

    I cannot agree with you on the 45 Colt with any safe loading being superior in power, range, accuracy or penetration to the 44 Spl with same 250 grain bullet and same powder charge which I worked up for both of 18.5 grains 2400.

    I can t ink of only one instance where the 45 Colt so loaded with Keith 250 grain and 18.5 grains 2400 would possibly be superior and that would be on a man at close range where the 45 would cut the larger hole and where bothhave more than enough penetration to go right through a man. That is the only place I can see where the 45 Colt would even equal the 44 Spl load with ame powder charge in its much smaller case. You do not get over 1100 feet from the 45 Colt load as against 1235 to 1250 feet for the 44 Spl. load. The 44 has much the better sectional density and penetrates deeper in shpoting big 2000 pound range bulls I found out, is much more accurate at any range than the 45 Colt and has it all over the 45 load at long range for bpth trajectory and accuracy.

    Using the pounds feet formulae for the two loads with the 45 Colt 250 grain at 1100 feet you get 37 pounds feet and with the 250 grain 44 Special at 1250 you get 44 pounds feet and that is about the way it compares on bulls or big game. If the 45 Colt could be loaded up to same velocity, it would equal the 44 Spl at close range but would lose out again at long range and might even beat the 44 at close range on a man where the larger bullet holes would be taken into effect.I proved all this to my own satisfaction a great many tears ago or I would still be using the 45 Colt. Trouble is cylinder walls are too thin and frame too small to take a proper load in the 45 andyou would haveto use 20 to 21 grains 2400 to equal the same velocotyh with same bullet weight in the 44 Spl.If you had the big Ruger Dragoon chambered and bored for the 45 Colt and used 20 to 21 grains 2400 or even 22 grains in it then you would getvresults superior to the 44 Spl but I doubt if they would even then beat the 44 magnum, as the larger the case the more powder necessary to give the same velocity of the same load in a smaller case. Likewise the larger the bullet the less sectional density in a given weight. Tyy it all out and I think you will find I am correct.

    As to that leading in the 357, Size buklets exact groove diamter and use Ballistic Lube made by J.M.Diebold, 11433 Partrudge Stn Coon Rapids Minn. Sincerely, Keith

GUNS & AMMO MAGAZINE • ELMER KEITH SHOOTING EDITOR | SALMON, IDAHO

June 26th 62,

Mr. George B Bredsten,
11155 Cypress Ave.,
Fontana, Calif,
Dear Mr. Bredsten:

    A one to 16 tin and lead mixture is about ashard as you can use and expect expansion even on deer, but a slight y harder bullet might give less leading tendency. I think if you clean with BoreKleen or Rices X-10 and X-20 that leading will be largely eli inted as those two with graphite soon im regante the steel until lead wont stock at all in all lead throwing guns.Adress Tom Rice,Palm Beach Fla, and H Tom Clllard, Box 3985, Detroit 27 for the Blu-Black outfit that sells the Bore-Kleen solvent,

    My bullet seems to work well through the carbine though you may have a little trouble chamberng first round unlessyou pull slide back and let go with a regulat spring tension,I have a hunch my bullet may work bette than factory in it as Ruger told me the throated the first ones long purposely to duplicate jump of bullet in revolvers and to my notion that is all wrong in rifles and now that they arecut ing short throats in the carbine they are getting much better groups ar und 3" at 10yard which is good enough.I gave my sons wife a remodelled and rebarrelled model 92 for the 44 mag for her deer hu ting in Oregon as they live at Roseburg,

    The 264 Winchester is a fine long range pest cartridge for coyotes eagles etc but I dont like it on game and if used on game should be Nosler bullet or Hor ady 160 grain with 57 grains 4831 with the 160 and around 60 grains with the 140 Nosl er, if we had a 160 Nosler would be far better load for the l ghter big game , should be a whiz on antelope however, but too small for elk and such game with any load unless placed just right,Your 44 mag carb ne o sixgun will take those deer n cely and you can eat right up to the bullet hole as I have been killing mine every fall w th 44 mag for some time now, big mule deer at that,I shoot deer to eat them not to blow em to hell with high velocity rifles if I can get close enough to use the sixgun and have killed two at 250 and 200 yards with the 4" S & W and several at shorter ranges withnit and the $6\frac{1}{2}$" S & W and he Rugers in 4 5/8 and $7\frac{1}{2}$"

    Glad you like the magazine and with the good staff we have think youbwill find its constantly improving, Best

Sincerely,
Keith

GUNS & AMMO HOME OFFICE: 5959 HOLLYWOOD BLVD., LOS ANGELES 28, CALIF.

GUNS & AMMO MAGAZINE • ELMER KEITH SHOOTING EDITOR | SALMON, IDAHO

Nov 22nd-62

Mr. George B. Bredstenm
Draper Hall,
Room 103A
6010 Jay St.,
Sacramento 19, Calif.

Dear Mr. Bredsten:

    I have heard nothing of this sixgun killing of elephant and it was not on our television programs.

    In the firstvplace killing elephants with a sixgun is some-thing in the nature of a stuht. George Neary Told me he was going to try it but I surmised he meant with a Ruger or Winchetser carbine and not a sixgun. I would like to know whether they took brain or heart shots as am doubtful of even my heavy loads reaching either brain or heart with a y certainty. He must have used my bullet cast hard of some mixture of tin and lead as it runs up to 250 grains and some moulds that are oversize could easi y cast one of 255 grains with soft metal, but how the devil he ever got any 2000 feet with that bullet weight is byond me and I would call that 2000 foot second statement a falsehood. No sixgun will stand the pressures necessary to send my bullet at much over 1400 to a possible 1500 feet. I use 22 grains 2400 and it goes 1400 or better from a 7½" Rger and will penetrate the thick hide and skull of huge hereford and Angus bulls alright but they are nothikng as compared to the skull of an elephant.It might get through to the brain from the side temple shot and also if poured right down the ear hole which is darn hard to locate exactly on a live elephant even at close range.If it will penetrate enough to go through heart they might have done it that way but I for one am skeptical and I designed the b llet and am responsible for both gu ns and loads for it.My 250 grain slug cast hard one to ten penetrates better and deeper in bulls heads than any factory load now made and have tried them all on bulls. However siad bullet must penetrate at least 18" to two feet of hide cellular bo e and hard bone to reach the brain unless sent down the ear hole and a man dont stand high enough to get the right angle. For a heart shot it would haveto penetrate around three feet of hide muscle and possible ribs to get to the heart. Id surely like to see the filmn on it.

    We had a wounded cow charge us a couple times while taking pictures of her wounded by natives in left temple and left hip, but I certainly would not want to stop here with a sixgun. I dont belive my bullet and best load would get through to the brain with any certainty but I may be wrong. In cutting o t my ivory killed with a 476 Westley It did not look like sixgun game to me.

                             Sincerely, Keith.

GUNS & AMMO HOME OFFICE: 5959 HOLLYWOOD BLVD., LOS ANGELES 28, CALIF.

GUNS & AMMO MAGAZINE • ELMER KEITH SHOOTING EDITOR | SALMON, IDAHO

Jan 16th-64.

Mr. Ken Lomont,
4421 So Wayne Ave.,
Fort Wayne, Ind.

Dear Lomont:
Glad to hear from you and also to get the targets from thos super accurate 8" S & W 44 mags. Your findings check with hundreds of onhers who also found my 250 grain bullet properly cast and sized and backed by 22 grains 2400 most accurate of all 44 mag ammo and will give longest barrel life as well. One outfit down in Florida wrote they had fired a great many ten shot groups at 25 yards, all just one ragged hole littlebigger than thebullet machine rest. Guess I designed even better than I lnkew back in 1927.

Air pockets in bullets caused by not fluxing metal enough or by moulds needing venting in my opinion. Also need the weight of plenty metal on the sprue hole to force all air out. Flux with lump tallow or beeswax every so foten and stir hell out of it and also check ,iulds may be trapped air and need some very fine cut vents near where air pockets occur be sure pot is full metal so weight will he p force all air out of moulds.

Cant figure your using 8" bbls for quick draw, go to 4" S & W for that job. Thos Jujuglars and other half jackets worthless and lead guns and never accurate. Fully jackted over bearing surface or my 250 grain slug only answer and I prefer my own bu let and 22 grains 2400 to anything. Wheel weights composition might be answer to air pockets. I like pure lead and tin best one to ten down to 1 to 16 for hollow points. Maybe your metal needs fluxing more often???. That or muld needs venting. Would be afraid of dunking ,ould in water, Might harden or shrink or change mould and damn dangerous if not throiyghly dry before using again.

I gave my 458 Alaskan to John Lawrnce in Africa. I used only 63 grains 3031 with 405 Winchester or 400 grain Barnes and think the 500 grain a bit too long and heavy for thse rifles and their actions that are supposed to be good pnly to 42,000 lbs.

For the 458 I think Hornady makes finest bullets of all both soft and solid. 460Weatherby very good if you want biggest possible 450. Get Iver Henriksen, 1211 So. 2nd St Missoula Mont to make it on brevex action or else a Wby rifle complete. Best case trimmer of all, is Trim-Mike Made by Micro-Precision Co. 2002 Burt St, Omaha 2m Nebr. Manybthanks for the pix of my living room and the guns, They are very good. Best for the new Year,

Sincerely,
Keith.

G&A MAGAZINE • ELMER KEITH, SHOOTING EDITOR | SALMON, IDAHO

Sept 8th-64

Mr. George B. Bredsten,
11155 Cypress Ave.,
Fontana, Calif.

Dear Mr. Bredsten:

The 4" and 4½" guns I have in S & W all cut my thumb with bottom cylinder latch so had the damn things ground off that is all the lower corner and on all three of my short S & W mags and also on my pair of 41 mags with 4" bbls. The long 6½" raises more in recoil and has never done this but the short guns drive straoght bacl in recoil and will cut groove in top side of my thumb so just had that corner eliminated as not needed anyway. Steve Herritt can make you some damn good reoswood or other stocks to fit uou hand and grinding off bpttom thar latch and polishikng will cure the trouble.

Wearherby romised to send me a 340 couple years ago but like a lot of his other ppomises never kepy so havehad no chnce to load for one However its just our old 334 O.K.H. with a shorter neck and larger powder capacity and .008" larger groove diameter. I used 73 grains 4350 in the 334 with 275 grain bullets by Speer and Barnes. In my two long magazine long throated mag muaser rifles with long throats I use the 275 grain speer and 76 grains 4831 and they will also handle the full case of 4831 or 77 grains nicely and also use 75 grains with the 300 grain Power po9nt Winchester wi h bases of bullets seated flush with base case neck. I would suggest the 275 Speer andthe 250 grain Nosler for your 340 Weatherby and you can start with 77 grains 4831 with either bullet and probably gp up to 78 or 80 graons.4831 is a s.ower better powder for them tghan the 4350 I had to use in our 334 O.K.H. My three 338s will all do under an inch at100 yds with Speer 275 and above loads. In the Olympian Browing can only use 74 grains account deep seating and the 275 grainbis heaviest this rifle w9th 12" twst will stabalize. The two mag mausers have ten inch twist. Think you will et best accuracy from the 275 Speer or the Winchester 300 grain Power po9 nt b t the Speer is much flatter at long range.

Soncerely,

Keith.

GUNS & AMMO MAGAZINE • ELMER KEITH SHOOTING EDITOR | SALMON, IDAHO

Jan 15th-65

Glad you like the book and will have another big book o t on rifles and big game hunting rhe middle of Feb as advertised in the Feb G & A.

For varmints and finishikng wounded big game the 41 mag would certainly be adequate and in fact is very little short of the 44 on killing power and is flatter in trajectory and seems tp penetrate just as well. However it is at its best with my 220 grain Keith bullet moulds by Hensley & Gibbs of SanDiego and Saeco of Pasadena, cat hard and sized .410" and loaded with 20 grains of 2400 with good crimp. This load beats the factory loads badly for penetration s I put one throygh a horse broadsde center of chest cavtity cutting rib on each side and threw up a hand full off mud on other side where it struck the sidehill. The factory 210 grain soft point lodged in off lung.I kike the 44 the best for my own use as want all the power I can get but the fact remains the 410" diamter against .429" is not much and ,y new bullet for the 41 has very good sectional density and peneyrates very well same as m 250 in the 44 but is flatter over long ranges. I would say get a 6" S & W 41 mag and think you will be happy with it, R.C.B.S. dies and Hensley & gibbs mould preferably and Saeco second choice, Saeco did not make front band quiet as wide as my specifications but H & G got it exactly right. I sold all my 357s but the first one given me by Doug Wesson when I worked with him on that load and Phil Sharpe claimed the credit for my work

You will have to ge5 a crimp die made for a very heavy crimp fpr shot loads, then load 5 grains B llseye and a slightly oversize card wad down on the powder tight and then all the 7½ to No 10 shot you can get in case of the 41 and a card wad on top with heavy enpugh crimp to hold it in place and best to drip some candle wax pver the top wad to seal ot for snakes. I never use shot in my guns preferring slugs and you can drop one in fast so long as is either under low or through a snake and he will instantly coil tghen you can take his had off with plenty of time at your disposal. A low shot thrpws dirt rocks mud or water on him and stings him and he will cpil, so I never monkey with shot in a sixgun but that is way to load them. Use 6 grains Bullsey in 44 mag and 6.5 in 45 Coit.   Sincerely, Keith

GUNS & AMMO MAGAZINE • ELMER KEITH SHOOTING EDITOR | SALMON, IDAHO

Feb 9th-65

      This is a good article except I do not agree with you on caliber and a 41 or 44 is a hell of a lot better for any big game shooting. Alsp for hol ow point use it is better to use a one to 16 tin and lead content that will expand but doesnot shatter as doe hard hollow point slugs.

      My 173 grain solid and 1 0 grain hollow point were designed for the 38 Spl and have to be crimped pver front band in the 357 Mag s7 W except their combat magnum and the Ruger will both take them properly crimped in regular crimp groove. They work well in the 357 in 38 Spl. Cases, Your case separations are due to headspace in that '92 rifle action and damn seldom occur in a sixgun where pressure throws them back against recoil plate. Most of this article covers about the same ground as I have for thirty years. It is a good artic l but where one editor dont need it another ight so you might try G & A with it or some of the other gun magazines.Guns may not want it because it is the op osite of their man and his half jacket bullets. Otherise it is about exactly as I have written for years.

      New book should be out in few days and you can get regular copy of Ken Bayless, Book Dept, Guns & Ammo or I will be able to furnish autographed copies spon as they send me a supply.

                                                  Sincerely,
                                                 Keith.

GUNS & AMMO HOME OFFICE: 5959 HOLLYWOOD BLVD., LOS ANGELES 28, CALIF.

GUNS & AMMO MAGAZINE • ELMER KEITH SHOOTING EDITOR | SALMON, IDAHO

March 20th-65

Mr. Ken Lomont,
4421 So. Wayne Ave.,
Fort Wayne, Inc.

Dear Ken:
Those are crazy small groups you shot with the SP-100 and sent them in for possible publication.

I have never had one of those replica Walkers for test so cant tell you anything about how accurate or longevity of the springs. Ooad same as my sixgun book and think the round ball on top of 60 grains FFG and a wad made by soaking an old and heavy felt hat in melted har tallow and then cutting wads, in top powder then the round ball seated down just below flush should be the load.

I have had lots of No 13 caps so they should be made by all soufces of supply including Remington. Best way to sig t the gun is wirh a small open dovetail in rear end of barrel and the regular or a new blade front sight . That damn notch in the hammer spur all too pften dont lone up at all or is off in elevation . Cant understand that one turn in 120 inches and should bot think accurate. The later Colts were cut with a gain twist and were very accurate with right load. Round ball always shot more accuratley for me than the conical bullets in all of them.

Think they have a special vermin licensein Idaho now but not sure and you may have to buy the high prices big gam license to shoot bear, Write Idaho Game Depy, Boise Idaho. They change laws so damn often cant keep track of them. The predators have cleaned up the jackrabbits and they arenow very scarce here but some down around Twin Falls and lots of chucks there also in t e snake canyon but only vermin left here in any numbers now. Wiol try get away for a day with you when you come o t maybe we can find somethong up Pahsimeroi that needs killing.

Bob Petersen our publisher got is record Polar bear wirh fibe shots in chest from the $6\frac{1}{2}$" S & W 44 mag and Norma spft point.

Idaho law says you have to have a hunting license to carry guns afield now. All the best and be seeing you. Have to leave for the N.R.A. convention next week at Wash.

Sincerely,
Keith.

MAGAZINE • ELMER KEITH SHOOTING EDITOR | SALMON, IDAHO

June 22nd-65

Mr. Chris Holman,
1135 Lynbrook Way,
San Jose 29, Calif.

Dear Mr. Holman:

    Often wondered what became of Capt Shank and those old Sharps I swapped him for a Govt. Sporter and some match ammo back in 1924. Wish I had those sharps now. Think you got the 45-70 with full length Cummins scope. I loaded 70 grains FFG and a card wad then a deer tallow wad about 1/8 inch thick and then the 420 grain paper patched bullet. That is the load used and wiped the barrel between shots after blowing my brath through the bore several times to moisten powder residue.

    Will be hom as far as I know when you get up this way. Been doing a lot of rifle testing latesly everything from 22s to 577-100-750. You might see my freind Steve Herritt at Twin Falls maybe he needs a machinist to keep his stocking tools in order.

    Please give Col. Shank my best and ask him to write once in awhile. I remember going over the range at Fort Harrison out of Heleba Mpntana shooting prone with sling and running it clean from 200, 300, 500, 600 and 1000 yards with that Sporter 30-06 Spfld he traded me. Fired ten shots at each range.

    Killed three bull elk with that rifle fall of 24 and found the 06 not so hot on elk so swpped it off and went back to my Sharps for a time for elk hunting until I got started with a 400 Whelen. Best,

Sincerely,
Keith

I see I did not write much better then than I do now.

Mr. Kent Lomont, Aug 12th-65
4421 South Wayne Ave,
Fort Wayne, Ind.

Dear Kent:

      Want to thank you for the slides and also the fine color prints of my present den and office. Could use more of these color prits of the den as these first that have been taken of it and you did real well.

      In all fast draw and hip shooting you will find if ypu lean into your target, focu your eyes on the target and throw your gun out at it exactly as you would point your finger you will make much smaller groups and hit from the hop a lpt more often than if you try tp do a back somersault to get your gun out as with butt to rear and shoot with gun alongisde hip. You should throw that gun at the target not hold it back at the hip if you want to hit anything and think the movies your Dad took of us working two guns at once will show you the correct stance and details.

      Had a good trip to Calif and got acquanited with our new Editor Mike Kesee and he is a real guy and one of the gang nd a shooter as well.Think the magazine will be even better now. Bob Petersen took us out on his yacht to Catalina and we had fun t ough fishing was lousy but Bob Speared an enormous shark that fouldd the rope from the spear head in the propeller and broke off.So we lost him. Rolled around on the ocean another day and noght after answering questions at the show for two days for albacore but did not get a bite myself though others caught 15 of them and I killed a couple sharks with sixgun.

      Looking for Wayne Leek of Remington their cheif desiger in Monday for few days so all for now as have a lot of letters still to write. Come see us again when you get out this way and in the meabtime get everyone to write in on these damn Dodd and Hickenlooper bills you can as we must lick that crazy deal.

Sincerely,
Keith

April 22nd-66

Capt. D.B.Wheeler Jr.
Speical Forces,
Box 334,
Claude,Texas, 79019

Dwar Caot Wheeler:

          The magazine had those knoves made to my design somewhere in Japan and gave the out as subscription premiums. They were not an exact copy but a half inch long and not as heavy as my original and I am not too sure of the steel. At any rate they gave the, all out and as far as I know no more re forthcoming as I think they cost far too much and the magazine lost money on the project.

          Those Gil Hibben knives are very expensive but also the best stell I have run into in an age and I belive worth their cost as you can have him make one exactly as you wish it and of any length weig t or shape which is something. My son was in Special forces for a time also a smkoke jumper in the Forest Service and I gave him one of those Jap made magazine knives and he likes it. You might write to Mike Keesee, editor of t is magazine and see if he can turn p one of those knóves for you or knows of one for sale. Best wishes,

Sincerely,
Keith.

GUNS & AMMO MAGAZINE • ELMER KEITH SHOOTING EDITOR | SALMON, IDAHO

Oct 31st-66

Mr. Ken Lomont,
Lomont Precision Bullets,
4421 So. Wayne Ave.,
FortWayne, Ind.

Dear Ken:
Never shoot until you are tried with any gun and your firing 500 to a 1000 44 mags a day is simply a damn fool endurance test and nver conductive to best work. I pack a gun all time and go for week or so many times wothout firing a shot and thebmaybe one or two at acat or flying bird or something and still keep my hand in. Like the plain clothes sxize grips best for my short fibgered heavy hands and no wood on back strap or behind trigger guard, except on little Chiefs spl. I too can shoot faster with 38 Spls than the 44s but you have movies I beliveof the poubding cans with two 44 mags at same time, and anyway why the hell shoot so fast with a 44 all you need is plant pne slug and look for another target for they dont need a barrage of 44s to stop a man like they do with little pip squeak 38s . You can recover from recoil whigle you are shifting to another target and one slug of my 250 grain at 1400 feet is enough for any man and most game if planted right.
Thought you would like Ed Bohlins fine gun belts and holsters, there are none better, Had an article in last Reloaded magazine on the 44 mags and also sold them one on the 41s. Best load I found for the 41s was 20 grains 2400 and my 220 grain H & G Bullet cast hard but Merrill of Merrill's reloading Service, Box 249, Libertyville, Ill likes 19 grains better and loads that for his cutomers. Jou can dind out which is best withn that fone pair of 41s with 8 3/8" bbls.
ou always have to hold up twice as much front sight with long barrels as with 4", account the longer sighting radius and the much letter angle when you hold up front sight over top rear sight. Guess freind Askins neverlearned to hlldup front sight or he would not have been using telephone poles as aiming points in his article debunking me in Shooting ti.mes in spite of his being natl champ at targets.I know I can make it damn uncomfortable for any man out to 600 yards with a 6 ½" S & W or 7½" Ruger 44 mag over dry dusty groundon still over cast day.I like the gold inserts better on front as so much more durable but red shows up better in some lights but damn plastic anyway.
Had a coronary the 31st Aug and in hospital on back 22 days and then mlnth home and just now getting on my feet.
obbered a very fat three yr old muley Sat with 338 at 250 yds with Nanacolas and Bob fraswr,They said they wanted a head shot o would not get their hands dirty dressing him so hit him in forehead and out between ears. 338 mag mauser 76 grains 4831 and 275 Speer resting over jeep hood.They di all the work for me and also got ,on on a noce two point so we have some meat hanging up to age and then into freezer for winter.
Send in arrucle to Mike Keesee our edotor for his perusal, Best,

MAGAZINE • ELMER KEITH SHOOTING EDITOR | SALMON, IDAHO

Jan 4th-67

Mr. Jack R. Tishue,
28 Vista Ave.,
Ferndale, Md. 21061.

Dear Mr. Tishue:

I have no record of y big game book being sold to or autographed to you or anyone in your vicinity so think must have been bought from some one else besides me. I keep a record of all and to whom sold and also autograph them to whoever buys them and have no record of such a sale. However if you will mail t to me with return postage will be happy to autograph it just as you wish and return.

    Dont have the address of the man who had a Rem rolling block made into a 450 Nitro-xpress not 475 butg he had new tool steel pins made and the firing pin bushed and said it handled the full British Cordite loads beautifully.

    Both Gollywood Guns shop and R.C.B.S. Oroville, Calif make excellent dies for all the bigBrit sh cartidges and Jack brickell, Oregon Ammunition Service Box19341, Portland Pregpn 97219 can furnish you loaded ammp and componenets ikn many sizes of the big British loads.

    Numrich has 45 cal ber barrels for these rifles and many parts as well.

    If I sold your book then I must have slipped as havent recorded it at all. but will sure autograph just as you wish so write it down on a slip and put ib front of the book. Get so many phone callsand callers etc I may have forgotten to autograph but have no recprd of the book.

                                                   Sincerely, Keith.

GUNS & AMMO MAGAZINE • ELMER KEITH SHOOTING EDITOR | SALMON, IDAHO

12th-72

    You got me wrong from that book Introduction, Am no kin whatever with Quantrell. Had an uncle who fought in Civil war Southern side, Oleander J Berry, who married Dads oldest sister. He was with Quantrell start of war said he found he was just a damn outlaw and quit hi and went to General Price and fought under him and was put out of commission at the battle of lexignton when rolling a cotton bale up to the fort which they took , he reached up over the bale to ram another ball down his old big bore Kentucky rifle which he used for sniping and a federal minne ball took him through roght arm breaking it and he was done for the duration. I am owever a deirect decendent on grand mother Keiths side from Capt Wm Calrk of the Lewis & Clark xpedition. Also Bill Keith an ancestor gave Gen Washington and his staff a dinner and toast in Madera wine the night beforethey forded the Delware, so guess am as much an amerixan as any but the indians'

    Iver Henriksen will make up my latest 338-74 Keith on this fine engraved Farquharson action.

    I dont want anythong to do with any bullet light than 250 grains in the 338 340 338-74 K and the 338-378 K.T. as that is light enough an not sodamn sure but the 275 Speer may even beat the 250Nosler for trajectory over 400 yds. Thos two are my bullets and ha e beennin correspondence with the head engineer of Sierra for a 250 or better a 275 B.T. match grade soft pount spitzer and they have invited me to see thm at the NRA convention and am also after Nosler to make a 300 grain 375 agaun.

    My son had tough luck several years with 358 Norma as those 250 grain steel jacket went through both elk and mule bucks broadside with no expansion, one elk and one deer he lost but gpt other two elk and several deer but that steel jacket too stoff as I wrote Sheldon of Norma and Ted finally sold the rile and I gave him my 340 Wby by Winslow which is a gol rifle as had another fine one from Wby with no free bore and premium Doug bbl and ten inch twist that shoots ingo one hole at 110 yds.

    Haveing ell of a winter and not enpuhgh big game left for seed and the winter will get most of them and the damn Game Comm sold us down the river with cheap out of state licenses and O'Connor fro, his latest blurb is as pp ular as a skunk at a wedding around here. Hope S & W gets your gun out soon. Best for the new year and maybe see you at Port and if tghey send me there.

                                                Ever, Elmer

Page two

Id prefer the Ruger with closed breech end instead of that hammer model myself.

My browning Olympian I measured and had 12" twist shot wonderfully well with 275 Speer and 74 grains 4831 C I mag but wou dnot stabalize the 300 grain and all tipped slightly at 100 yds and wortheless at long range went all over beyond 400 yds. Need 10" twist in all 340s and 338s.

The Remington action is long enough so you can have barrel throated to take ong seated bu let and I have two mausers with long mag actions, long throats and seat base bullets flush with base case neck and they handle 76 grains 483! and the 275 Speer perfect. You could have Iver Henriksen, 1211 So. nd St, Missoula, Montana who made my rifles make and fit his Premium Douvlas tube to your old model 70 if it is a mag action or to a Rem 700 and have same long bullet seating if throated for it as he did for me. He specializes on this caliber and is one of our best gunsmiths. Id have Iver rrbarrel that model 70 as cheapest and best bet but if you get a Browning you will have to stock with deep seating and 275 grain max bullet weight.
I dont have any use for those damn Western 44 mag loads way too heavy for any sicgun and I wont shoot em in my fine guns have even 44 mags three rugers and four S & W. in 44 mag.
Had two paid of those derringers two in 357 and two in 45 Colt and still have one but action too soft and goes haywire and wont recommend em better use a Chiefs S & W andbe sure of the damn thing firing anyway.

You sti 1 type better than I as I get going to fast and pile up tupe and big fingers never meant for this machine, wish I had one of the new ones that has old type on a cylinder as cpuld not get two letters on paper at same time MAYBE///???

Am damn sorry tomlearn of your accident but hope you can save enough of that hand to keep shooting and hope to see you both out here next summer. I am getting str nger daily but has been a long haul. Will be back to NSGA show at Chicago each day starts the 5th, maybe you can run over for it. "ere is to be at Navy Pier at least Sp Harm"illiams of Browning wrote me lately. All the best and better go light pressure on that Single shot 460 until you find what that action will take.

Sincerely,
Keith

Elmer

GUNS & AMMO MAGAZINE • ELMER KEITH SHOOTING EDITOR | SALMON, IDAHO

Feb 21st-67

Mr. Jack R. Tishue,
28 Vista Ave.,
Ferndale, Md. 21061.

Dear Mr Tishue:

    I Dont expect everyone to agree with me but it is funny how many who criticize me later and after more experience come around to my way of thinking.

    I have a supplyv of my Big Game Hunting book and can ship you one at once autographed to you on receipt of $ 12.50 prepaid to you .

Sincerely,
Keith.

Want this book

April 11th-67

Dear Ken:

Recei ed the 500 grain gas check bullets O.K. and they look very good to me. The factory 510 grain load goes only 2130 feet and wonder if I cannot get about same veloc ty and hold the rifling with these. Will find out when my new Champlin and Haski s rifle gets back from Enid OKLA I went down there and he ped this form design the most moder of all bolt rifles and the pulot ,odel we had up here shot under and inch at 100 yds with factory 510 grain soft nose. t has a 12 groove Sharon barrel and I belive will be best of my three 458s for use withn thesesl ugs. Going try it with 60btp 70 grains 3031 or 4895 and belive they will hold yhe rifling. Can run a wad down on top powder to further seal the gas.

How is that hand comibg by now, sure hope it dont handicap you too much. I am getting little stronger every day think and shooting nd fishing. Come o,t and we will do some more shooting this summer. ,agazine work has kept ,e too busy to get into any mischief lately but have fun fishing and testing new stuff right along. Recommended you to everal for bullets and will keep on doing so. I never get enough pix nd magazine wants more of me shooting, Do you have any of us at Bench rest or shooting sixguns?

Will let you know hwo the bog slugs go for accuracy when I get my rifle back as several things had to be corrected and they are going restock as got a damn castvin stock on it first which is all wrong for me. Best to you and your Dad,

As Always, Elmer

April 16th-67

Mr. Ken Lomont,
Lomont Precision Bullets,
4421 South Wayne Ave.,
Fort Wayne, Ind. 46806

Dear Ken:

You have a rifle for factory loads until such time as the Norma outfit put some brass in those case bodies. No fauly of the double rufle at all that I can see just lousy thin brass. I have some Remigton 45-70 not asbad as yours but had some head separations first firing in a good sound '96 Winchester with no headspace with 53 grains 3031 and the 405 grain soft point and this 45-70 brass like yours for the 9.3X 74, thin as paper.

Glad you are shooting again after that 450 Alaskan blow up. You will simply have to shoot those 9.3X 74 cases about twice and throw away.

I have some 9.3X 74 ammo on hand I paid a hell of a rpice for onee for a Farquharson that I sold, but dont know how good the brass and presume Berdan primers. I have two double rifles for the 400/360. a Best Westley and a Box lock Purdey and cases stand up well.

Briig that one out when you come but am sure is just brass trouble. Like to try some of your 500 grain hard cast gas check 458 bullets also as have three 458 Wibchesters now. that is rifles for that load a Super grade 70, a finemauser by Henriksen that cuts clover leaves at 100 yards and a new Champlin and Haskins rhat I did a lot of the design on that wlll be here shortly.

Phil Robinson had a point mould made for my 44 Spl and mag bullets cast the tip whole front end of pure lead then puts this in mould and casts one to ten tin and lead body around it and works and expands baeautifully and holds the rifleing and came out at 250 grains. Be fine for deer I think. All the best,

Sincerely,

Keith

GUNS & AMMO MAGAZINE • ELMER KEITH SHOOTING EDITOR | SALMON, IDAHO

May 24th-67

Mr. Ken Lomont,
Lomont Precision Bullets,
4421 South ayne Ave.,
Fort Wayne, Ind.

Dear Ken:
    Will try both the flat point 535 grain gas check and the 500 grain roundnnose in my 458 when Champlin & Haskins gets it back here/ It has a 12 groove sharon barrel with one tunr in 18" same as the old Sahrps 45-120-550 that used to sp n the 550 grain nice;y and still does so should andle t e, There was some tings not right on this first rifle and somehow they got it tsocked cast in so have to restock and then I wil ry 70grains 3031 and 4895, think can work up to that with thse bu lets if they dont lead and hold the twist O.K. If so can get some mighty good game killing loads and no barrel wear. Enclosing C & H folder.or brochure.
    If that flat point dont ypset to fill full length will be O.K. but if it does then will have to stock with the round nose and thing lynotype best for these gas checks anyway as they sure work in the 375 H & H with around 47 grains 3031.
    Ionce pyt 500 rounds of high speed through an aluminum Chiefs for Karl Hellstrom and an equal amount through a centennial hammerless 38 Spl theChiefs weighed 10½ ounces and I cpuld not fire over 50 rounds with eithr gun at a time and hand sores as hell after each but proved the guns could take factory high speed. Hellstrom gave me a fine 44 Spl 1950 4" target for the work. Put a bigger Herritt grip on the chiefs and then could use with comfort but no way for my big hand to grip that tiny Chiefs grip to keep it from poubding web of hand.
    Dont know where you could get once fired 10 mag cases unless from yhe ballistic lab atRemington where they no doubt have them from test firing.
    I used 52 grains Herco years ago but with only 2 oz of No 3 shot. A freind wroye he had a darn good load of 40 grains Unique and two ounces heavy shot with 60 pound wad pressure and also 38 grains Unique and 2 1/5 ounces No 3 and 6 pound wad pressure and said beat factory loads badly. That Ithaca over 400,000 has got to be a rechambered super ten as mine no 500,000 is first mag ten ever built and for old major Chas Askins and he sold iy to me when he got to old tonstand tsvrecoil.It has been my best shogtgun and still is for that matter. V.M.Starr, Eden So. Dak is best barrel man I know on these ten bores or other shot un chokes but he cusses me for sending him Mag ten people accou t therecoil.. Patterning mag tens comes under the heading of hard work. If t atvus a heavy frame Ithaca asmost tenswere should be O.K. anyway for the big load. Only trouble is the mag ten is or should be over bored and rechambering the older smallerbored ones gives more pressure and poorer patterns, most of the old guns over cboked for the big loads. Starr could probably rebore.

Page two.

Want you to take enpugh action shooting pix this summer to do the magazine for a year, They always want more pix and no one here can do proper job most of time.
First mag ten loads were 52 grains Herco and two ounces as I remember so they must have used a different lot of powder then that wasslower burning. Dont know when Reloader will run the 41 mag article and G & A has LaChuck to write on sixguns now I guess.
Brass cases are thinner and you nned oversize wads but they will develope less pressure than any typepaper or plastic cases in my opinjon. You have to watch out on all these mag tens other than Ithacas over 500,000 for if bore is saller and the real ones were all overbored so they are between 8 and ten gauge really about a 9 and of smallerbores then the loads right for the pver bored ones will be far too heavy in the rechambered superten of oH vintage.

Have noticed years ago about 35 to be exact that 44 apl loads with ,y bullets and No 80 powder built up pressure after being loaded a year and t ink it is as you say bullets getting harder and causing more resistance.There is a hell of a lit none of us know gyet about ammunition etc yet others burst out in print with no knowledge at all and tell you howto do everything.
Phil Robinson had Saecp make up a soft point mould for my 44 bu lets and casts the point of ure lead and then casts the one to ten tin andlead body around it and it works and makes a real soft point, same as we used to do years ago with 38-55 and 45-70. In 250 grain weight beive wil prove best deer bullet of all for th 44 magnums. I wrote it up for my column, but have written up a hell of a lot of stuff never used at all and yet they run stuff by men with little or no knowledge of their subject. Editor has to try select what he thinks readers will want and diversify it to try to please em all and I sure dont waay is job, as impossible to please em all.

We will fly down to Santa Ana Claif withSpeers for the Santa Ana Gun rolm show the 27t July and rest of time will be here far as I know. All the best and thanks for the bullets dont thibk will work too well in my 70 458 or my Premium Doug Barel 458 by Henriksen but this Cham 1in and Haskins 12 groove should handle t em perfect, will see.

Sincerely,
Keith

Elmer

July 12th-67

Mr. Ken Lomont,
4421 So. Wayne Ave,
Fort Wayne, Ind. 46807

Dear Ken:
Think you could best ship your gear out by Garrett Freight lines and they can hold itg here in theor big ware house for your arrival next year. Should be no problem at all renting a car or small truc for your trips. Jacks all gone from Pahsimeroi now but may come back some by then, eagles got last of them. Also had he 1 of inroad of coxes that did not help matters.

The C & H Keith grwade goes at $ 1000.00 and worth it and the Octagon bbl I figue heats up slower and better disperses heat than a round barrel and is as accurate or more so than any round to my notion and looks a hell of a lot nicer. Three of us fired three shot groups here withn the one pictured on the folder and Don Martin got his three in 9/16" center to center= widest holes at 100 Yards, I got mine in 3/4" center to center but magazin quoted mine group as 7/8. Brian Shanks got a 7/8" group center to center and t is in puffy wond so know she will shoot. Some little incidentals not right on this rifle so they have it back there and buioding me a new one. The new action made on the big precision tape mac ines and will be better than those they hogged out on their milling machines they tell me and wanted to build another one for me but that one shot like a house afire.

Les Bowman heard me tell some of the boys back at Remington that I was working with C & H on a new rifle so he hied himself down there and promoted himslef a rifle before I went down to work w h with them on this Keith grade. He had an article in July GUNSA, but guess my article in Aug G & A will give you the dope. Think you would like the 458 C & H even beter yhan the Wbys, I know I do and while Weather ys fine rifles at tikmes not in class with this one. Want to find put what the slugs you sent will do soon as get a rifle back here. Have my other two good 458s though and can work with them if can only get time but had lot of company and also Mike Keesee the editor was here and took pix till he ran out of filmn for future articles.

Hope the last operation will better that hand of yours so you can shoot, bug better use the right for the sixgun and save that left to support the rifle foreend from now on. You are doing good with that little chief. You can only demonstarte o the darn folls what a sixgun will do you cant tell then and half of tghem wont belive gheir eyes when you do make some long sh ts for them. All the best,

As Ever, Keith

Elmer

Sept 14th-67

Mr. J.P. Tishue Jr.,
28 Vista Ave.,
Ferndale,Glen Burnie, Md. 21061.

DearMr. Tishue:
           I agree with you on one th n the 358 Winchester
is a better deer gun than the 30-06 especially with 250 grain
bullet load. Hav ng killed my 47th elk for my own meat two years
ago p us a hell of a lpt of crips in 30 years guideing, plus
a couple hundred deer, I have my own ideas. Sure a high velocity
small bore that getsibto chest cavity or heart kills far quicker
than a big rifle with slow heavy bullet in same placemnt because
it simply explodes inside and also blood shots about half the meat
of the shlulders, while a big slow slig cuts celan nice wound channel
clear thro ugh and you have to wait for the animal to die of hemhorrage.
I have had them run 200 to 400 yards with a 350 grain 400 whelen
through behind shouldrrs, mule deer also a 45-70, but they wwre bled
out clean when I trailed them up and I could eat the bullet hole.
         Raking s ots however are a different story and a light
high vel bullet will /ften blow up in a ha, and never get into
the boiler room. Seven elk shot out of S elway lodge onr all with
a couple 264 Winchesters with 140 grain, all broadside shoulder
shots, all went down but all got up and got away with broken shou
lders and were never recovered in the maze of elk tracks. If you
want them to drop on the spot ypu have got to hiy brain or spine
and this goes for elkand deer both as well asbear.
          THe 333 O.K.H. is a ine cartridge and best to get the
barrel 338 now account bullets. Use with Winchester cases up to
60 grains 4350 with the 300 grain rpubd nose B rnes two diameter
or the 300 grainW nchester for elk and the samepowder charge works
well with the 250 Nosler or for an all around bullet the 275 Speer
This 06 case wont give as high vel as the 338 mag case which is just
our old 333 O.K.H. belted in .008" larger groove diamter and you
wont get as qucik expansion but it will work on all Amercan ga me
very nicely. However wrather than a reloading problem with 06 cases
I would suggest you ust get the rifle made up in 338 mag caliber
Get a Browning an old Model 70 inchester orbhave Iver Henriksen
1211 So. 2nd St. Missoula, Montana make you one on a mauser actipn
or whatever you have. Fpr the 338 use 74 grain 4831 behi d the
275 Speer and 75 grains behind the 250 Nosler and 70 grains behin
the 300 grain Wunchester bullts.
           For your wife if you want to get her a real gun better
do like my wife and get her a Model '99 Savage in 258 Win or
else the old light weight model 70. Rhis makes the best light
weight gun for a woman I know that is still adequate for all
species.My wife has the light weigytv70 and also a '99 new
model Savage and has clobbered her game with both and she is
also a small woman.I let her use only the 250 grain bullet load.

Page two.

The 44 mag either sixgun or carbine will kill elk nicely with braodside shots fairly high bebind the shouler buy dont expect them p go down right away as they can take two or three and stand around or run a good ways before they fill up with blood andgo down. I know one man who has killed some 25 or 30 with a 6½" S & W 44 mag but he is an old hunter fine shot and works in close andplants the 250 grain Keith bullet with 22 grains 2400 and gets the job done. If you freind wants to kil them quicker however and dont like recoil suggest e get a 358 Winchester with 250 grain load only same as your wife. The 350Rem with 250 is also adequate but I urded Re, to bring that rifle out in 358 Win isnated of they big short mag,Their cartridge is O.K. though of made up for a longer agazine rifle so you can seat the bullet out farther and about equa the 35vWhelen. or beat it.Best 44 mag caribe for accuracy is the Marlin 336 and have tested a lot of them. Have not had a '94 Win for test as still not in productio or on market. The 44 marlin s good if we had a heavier bullet. Hornady has just brought out a 265 grain but that is but lutrle better than the 240 grain, Use53 grains 3031 with this bullet for 2200 feet in the 444. It is a short ranged load and high trajectory and the 350 Winchester with 250 grain better if any considerable range in volved though the 444 better at up to 100 yards.
  Speer was working on a 340 grain bullet for the 44 and if he brings that wat would make a gun of it but dont like that short 240 grain pistol bullet in the big cartridge.
  Glen McFarland, Carmen, Idaho can give you as good an elk hunt as anyone and has a very good territory. Also Rolla Briggs, Box 91. Salmon, Idaho can fly you inyo th SelwayLodge where I hunted for years. McFarland has my old elk country here out of Salmon. Joe Scoble, also of Salmon can also give you a good elk hunt. You can write them for prices. Think I811 go put with McFarland or Briggs this fall. I wont recommend anything less than a 250 grain bullet nor 33 caliber for elk.

Sincerely,
Keith.

The 375 H & H is also a hell of a good all
ar/und rifle for everything as well as the 338.

Nov 11th-67

Mr. George Bredsten,
1527-V6 Wilder Ave.,
Honolulu, Hawaii, 96822

Dear Bredsten:
You have as good a police weapon as any man needs and the fact is the single action points better for any fast hip shooting than any other gun and also the five rounds are all that re needed in most gun fights if you plant them. Any single action man can get nfirst shot as fast with a S.A. as any gun and I belive I am still faster fo first shot with a S.A. draw and hit up to 15 yards. The only drawback isslower ewloading as any single action man can cock the gun as it raises in recoil and before it can be pulled down on target again. Some critics say you cant get n second shot fast enough and my answer is why the hell a second shot shlu d be needed if they use a gun an plant the f rst lne un less more than one man is shoot ng at you. I pack a 4" S & W 44 magwith my heavy loads and have for years. about only dvantage however is in six rounds and fastwr reloading.
The 44 mag 4 to 5". is best police weapin in world with my heavy 250 grain slug and it cus just as clean ahole as any wad cutter and carriedmore weight and shock. I have killed a hell of a lot of big game with the cartridge everything even elk and caribou and bear and found ut kil d better than th 308 or 30/-30 under 100 yards if planted in chest of an animal.
The 41 mag is next best in S & W and Ruger 4 5/8" as a peace officers weapon and Amarillo, San Francisco, Ventura Calif and many more cit es have now eent yl the 41 mag as standard polic weapon and all cities and sheriffs officees s uld adopt either it or the 44 mag and gi e them men the preferance of which they want to carry. t will take time but would save a ell of a lot of fine officers that are killed in kine of duty every year. I have had thousands of cases brought to my atten t ion over theyears where th 38 Sp failed miserably and often after a gun full of hits well placed athe officer still g t killed. Your outfit has th sense to er an officer use an adequate gun as the officer is always at a disadvantage and has t o take the second shot so to speak andmy sympathy s with tghem not the damn crooks. Have been an officer a ood part of my life.You cant go wrong on your selection and tha gun will rake a lut 1ore rounds than will the fine S & W and still stay in perfect shape. If you are used to a good gun stock to i n and it is just as good for uniformed wear as well to my notion. Bestwishes,

Sincerely,
Keith.

GUNS & AMMO MAGAZINE • ELMER KEITH, SHOOTING EDITOR | SALMON, IDAHO

Nov 12th-67

Dear Ken:

Thanks for your good letter and all the dope. Am writing up your mag results at 100 yds for my column. The 44 is tops and the 41 second and the 357 a poor third for accuracy is my findings also. 41 seems flatter over long ranges however.

Flared bases and too short bbl in the 357 is cause of its inaccuracy. Bullets have to be fired. Wife has one shoots good t close range but not so hot for any seruous work at any range so she keeps it under bed for possible social use. If you want to hit and kill game or ,an tghe the 41 and 44s are tops and the 44 best of all.

Tried the 500 a d 525 grains bullets with 60 grains 4895 in the C & H 458 and all t pped and shot allmover the paper will try agin and cut load down to 50 grains. Has 12 grooves and nkt very deep rifling as was rough but straight Sharon bbl and they lapped it. Will stay in a half inch at 100 yds with "em or Win factory 510 grain soft nose just curs clover leaves if held perfect, but only made onetest with 60 grains 4895 as dud not have tikme for more.

Remington took us up to Maine for seminar and as far as shootin concerned was a washout and we killed a frw scaups and merganswers only, Have to go to Rome italy and then Portugal on Wibchester seminar last of month and look for plenty bird shooting there on that trip should be back by Dec 10th, long trip this year

Killed elk 385 yards wit 458 and 510 grain soft nose rang post and cross wire both up over withers and held too high nd would have missed but he swung his head aroubd over withers just as rifle cracked and it took him back of neck andout throat 3/4" exit hole and severd spinal cord five nc es from skull. HVE TO GET A COUPlE bucks yet is fall. Hit the damn wrong kep and locked in capitals.

Hope that"ewmaun mag tne works out O K. never know. The choke all depnds on what the bore is behind it. My mag ten has had forcing cone all removed and tapered up barrel and just a shouder thickness of the case at front end chamber. Is over bored as they should be and dont know measurements inside as haveno way of getting them. Ten mag bore should be .775" and full choke .739" There were some ten mag ithacas advertised in Shot un news think one last issue so check that paper put every issue and y u can find an It aca but had letter from man in Canada with an Ithaca that g es 55 percent sonyou never know. Those rechambered tight 10 bore barrels for standard ten going less in kreo diameter dont handle the big load ri ht. V.M.Starr, Eden So. Dak best barrel man I know to make them shoot but he cusses me for sending people to him accunt recoil of the big guns when patterning. I found I needed 25 foot lead on mallards and geese at 80 yards. Looks like .360" best amoun of choke but every gun a law unto itself. I had mine double also and had to have second sera set harder, Best, ever Elmer

Dec 13th-67

Mr. Jack Tishue Jr.
28 Vista Ave ,
Fwrndale, Md. 21061.

Dear Mr. Tushue:
You seem to have aheard a great many lies about me by peop,e no doubt hwo never even seen me ket alone hubt with me. I quit quideing when I was 50 years young after 30 years to do somehunting on my own and beacuse was gettikng to old for thatracket. Have bugled up many elk but no elk hunter ever bugled me up. K lled one mule buck t 600 and several at 200 to 225 later w th 4" 44 magnu, and all before witnesses and a good many at close range with s ame and other sixguns.

The world is full of liars and we have a goo supply among Americas gun writers I have found alsd also many that will plagarize anathing you write.

The 50 grain bullet may be a bit short and light for the twist of your 300 Wby for best accuracy, You will have to c eck and find out 80 grains of 4350 is a very good load for it wiyh 150 grain bullets but if it is free bored am sure a longer bullet will give greater accuracy and I would prefer the 180 grain bullet with 78 grains 4350 or 81 grains 4831.

I have quit using 30 caliber rifles for most of my big game unting as I much prefer 338s and 340s for any long range ork even on deer as the heavy 250 and 275 grain bullets have a lot more killing pwwrr at at long range when I have to make such shots. est load for the 44 mag for me at least is 22 grains 2400 and my 25 grain bullet. It has killeda lot of deer and just slips throughbbjt if in lungs they soon stop and ble d out. You can also use same powder load with my 235 grain hollow point cast one to 16 tin and lead and get good expansion up tol 100 yards and this kills a lot quicker on side shots on deer. The Ruger 44 mag will stand mpre heavy loads and more abuse than any other sixgun ever made and is a darn good gun.

P.S. R.W.Thomson and Mrs Thomson witnessed the best long rang sixgub shooting I ever did both sitting and flying game with a 4" 44 mag. Ask him about it some ti me. His address is Colorado Sportsmans Center Woodbine, New Jersey.

Sincerely,
Keith.

Drc 14th-67

Dear Ken:

Got your copy of G & A for BigGame hunting off to you yesterday autograped to John Halter as requested. However they are $ 12.50 a copy instead of tn and y.u can send ,e the rest when you get the book or later.

Had good trip to Europe and some good fast and very tough wing shooting and am still t.red.fr m the t r p and a mountain of mail to get lut besides some rush articles as well so will have to cut this short. Will look for you out next summer but don't know ab ut using two to three dollar 577s on jacks, havent enough for that purpose. Have three 577s however.

My two 338 Browings both had 2" twist traded off first and still have the Olympic and it will do about 5/8" or less at times wi h 74 grains 4831 and the 275 Speer but tips all 300 grain even at 100 yards and the other one did also as they have a crazy 12" twist and should be ten inch. If that old 338 wont spin long bullets bet it has also quit grouping with short ones asthe long slugs have much the best chance of brging a shot out throat. Iver Henriksen, 1211 So. 2nd St. Missoula can rebarrel wi h fine barrels for ou.

Your 338 is certainly shooting and I have a very high regard for all Browning guns/Getting over the damn coronary. Best for the coming season and in haste,

As Ever,
Elmer

MAGAZINE • ELMER KEITH SHOOTING EDITOR | SALMON, IDAHO

Jan 18th-68

Mr. Jack R Tishue Jr.,
28 Vista Ave.,
Ferndale, Mr. 21061.

Dear Mr. Tishue:

You book was autographed and shipped back yesterday. I n.tice it arriezthat Edited and Re-Write by John Lachuck on front page hen t hat one armed bandit never wrote a single paragraph or edited a sentence of my work. "e and Bayless did mess up all the captions used lot pf pix I did not want in the book and turned down many I did want in it particularly of every game species. I never saw any galleys of he illustrations but cut ten pages of crap out of the text that LaChuck attemped to get printed and ride my name to fame. They pr mised to puy the sticker over this on every book as I have done on yours, but are no6 doing so and they wont pribt any more books by me on this kind of a deal. One of the most undercover stunts I ever had pulled on me.

Those new vibram soles I beliesthey are called are used in heavy cleated fom on their loggers and a smooth pattern on the best pil tanned packer shoes I designed for White . They make the best hunting boos I know of and I use their packer for all dry weatherhunting. These new soles badly wotwear leather and are good on rocks as well.

Have seen some of Biesens srocks and they loo ed goo but Henriksen told me he had one Biesen rifle in that he had to rebed before it would group at all, I know Gale & Skip Bartlett, 23004 West Lancaster Road, Lancaster, Calif and also Iver Henriksen 1211-So 2nd St, Missoula, Montana cant be beat on stocking anything and Iver s one of our best rifle makers and turns out tack hole jobs. Champlin & Haskins are bow usingShilen barrels andpraise them very highly, I havent seen one yet but will when I go dow to the Dallas gun show w th them in March. Circassian and French getting very hard to come by and Al Biesen may have some. Henriksen and Bartlett had hard time getting any suitable for fine stocks lately.

Sincerely,

Keith.

Jan 24th-68

Mr. Ken Lomont,
4421 So Wayne Ave.,
FortWayne, Ind. 46806

Dear Ken:
First the scope, be sure there is a gap between ends of the lock rings so screws set up tight, I have even dented these aluminum tubes with too much pressure. Clean all screws with alcohol or gas also scop tube and inside rings. then shellac the rings inside and also the tube at contact and it should stay put. When scope rings are a bit long and come togheter at ends I have used machinist tape aound the tube and then shellac and it has held for me. Also on a 458 Henriksen Mauser. Have had two 338 Brownings and both 12" tiwst should ha e neen 10 " as they both tipped the 300 grain at 100 yards and shot wildaas hell out at 500 but 275Speer and 74 grains 483k and CCI mag primers shoot wonderful one big hole at 100 yds and also out to extreme range, 275 about limit of the 12" twist Urged Brownikng to change to tne inch but no luck.

Long barrel sixguns often print different with different loads account longer barrel time and gun recoils up and back or down and back and bullet leaves muzzle at different point in vibration node and recoil becuse of different barrel ti,e that is length if time it takes to go through thetube. This is constant with nearly all long barrel guns as opposed to short barrelled sixg ns. The old 44 Spl seems to shoot different loads to same point of aim better than the 44 mag. The 6½" and 7½" shoot different loads to different places with same hold much more than the shoryer 4" guns has always been my experience. Also load variations show up more in different points of impact with long barrels than shott barrels due entirely ro rhe time element and position of muzzle with relation to target at time bullet emerges.

on huge bulls skulls my 250 grain hard cast solid penetrated more than ajy factory load including the Norma steel jaclet soft point when it centered back of brian it went on inyo the neck through hole in spinal cord back of skull. Winchester barely g t into brain and Remingto n always got ingo brain b/oth the lead gas check or part jacket and the soft point and Norma always got into brain but stopped there all expanded far more than my hard 250 grain which ust battered up nose a bit. On side brain shots went to hide on other side big bulls and never failed to dop em. Shot one 1800 lb bull in forehead with the damn S & W Jet. He just stood there then lowered his head and raised it three times, then shivered and fell on his nose. Gave him a 250 raun 44 to be sure and when we cut head apart found the 22 Jet had blown up in brain that is stoppedthere what was lfet fo it. Do t want any Jet for big game for my part. Traded the damn thing to Red Bell for an old '97 rench gun as blasted my ears every shot. Will be at the NSGA show and Stay at Joe Merril's in Libertuville, See you them, Best

Elmer

MAGAZINE • ELMER KEITH SHOOTING EDITOR | SALMON, IDAHO

Jan 30th-68

Mr. Jack R. Tishue,
28 Vista Ave.,
Ferndale Md. 21061

Dear Mr Tishue:
    I saw the bum write-up by Raffin in Rifleman. He had to try and find some fault and the silly ass does not know tghat shotgun ve ocities have changed very little in 40 years and I doubt if more than 4 feet difference in velocities of stand rd loads 6f 40 years ago and now. Also he seems tp think all old barns are sacred when ghey are fallong down all overmost of the country I have lived in and guess he is just a liuttle Brooklyn boy like Wally Howe that never grew up. Certainly he just sprouted his wings in the Rifleman staff.
    I cant find anything in the new Feb Issue of G & A that Ackley wrote ab/ut me or accused me of. I saw all I wanted of that lad at Pgden arsenal and went down to his shop ro kill him and would have done so if Karl Jugler had not grabbed the wrecked Enfield barrell swuhg to brain him w th. I know all abo/t the lad and willnpt be guilty of tellagg a lot of lies as he has about me everywhere he goes. He is not my idea of a man.He pulled every stunt in thebook on me at Ogdenarsenap and it apb back fired and he was fired from the job.
    I never recommended a 30 carbine for anyy ing larger than chucks and jacks while the 44 mag has proven a better killer on everything from elk to moose and big bear under 100 yards than the 30-30. Ack ey said a 45 auto was no good over 20 yards and arguments got so strong th Col has us out to the range and I emptied one at a small snow drift at 250 yards, going low first over second shot then next 5 in it and then another 7 shot clip all in the snow drift about one foot high and two feet long, then Asked Ackley to go lay down in the snow and let me shoot a clip at him. He dont tell these things that happened.
    Our Dup ex loads wwre origianlly one p wder but the tube fired the front end of charge. Later I did use slower powders forward and fasterin hell of case for even more velocity but patd was based on one powder. Your friend listened toF.C.Ness.
    You cannot beat a 338 or 375 H & H for an all around rifle butI wantg no dekicker or com ensators as most all of them throw the muzzle blast back in your ears and deafen yhou and Id far rathertake a little recoil than have my ears ruined.The 375 has same recoil as 12 bore duck load no more so why worry ab/ut it. I do it use any 30 caliber on game larger than 350 pounds and for elk will not hunt with less than 33 caliber nor less than 250 grain bullets and killed my 48th elk for mybown meat last fall with a 458 at 385 yards one shot. The 333 O.K.H. or the 338 O.K.H s a darn fine cartridge for everything and for your wife that and the little 358 is also a good ladies cartridges with 250 grain bullet.

                                            Sincerely, Keith.

GUNS & AMMO HOME OFFICE: 5959 HOLLYWOOD BLVD., LOS ANGELES 28, CALIF.

GUNS & AMMO MAGAZINE • ELMER KEITH SHOOTING EDITOR | SALMON, IDAHO

Feb 20th-68

Mr. JackR Tishue Jr.
28 Vista Ave.,
Ferndale, Maryland, 21061.

Dear Mr. Tishue:

You copy of the book is now autographed as you wished to Sgt Britt a d will be in the mail today. I also put a STCKER OVER THAT ONE ARMED BANDITS NAME John LaChuck who never re-wrote or edited a single paragraph in my book. He did try to inject ten pages of his crap in it that I could from the galleys but they never sent me any galleys of the illustrations nor front page no captions of illustration with the result they are badly mixed up and many photos of record species of big game I wanted published are not in the book but a lot of p ptos of my ugly mug loadings 577s that were not wantedor needed.

The 340 Weatherby is a darn goodlomg range catridge and better even than the 338 which is our old 333 O.K.H. .008" larger diameter bullet and the 340 Wby is our old 334 O.K.H. with slight shoulder change an shorter neak. It is the best long range cartridge short of our new 338-378 K.T. now being made by Champlin & Haskins as we necked down the 378 to 338 and I cut the shoulder back one fourth inch and also the case neck to bring it in line with bore capacity and we get 2008 to 2047 feet average with the varuous 250 grain bu lets and 2869 with 275 Speer nd 27590 with 300 Win power points all with pressures of around 54.500 PSI give or take a few feet and most uniform velocityies and pressures Bruce Hodgdon claims of any of our bog rifleloads he has chronographed.

All the alberta guides I knew havedied off and am not familiar with the present crop nor do I know who to send you to there.

Sincerely,
Keith.

GUNS & AMMO MAGAZINE • ELMER KEITH SHOOTING EDITOR | SALMON, IDAHO

March 1st-68

Mr. Jack R Tishue Jr.,
28 Vista Ave.,
Ferndale, Maryland. 21061.

Dear Mr. Tishue:

The Churchill is a fine gun have woned a couple of them. However the bottom flats of the barrels should be stamped for 70 grains Cordite and 480 grain Max if the 3¼" straight Cordite rifle and the o her rwo are the old black powder 450 and the 500/450 bottleneck now no longer made. If the rifle is for the straoght tap er 450 3¼" cordite and stamped for the 70 grain charge in good condition would be well worth the price but the black powder iles worth ess than half that andthe 500-450 b.ttle neck you would haveto make cases from 465s or 47s and then ream the necks thinner.

I have not had as good accuracy from the Ferlach over unders nd dont like an over under in a double rifle have to open them too wide and much prefer a good s de by side used English double also latter has better sights.

Bill Piznak and I designed that new BSA action a good many years back and write many length letters and made many drawings and we were to get one of each of the three length actions in complete rifles for our work but their representative wuit and went to Canada and I have never had one even for test. I do have a Sako 222 that looks like the action we diesigned for the BSA outfit so wonder if a copy or they had BSA make them. It is considered a very good rifle but I have had no experience with it as above stated in spite of helping design the darn gun. Should make you a good rifle and Iver Henriksen can stock it to suit but better buy a good French blank of Keith Steegall as Iver has been having trouhble getting fine wood lately.

Havent heard from DickSimmons in an age He was a sheriff in Wash. last I heard from him dont remember the town or county.

Sincerely,

Keith.

March 24th-68

Mr. Jack R. Tishue:Jr,
 28 Vista Ave.,
Ferndale, Md. 21061

Dear Mr, Tishue:

      Persuant your letter of the 15th and your phone call lately, I have no objection whatever to Winslow using the same pattern of checkering on your rifle as he used on mine, Up to them entirely. They make a beautiful rifle but all I have seen including mine I would li e better if they would make the small of stock much larger at least 5" in diameter as I hate these small springy skinny grips in back of action. Enclosing brochure and price list of the new Champlin& Haskins Keoth grade rifles I designed externally add they already had the best action I have eyet seen in a bolt gun. They are turning out beautiful rifles and if you get 340 Wby or our new 338-378 K.T. suggest 10" twist and np free bore and magazine and throat long enough to seat the 275 Speer bullet with base bullet flush with base of case neck and n.t driven down into powder chamber as is necessary woth many 340 Wby rifles. Its a hell of a good load for long range and only our 338-378 K.T. will beat it woth 250 grain at over 3000 feet and normal pressures.

                                            Sincerely,
                                            Keith.

GUNS & AMMO MAGAZINE • ELMER KEITH SHOOTING EDITOR | SALMON, IDAHO

July 8th-68

Mr. Jack R. Rishue, Jr.
28 Vista Ave.,
Ferndale, Md. 21061.

Dear Mr. Tishue:

You were very lucky to buy three old model 70s and in such a good all aroujnd caliber as 375 H & H. Four Alaskan Sourdoughs and I designed that old model 70 long agao and its still a good rifle, OnlyChamp;lin and Haskins action beats it to my notion.

We just got home crouple days ago from the Winchester Buffal Bill; celebration and corner stone laying at Cody Wyo and have a raft of mail piled up and so darn many callers the last three days have to write in early mornongs.

No-shok pad are good and I used them for years but Frank Pachmayr has out an even better solid pad now in different colors as well and C amplin & haskins are using t em exclusively Clayton Nelson their foreman delivered a new 338-378 K.T. to me yesterday and its a beauty and all to my design.

Will be here as far as I know last of August so drop in if you get out this way. Cant agtee with either of the Askins families on their writing on sixguns lately, they seem both to have gone small bore 9 ,M or under and harlie even stated in print that the 41 mag had doed a borni ng, when facts are that both Remingto on ammo and S & W on the guns have been badly back or ered since the 41 ma s inception.

No darn muzzle braks for me as they wi l ruin your ears and Id rather take the recoil of a rifle than have my ears pinned back every shot until the hurt for weeks and I cant hunt with my ears plugged.

There is only some five to ten percent pf cummounits in our top bracket in Govt trying to push these anti gun laws down our necks and if every jothers son who shoots will fi ht them at every opportunity we can lick them and also vote them out this fall and that goes for a lot pf our fat tailed congressmen as well.

Sincerely,
Keith.

Aug 2nd-68

Dear Ken:

Would like a bunch of glossy black and white prints of the double rifles and the Champlin & Haskins rifles, soon as can get them as need them for my African book to illustrate the rifle chapter. Truman Fowler is g/ing tg. publish it and we are adding final touches to being it up to date.

If you took any of my african game heads that would also help to illustrate it.

Been so darn busy since you were here havent had time for any shooting. We broke up and toom the huge old coa; stoker furnace out of basemenn and put in an electirc furnace humidifier and electric air cleaner so am done heaving 13 tons coal every winter.

Hope you folks had good and safe trip back and looks like we got some of rhe anti gun crowd licked but imagine all the damn rms companies advocating xagixix stopping mail order sales all long guns and advocating re istering gun owners and Win, Ruger, Rem, Hi-Standard and Colt all went in on it, the damn fools . They cant seem to realize its ure communism at work. So we will have bigger fight next year looks like.

Pictures should be 5X 7" and be gladto pay for them as need those C & H and double rifle pix bad. My 338-378 K.T. will do about 5/8" at 110 yards wimh 275 Speer and 99 grains 4831 load I sho in it last. Ken uou better sell off some lesser guns and have them build you a Keimh grade ib whatever caliber you want 338 375 H & H or 458. They are now making worlds finest bolt action rifles of that I am sure. All the best and must get back on this pile of gun inquiries,

As Ever, Elmer

Elmer

GUNS & AMMO MAGAZINE • ELMER KEITH SHOOTING EDITOR | SALMON, IDAHO

Aug 16th-68

Dear Ken:

Sure want to thabk you for thie pix. However I need some black and white of the double rifles assembled as we took a bunch ut dont know if were color or black and white but need some in B & W of the double rifles alone. The three cased ones came put good and need cpuple more of the 375 H & H outfit.

Want these for the book and coule use some more prints of the 338-378 and 458 laying on the bear head alone and that one shot of the two rifles and knoves from above asthat is very good.

Guess you folks got home all O.K. and only wish I had hadmore time with you also I was under the weather a bit when you were here from kidney stones.

My 338-378 will hit end of a cigar every time at 110 yds same as the 458 C & H rifles and think you would do well to sell some lesser guns and have the build you a keith grade in 338, 340 Wby or 338-378 K.T. for your all aro nd long range rifle for all of the game on this continent. Believe ot is the est holt action rifle yet produced even if I did design all but the action. and the shotgun safety and extended tangs top and bottom also my design. Am going to hunt with the 338-378 K.T? this fall.

Got my electirc furnace in and star ed it up yesterday as has been cold and raining to beat hell for three days and sure orks fine and wont ave all the dirst from burning 13 tons slack coal this winter.

See they finally run the wite-up on your 450 Alaskan blow up in last siisue. I had quiate an argu,ent with Joyce Hornady on this and his 265 grain 444 Marlin bullet and he even drove bullet down on primed cases and sent them to me and could not ignit primer but I think he will sooner or later get one to blow up also as his soft point is so small contact cap direct only. I know damn well I wont load andof them and that 444 is going be a joke anyway if the dont cut it with a 20" twist and use a 350 grain slug at 2000 instead of that crazy 240 grain at 2400. I notice many game head pix were taken too close and corpped horns etc and also see that you should have had ladeer and g itgen upl level with them. This photography is a busjness all is own and a dan tricky one. Our best yo you all and hope you can make it out next year as I am seeong a good any young jac s lately but wont shoot em want em to increase and come back and maybe by next year we will have them in numbers again without hunting for them.

As Always,
Elmer

GUNS & AMMO HOME OFFICE: 5959 HOLLYWOOD BLVD., LOS ANGELES 28, CALIF.

GUNS & AMMO MAGAZINE • ELMER KEITH SHOOTING EDITOR | SALMON, IDAHO

Box 1071

Aug 16th-68

Mr. C.K. Carroll,
1910 West 1st Ave.,
Cplumbus, Ohio, 12.

Dear Mr. Carroll

      Capt A.B. Hardy bow long gone designed that uttle tab of leather for the firing pin of the S.A.Colt sixgun. I designed No 34 and No 120 holsters for George Lawrence. You can take a piece of not too thick leather and cut it to the width of the hammer cut in back of the S.A.Colt frame and either sew or rivet one end to the front of the holster on the outside, then bend it over and slip the gun in holster cocked and mark where the hole should be and punch with leather punch and thus put this safety strap on any open top S.A.Colt holster. It holds the gun in the holster until the coking motion is started and needs no retraction spring as with Bohlin straps over hammer spur, as it simply clear the gun as that tapered S.A.Firing pin retracts from the hole and it is then s afe to carry six rounds in the old gun and a method I used for years.

      Hpwever dont you realize S.A.Colts are now obsolete, Read Askins in the September issue of G & A. Also all revolvers according to Sr. and Jr. Askins now obsolete .I thank a damn lot of peace officers and oshers as well will notg buy this tripe on a 9 M M auto being the only hand gun for game or defense useage. Guess the edotor run this to stir up controversy, can see no other reaso and I would have thrown that article in the basket. No hand gun points as well from the hip or is any faster to get in action for the first shot than the S.A.Colt and Ruger sdngle action and any test by competent single action men will demonstarte this fact. Hpwever guess we are all old foggies now according to these late Askins artucles. Get a Lawrence 120 Keith Holstwr and add that safety strap yourself is easy done.

      Bpth Colt and Ruger single actions veru popular here and in most of the country, The S & W double action 41 and 44 mags superior for officer use for one reason only andthat is the speed of emptyingvthe emptues and reloadng the gun. In a gun fight you only need one slug for each oppanent if you use a gun instead of a 38 or 9 M M pop gun and you have p,enty ti me to cokk the gun again as you return it from recoil. The hammer sipply slips down under the thumb asthe gun recoils.

      Any outfit jumping civilians as you experience would not live long in my town I can assure you, and you folks back there better go heeled regardless of the law. The overall picture of all this anti-gun crowd and their legislation is simply communism and their united and well paid efforts to disarm America, create racial trouble scatter our forces all overthe earth and ultimately to come in with bombs and paratropps and take over this country. Crime is worst where gun laws are most in vogue. What we need is to arm every citizen and teach them to shoot and crime would practically dissapear over night. Best

                                              Sincerely, Keith

 MAGAZINE • ELMER KEITH SHOOTING EDITOR | SALMON, IDAHO

Aug 16th-68

   Agree with you 100% on these samll calibers on big game. The two small bore addicts you refer to are both probe to both falsify and exaggerate. I sent O'Con mor and Doc DuComb of Carlyle Ill on a hunt with Westley Brown in B.C. years ago and bpth Doc and Westley wrote me of the two of them Oconnor and Doc putting 17 rounds from their 270 and Docs 30-06 in one small black bear before he expired and when I brought it up to O'Conjor he said was a damn lie so I asked him if he considered Doctor Ducomb and Wes Brown liars and he walked off.

   In 30 years guideng I have seen so many cases just like those you descrive that it is sickening. Eveb the best 30 calibers fail all to often at ranges over 300 yards for me and I now hunt prac ically all my american game with nothing less than the 333 O.K.H. 338 334 O.K.Y and the 340 Wby and will now use the 338-378 K?T. from now on. I found long ago that a 250 to 275 grain 33 caliber slug was much more reliable on anything at any range than any possible load from the small bores and very often wasted less meat. I dont agree with either of the gentlemen on anything and after O'cpnnor turned a dman auto lpaded shotgun on me while he cjacked oit a shell a d let it go back to battery whule turnedon me three times I want nothing to do with either or ever to shoot with either of them if I can get out of it. They dpnt add up in my catalogue and from what a bunch of Wyo guides told me at the Winchester Buffalo Bill ceremony at Cody this July I guess a lpt more have the same ideas as I have come to.

   That Norma 240 grain 44 mag will penetrate but expands less on contact with game than any of the other available soft poins and the Remington next and the hollow soft point winchester expands he fastest. You simply did not get that bear through lungs and I'll bet bullet hit slightly off center and w ent between rib cage and the shoulder. I did same thing in Alaska with 300 H & H mag 220 grain Norma and chaeed that grizzly three miles and hit 7 out of eleven and then the guide finally finshed with two sixgun slugs at close range. Have seen 270s go between shoulder and rib cage and game get away for a tikme several times.

   We had a 264 at Selway Lodge one fall and 7 elk hit in shoulder braodside with factory 140 grain all got away andnone recovered, Some elk gun d say. Sid Hinkle who ran the lodge calls it a squirrel gun and he is abo ut right. I have three 7 M M Mags 4 300 Mags and yet for some tkme now have done all my hunting with 338 whish is our old 333 O.K.H. Belted with .008" larger bullet and rhe 340 Wby which again is our old 334 O.K.H. wit larger bullet and

GUNS & AMMO MAGAZINE • ELMER KEITH, SHOOTING EDITOR | SALMON, IDAHO

Aug. 22nd-68

Dear Ken:

Received the batch of color prints and the congressional record on these crazy anti gun sermons. O.K. Many thanks and you will get the first copy of the African book I get my hands on. We hope to get it out in time for Xmas sales. Sent the best of the double rifle pix on down to Truman to put in the book a d need more especially B & W and Color of the double rifles and actions and would like couple more of that 375 H & H in its case. That is a good shot. We are planning on a lot of color pix in this book. No use printing up any but the best shots however. The best of the Champlin & Haskins rifles is with me holding them and the olne flat pix of the twp on he bear with my three Draper knoves between them The pne taken from one end of the rifles not worth printing, but the other is a peach also those of the guns laying on the polar bear head.

Your tests with the 41 mags proves outmy 220 grain bullet same as your 44 mag tests have long proven mu 259 grain the most accurate. Cannot expect to get the finest accuracy from the soft tip two piece cast bullet in soft point unless it was swaiged and cant be donw ith grooved bullets very well.

Think if cast bullets dont upsetvin cylinder throats, they should be near a snug fit there but the throats have to be small enough to be in some relation to tghe groove diameter. That is trouble with most 357 and 38 colts damn groove diamter is usually .354" and cylinder throats .360" and that simply wont work for fine accuracy. If you 44 mags have .430" barrels groove diameter and your cylinder throats around .431 to.432" you might get even better accuracy with a .430" sizeing than 429".

My Browning Olym ian does one big hole group at 110 yds with 74 grains 4831, CCi mag primer and 275 Speer. Brownings are always darn fine rifles. For some reason my 160 grain hollow oint 38 has slightly outshpt the 173 grain solid. Most accurate 38 Spl load in any 357 that I have tried was these bullets and 13.5 grains 2400 in 38 Spl cases with proper crimp and is only bullet that wi l shoot frm 38 Spl cases in the 357s. That load badly beat the first 357 factory loads for accuracy when I testedone of the first guns way back in late 30s.

In that 44 Spl you can use the cut down mag brass with around 17 grains 2400 and should do O.K. very accurate with my 250 grain.

Your Ind Rep is a darn good man butg this govt is loaded with Russian commies make no mistake on that score or else they would not foster these crazy abti-gun laws Hope you land the arco job and we can do some shooting together then, also hunting. That was commy work loading those guns at the show. Thin the Check invasion will cool poff a lot of the doves in the demos. Unless Nixon and Wallace get their heads together may go to the house for presidential selection. Best and send the double rifle photos soon as you get them.

As Ever, Elmer

Elmer

GUNS & AMMO HOME OFFICE: 5959 HOLLYWOOD BLVD., LOS ANGELES 28, CALIF.

Sept 19th-68

Dear Ken:

The gun pix were just what I needed and have sent them on to Fowler for inclusion in the book and he hopes to get it in the printers hands very soon. Want to thank you and Dad for them and will get a copy of the book to you soon as they are out. He plans on abput 40 pages of B & W and full color in it at least.

Wall they put over the long arms on their damn restrictive anti-gun law. In my opinion they should have put a very high prohibitive tariff on all imported arms under $ 50. value and would have done a lot more good than any anti-gun law.

Read the Oct issue of G &A my column and let the edotor knww what you think ofit good or bad. Johnsons outfit will now probably put me on the FBI most wanted list but if the shoe fots them let them wear it.

See a senseless elk rifle article on same issue, bet that lad has killed all of two or three elk in his life so knows all the answers. Have a batch of letters to get out this morn and the grouse season opens Sat and want to give the dogs some exercise and also eat some fried chcicken for a change, so all for now but keep in touch. Have a letter here now wanting some 44 and 41 and 357 mag ammo loaded so will refer him to you from Bob Newsom , Box 607, Columbia, Miss. Our best to all,

As Always, Elmer

Elmer

GUNS & AMMO HOME OFFICE: 5959 HOLLYWOOD BLVD., LOS ANGELES 28, CALIF.

GUNS & AMMO MAGAZINE • ELMER KEITH SHOOTING EDITOR | SALMON, IDAHO

Oct 9th-68

Mr. Jack R. Tishue Jr.,
28 Vista Ave.,
Ferndale, Md. 21061.

Dear Mr. Tishue:

Our 285 O.K.H. was on the 06 case and with 55 grains 4350 in Duplex teubed case with 180 grain Western Tool & Copper Wks. Bullet that I designed gave just .5" midway trajectory at 200 yards over a 400 yard range as against 7½" fpr the Western 1,0 grain B.T. factory loaded 300 H & H magnum and a flat base bullet in the 180 grain 285 O.K.H. Then on steel plate the 300 magnum went three foruths way through at 20 yards and the 285 O.K.H. load blew a big cork out of the 5/8" plate and at 50 yards he 285 O.K H. Duplex 180 grain flat base still blew corks right out of the plate and the 180 grain 300 H & H Western boat tail load only went half way through. Figure it out whether I or the famn NRA
staff is correct.
The shoulder shot just as freind ryalor syasis most deadly of all broadside body shots but also s;9ils some meat, but of no pnsequence in africa, here on deer or elk , prefer to stay off the good shoulder meat but inafrica shoot for center of hsoulder in line with spineveer time if you can get that shot.
Best 375 H & H load I know is 37 grains 4831 with mag primer that gies according to Hodgdon 2649 feet and nosler bullet preferred if you can find any now and the other 300 grains wil do with same load.
My Big Game hunting is now off the market and have about a dozen copies left and that will be all and Rifle for large game now brings $ 75. a copy if you can find one of the 2000 printed.
I have a shipment of Sixgunsprmised to be shipped the 9th today by Stackpole but they have made promises before and tried to farm this book out and only printed 1000 of this third edition and price has been raised to $ 12.95. That small edition wont last six months as I have twelve paid orders on hand now waiting their shipments arrival that they poomised a mobth ago. If you want a copy Sixguns better grab on of these.
I have been Western Agent for White Hubters Ltd Africa since 1957 and know it is one of the finest outfits in Africa. Enclosed is their brochure and Price list. I get ten percent on booking and price just the same to client whether he books direct or with me. They can give you as good a hunt as anyone and if you book well in advance they may be cable to come up with a rhinp license from the Gam dept to kill one that is causing native trouble. Be glad to book you up but suggest you book at least six months in advance as they are pretty well filled most of the time with european hunters as well as from the sites, Best
We require one foruth down.   Sincerely, Keith

GUNS & AMMO MAGAZINE • ELMER KEITH SHOOTING EDITOR | SALMON, IDAHO

Dec 13th-68

Postmaster,
Claims & Inquiry,
Baltomore. Md. 21233

Gentlemen:

The enclosed addressed piece of paper you returned was the outer cover or shell of a regular book card board box and I shipped JoanV ishue a copy of my $ 12.95 book Sixguns in it.Somwpne in t e postal service evidentlu swiped this book and how the mana ed to peel the outer covering from the box is beyond me
 The boom is a large one later than this sheet of paper an the box had ends that folded over several ti,es to prevent damage and they even left some of the taperwith which I tapped the open end of the box closed after folding the heavy card board to form an end cushion.

I have shipped hundreds of these books but this is the first one to go astray in the U.S. I wish you would write or call Mrs.Tishue there and see if he seceived the book and som one peeled and returned this wapp er to the P.O. The box qas ovwr an inch thuck and full size or slighrlylarger than this addressed cover and you can see the corrugation of the card blard on the back.

Sincerely,
Elmer Keith

The book was autographed on first page
to Jack R. Tishue.
           Also with my signature

G&A MAGAZINE • ELMER KEITH SHOOTING EDITOR | SALMON, IDAHO

Dec 18th-68

Mr. Jack R. Tishue Jr.
28 Vista Ave.,
Ferndale, Md. 21061

Dear Jack:

Your wife ordered a sixgun book from me which I autographed and mailed and when I came back from the east the 12th I had a letter from the lost and found P.O. Dept in Baltimore, Md and they enclosed the surface of that card board mailing carton with my name for return and Joan V Tishue and stamps cancelled and looked lkke some one had carefully shaved or peeled the paper from that heavy card board book box and even had the paper tape still sealed on one end where I had sealed the carton. I told them about the ook and the size of the carton ec and returned it all, so let me know if she received the book or not as ooks like some of our good democratic postal employees went to a hell of a lot of troible to steal it.

Now for elk versus horse, much the same except elk have much high boss ribs tghan horses over the withers andthe skeletal structure is of course very different but both require a lot of killing and onlu heavy bullets of not less than 33 caliber nor less than 250 grains weight should be employed in my humble opinion.

Glenn McFarland does not guide for goats I belive though a few in his district but do not know if open or nog but if so he can get then as are on bpth twin and west fork in his distrct. AlsoErvMalnarich of Hamilton, Montana can get uou goat and elk as he hunts Idaho where both occur, also Rdlla Briggs of Salmon, Idaho.

Let me know if that sixgun book arrived or if stolen and if you have heard from the P.O. dept in Baltimore where the paper outsideof that card board was returned to me from.

Sincerely,
Keith.

GUNS & AMMO MAGAZINE • ELMER KEITH SHOOTING EDITOR | SALMON, IDAHO

Jan 8th 69

Mr. Jack R. Tishue Jr.,
28 Vista Ave.,
Ferndale, Md. 21061

Dear Jack:

Am afr id your wife balled things up a bit as this is now two shipments of your shotgun book and also two shipments of uour copy of Sixguns.

She ordered Sixguns and I s hipped it before Thanksgiving, then funally got a letter from the Baltimore lost & found Dept and they returned the thin skin of paper off the face of the book carton containing the address Joan V. Tishue Rt 216, Fulton, Md 20759 and my return and the cancelled stamps, wantong to now what was in the package, so wrote them air mail and told them the sixgun book was in the package and to send it to this address if they found it as it clearly showed somepne had cut the face f that book carton with a knife and peled it off. Then a few days ago I got the damn booo back agin re acked by the P.O.O. dept and my leyter and the face of first carton, so recpacked and put my letter and the face of carton of first shipment in again and addressed ir the zame way but insured and a return card so have now spent some money trying to get that book to you and to date have had no return of the return card no answer to a letter I wrote same time to your wife.

Next when she ordered the Sixgun book she did not say to who, tp autograph it so signed it and left open and now have autographed it to you and returning today to your address of 28 Vista Ave, Ferndale, "'d 21061 and wish you would check on hat damn Fu ton P.O. and get the sixgu book as think your wife ga e me wrong address. Anyway have done my best and shipped both books twice and insured the last ri es so let me knww if uou get them.

Have 105 orders piled up with che ka nd money prders here now for Safari and expect it any day as damn printers got the hong Cong and help up on it and was ro,ised the 24th Nov and they finally printed it the 24th Dec and is now in Salt Lake at abindery and am expecing copies any day now. Your order must be in this pile and if so wull go put soon as I get the books.

Les and Jack are two gentlemen I wqish all the luck in the world but also wish never to be around either if I can avoid them as neither measures up to my standards. Best wishes to you both for the New year and please get the same address for both you and wife so wont ball up next shopment,

Sincerely, Keith.

P.S.

Springfield action too recent for 338-378 K.T. Only Weatherby Brnd Chamberlin + Kalbert or old Lorky Vary in dinner will handle it & using recommencent Enfields — now The new 338 Wm action with third Lien lugs. E.K. Too magnatory Navy C.

MAGAZINE • ELMER KEITH, SHOOTING EDITOR | SALMON, IDAHO

Jan 25th-69

    Agree with you 100% on those small rifle calibers on big game. I will shoot game with any man rifle shotgun or pustol and I have never yet seen the man who can always place his shot under average hunting conditions and have trield up and finished so damn many animals with my sixgun and also lost plenty from small ore addicts I wasguideing that I long ago soured on all small calibers and will hunt elk withn nothing smaller than 33 caliber and a 250 grain bullet and woukd rather have my 44 mag sixguns on k than any 270 or 264 or 6 M M believe it or not as the sixguns will penetrate and even with big calibers you will have unaccountable failures sometimes but far often than when using those needle blowers. Trouble is some of these new authorities neverkilled a fraction f the hundreds of game they c aim I have killedsomething over 300 not countkng crips in guideing and I learned back in the 20s that 30 calibers were not elk rifles.I hunt mule deer here bow with my 338s 340s and our new 33x-378 and find it ills a long range where the little 30 and smaller guns make the jump andkick at their belley and often get away even with good lung shots due to bullet not expanding.The 340 Wby just our old 334 O.K.H. and was best long rangerifle exta t till we brought outvthe 338-378 K.T. and that beats it also the 378 Weatherby beats it.

    Several have written me of using the 378 case full ;ength in 338 and Hutton claoms 3250 with 250 grain, we got justvover 3000 with 250 grain in the 3380378 K.T. and 103 grains of 4831 still dont fill the case to base of bullet so you wouldhave to use a slower powdwr but Hodgdon said our case was perfect for 4831 and he should know. You will need Weatherby Brevex or mag mauser action old one for such a round.

    350 Rem from the 700 make a fine rifle is you open hroat so bullets can be seated out and use 275 Sperr and 250 Nos;er and Rem corelokt. the little 358 with 250 grain is far better on el, moose and big bear than any and all of the 300 magnums. No wuestion in my mind but that if O'cpnnor and Bpwman shot a fraction of the ame they claim wthn270s and smaller that they lpst two br everyone killed. I checked with all the guides here for four years and they concensus was that users under their guidance with 30 and msaller callibers always wounded and lost two elk for evey one killed they got.   Not slated for Houston but am for the NRA at Wash I guess/

    17 calibers for the burds, Charley Oneil asked me to work with him on the first one back in 1942 and I to;d him would avenothing to do with it and I asked Ackley to make the first barrels which he did. Also told Remington their 20 caloberbottle neck rim no good and notice they have never brought ft out;

                                  Best, Sincerely, Keiyth

GUNS & AMMO HOME OFFICE: 5959 HOLLYWOOD BLVD., LOS ANGELES 28. CALIF.

GUNS & AMMO MAGAZINE • ELMER KEITH, SHOOTING EDITOR | SALMON, IDAHO

Feb 7th-69

    Steindler asked for a review copy of Safari and I sent him one also sent one to Neal Knox and Askins, so guess they will cover them for those magazines if they wish. Bpkm is selling like hot cakes now.

    Our 338-378 K.T. is still overbore capacity for 4831 powder and the full length 378 case with a quarter inch longer powder space ever so much larger but Bob Hutton claims they are getting 250 feet more with it and some of those very slow ball powders. or 3250 with 250 grain where we get 3009 feet with 250 grain and 103 grains 4831. Might be still better if powder is right but Bruce Hodgdon who did our chrong work said our case perfect for 4831 and no powder would beat it, but the longer fukl length case moght be even better. The 340 Wby just our old 334 O.K.H with larger bullet by .008" If necked down further our case would be much too large for bore capacity inless somevery slow ball powders used in my humble opinion. Our ctg killed 21 head african game wart hogvto buffalo and no lost wounded game for George Gelman of Bakersfueld Calif. He is very enthusiastic about it for allafrican game with solids fpr the big stuff.

    You c n put ckley in the same class with O'connor and Bowman in my bokk also they are three men I wish all the luck in the world but dont want to be around any of them myself at any time. They have contributed to more wpunded andlost game than all= other mediums put together. They none of the measure up to my standards of a xixexx man. At least my design work in firearms, scopes sights cartridges, rifles and sixguns overthe past 40 years has put hundreds of workemn to work andkept the in jobs so feel I have contributed slightly to the economy of the counyry and also o game conservation by my aartridge recommendations. Dont know what if anything yhese men have donein that line ???? Best

                                            Sincerely,
                                            Keith

Feb 11th-69

Dear Ken:

Been too damn bus7y to keep up all correspondence. Congratulations on that fine boy and I know both you and the good lady are happy about that.

I was not scheduled for the NSGA show by the magazine but they have me slated fpr the NRA show.

My Sharon Bbl C &BH ri le has 18" twost and shoots one hole groups win 500 grain factpry but went all over the paper woth the bullets you sent and keyholed badly 60 grains 4895.

Weather been too bad to try more but those long test you run indicates that metal used in bullet you sent may be cause of the inaccuracy and maybe not hard enough to hold riflong. Gave some of them to Dick Leach wbo has my fine old custom 458 Win and he is going run so,e tesrs also soon as weather permits.Been mild here as compared to all around us but too cold and snow for testing for us to get to the range.

Sounds like that Monometal may be tha snwwr and 4831 powder as I dont have any of the H57. Like ro try some of your 500 grain from the new metal in this rifle someti me also in my other Henriksen 458 with remium Doug barrel that also cuts clover leaves at 100 yard s with factory 510 grain.

Sent uou a copy 1f the book soon as they came out were delayed by the HongKong they sayed.Let me know how you like it Wish you lived here where we could get some testing done rogether at times.

Intend goingvto Africa in Sept for month on or after a bog elephant each and I also want a big buff and he a leopard. he has been over three times and we are going tpbthe Galana distccit south of the Tana which is considered best country for big tuskers.Will take my 577 W.R. and either the C & H 338-378 or my fine Hoffman 404 the latter of it is to be close range bush country.

Cone tol mount as stood up well on a 300 Win mag and also on my 338-378 K.T. sp far and is neatest streamlined of them all but is hell to get scope set level when puttibg ut yogether asthe darn rings are hard to adjust for vertical and whenclamped change but once all is locktited in place has done wonderfully well and I think will take anything as recoil of this 338-378 as aharp as any can be with 100 grains powder and 275 Speer.

The S & W is th finest of all sixguns but simp y will not take the pounding of heavy loads near as long as a Dragoon Ruger and we will siply have to put up with that fact. Our best to you the wife and Dad and let me hear from you.

As lways,
Elmer.

GUNS & AMMO HOME OFFICE: 5959 HOLLYWOOD BLVD., LOS ANGELES 28, CALIF.

GUNS & AMMO MAGAZINE • ELMER KEITH, SHOOTING EDITOR | SALMON, IDAHO

March 6th-69

    I designed the Keith grade C & H rifle externally though Jerry designed the action and it is very good. Liked him very much and was sorry to hear he pulled out of C & H. Dont know reason but suspect he and old Joe Champlin didnot always ggree. He hpned me some mobths back was going start a new compnay and had somebetter action ideas. Have heard nothikng from him since but he is a worker and a damn good designer.

    If he gets right backing may go places dunno. Have seen so many ome and go in the years gone by iincluding Goffamn arms co that made the inest rifles before C & H.

    April issues of Gu/n World not out here yet but wull get a copy nd if you pamned that knothead bill askins so much to the good as he has it coming. I would never have printed an article such as the pne you and others described, benn too busy to look it up but guess he panned me and all long range shooting which only shows his ignorance. Ignorance is bliss.

    Good luck on your column with Juns magazine. I worked for them four years. Best,

Sincerely,

Keith

GUNS & AMMO MAGAZINE • ELMER KEITH, SHOOTING EDITOR | SALMON, IDAHO

March 18th-69

Mr. JackR. Tishue Jr.,
28 Vista Ave.,
Ferndale, Md. 24061.

Daar Jack:

    That article is sure garbage alright and typical of a lot of printed matter these days in every field ofendeavor.

    4227 raises pressures for velocities. An old Fraind of my earlier days once worked up a lot of 44 Spl load for his triple lock and wound up hunting for a new cylinder for the gun with 4227. I am well satisfied with the dirty 2400 as has served me well for a damn long time and done my best long range sixgun work with it for years. 22 grains 2400 and my bullets is enough and nothing gainedby going either higher or lower.

    Yes am scheduled for the NRA convention, will try get here for the morning ol the 29th and already wrote for hotel room. Best

Sincerely,
Keith

GUNS & AMMO HOME OFFICE: 5959 HOLLYWOOD BLVD., LOS ANGELES 28, CALIF.

GUNS & AMMO MAGAZINE • ELMER KEITH SHOOTING EDITOR | SALMON, IDAHO

April 14th-69

Mr. Ken Lomont,
4421 Sout Wayne Ave.,
Port Wayne, Ind.

Dear Ken:
Many thaks for the pix and also the chronog sheets on the sixgun and 458 loads. When I first hadthe hollow base 235 grain 44 bullet moulds made I put three out of five through a 5 gallon gas tin at 300 yards with my old Roosevelt 44 Spl single action and later found that hollow base will take a trifle more powder account pre air space about one grain more and was extremely accurate at very long ranges in the 44 Spls.

Am out of Fed license copies must get more made. Damn this crazy law. The commines want to totally disarm us and that last adminostration was wel composed of them so they can take over and know where ever gun is in the country and also stop reloading. Noticed several of the NRA directors wearing their guns right in the hotel at Wash and an FBI slapped me on the hip and asked where my gun was, told him lockedin my room, He said youdont need to lock it up here we know you. Evodently from what the Wash D.C. and N.Y.C cppos at the convention told me they are not in syampathy with the damn law at all. They know an armed citizen is often a very good back up for them in time of need. To me the showseemed better this year rha two uears ago and semed an entirely different atmosphere and for the best. Everyone up in armson the new gun law and rhink we should all work for outright repeal and also get rid of every damn egialator who voted for it next election. Mansfieldof Mont will get his next election they assure me.

I got a 5" 44 mag S & W for son Ted from Harris of Chi and he likes it and I do also also gave im a 5" 44 Spl 1950 target and S & W are su posedto be building me a 5" this last year and Doug Hellstrom thought it had been shopped so maybe will get it one fo these days. Makes avery useful gun for all around work not quite up to the 6½ for long range or game but darn near it as your tests prove. The 4" however is a handy fast police gun and a damn good one.

Got a beautiful perfect ibside fukl side lock Springer double ejector 9.3X 74, Zeiss Zeukvier detcah scope but so far have tried three makes and two bulletweights factory loads and all shot wide left bbl up at ten colock and the right low at 5. Got some Norma case and bullets finally for our primers and dies so will have to work a load I guess. What worked best in your 9.3X 74?? This gub fully engraved nd made as copy to a Royal H & H and all locks gold plated bolts and ejector locks. Got to get it on the money and use for my timber rifle for both elk and deer.

Leave here the 28th Aug for NYC and next eve on TWA flight 150 for through flight to Nairobu to put in a month for big elephant with Fowler on the Galana between the Tsavo park and Malindi. Hppe we can findcpuple100 pounders. Best, Ever,   Elmer

GUNS & AMMO MAGAZINE • ELMER KEITH SHOOTING EDITOR | SALMON, IDAHO

May 17th-69

    Got a kick out of Glanzers cartoon. However that guy os a nut spent several days develing Judge Martin and I andtoo, him out and shot with him and wanted my loads for the 357 with my 173 grain bullet for his ruger, told him 14.5 grains 2400 woth this bullet, then he loaded up with 17 grais and sent me acopy of a letter he wrote Bill Ru er telling hikm hisgun was ko good as the base pin had frozen in it and could notg get ot out. Told him he was damn kuck he was shooting a ruger and that better sprout som wings right soon before he made the promisedland with such crazy loads.

    Inhave no use whatever for any bullet loghter than 250 grains in any of the 338s. tried the light stuff long a o and good for 300 yards woodchucks but boows up badly on heavy game and drifts badly in a wind and does not have the pnetratuon also loses celocity and energy too fast. Luketheb275Spper best so far and the 250 Nosler has also done well the Nosler opens more at long rangethan the Speer but both have done roght well for me at long range.

    Never tried anu 205 as been right well satisfied and geting grpups often under a hlaf inch and many under an inch with 74 gr ins 4831 and 275 Speer and 83 grains 4831 and 250 Nosler in the 340 Wby also a quarter inch centertoc enter group with factory Wby 250 think Hornady rou nd nose in the 340 Wby for six shots and that is good enough for me. Used the 74 grain load withb275 Speer in the 388 s

    Been using 95 grains 4831 lately in the 378-338 K.T and also shoots very small groups in my C & H rifle. Clobbered three mule deer last fall first 400 yds only head and neck shoing above sage got him throu h base neck, sedond 300 yds high lung shot thrird 500 yds went over first shot as did not have tkme or change to judge range and sedond through lungs used 275 Speer and 98 grains 4831 Norma brass soft and have ad some extraction troubles so cut chg to 95 grains and will see how that goesbug big loads very accurate.

    Id like to see Soerra bring us out a soft nose boattail in 338 in 250 and 375 grain. Geroge Gelman of Bakersfiled killed 21 head African game mostly one shot from wart hog to buffalo woth the 275 Speer and 99 grains 4831 and CCI mag prixmers and notuing got away and his white hunter has orde red a similiar Keith grade 33 -378 K.T. Think wikll,send Glanzers cartoon on to bob Thomson at Glenwood Springs s he should also get a kick out of it anyway.Best

Sincerely,
Keith.

GUNS & AMMO HOME OFFICE: 5959 HOLLYWOOD BLVD., LOS ANGELES 28, CALIF.

GUNS & AMMO MAGAZINE • ELMER KEITH, SHOOTING EDITOR | SALMON, IDAHO

May 22nd-69

Mr. Jack R. ishue Jr.,
28 Vista Ave.,
Ferndale, Md. 21061.

Dear Jack:
    Am mailing your copy of Safari today, Thanks.
Dont knowa thing about the Alaska Sleepong bag but do k ow both Woods and Bauer are very good and dependable. I have an old one madeby the company that sold out to wood and later became the woods co so must be 50 years old but with a new blanket liner is still doing yoeman service.
    You cannot get s;eed out of cast bullets but uou can load Ideal gas check bullet No 375449, wi h 45 to 47 grains 4895 or 45 grains 3031 and get a very acfurate load that will go into one inch at 100 yar s in most 375 rifles H & H of course if you cast the bullets of ure typemetal from the rpinters. Takes a hard bujllet to hold the rifling. This is best reduced load I know for the 375 H & H. Try it.Best

                                              Sincerely,
                                              Keith.

May 26th-69

Dear Ken:

Glad to get your letter and all the 9.3X 74 dope. Havent had time to work with this rifle but as bores are new and it shot well with some German stuff the former owner said think will get a load without trouble with the 285 grain and 3031 will start at 52 grains that shot well in one I tired and wprk up. Enclo ing apicture you will understand and appreciate.

Am now workKng yp loads for the 404s we will take as light rifles and loaing a 120 rds for 338-378 K.T. for our plains rifle for Africa and we will take two fine jector doubles in 577 so that should be good medicine. Huge herds of elephant down there on the Galana where we are going betwee the savo park and Malindi on the coast. low hot dry bush country and if dry season as should be elephant will be concentrated. tony dyer took one snap shot out of his plane down th re and there are at least 600 and maybe 800 elephant in the one snap shot. Soo we should get a couple old busters in a month, want a big buff also if time permits and can find one.

SENtKrpvoza cp y of my fifearms ermiy and the Feds sent me ap;lication blanks and sent metne buck check so maybe will renew or return my check . Old pne good though July as I remember.

Have seen barrels shot out for boattauls that still shot fair;y well with flat base, longer bearing surface and better gas seal but should not string up and down unles poor bedding at tip forestock.

Dont like hard cast bullets in big riflesfor game if brittle but if soft enough to hold together would work and in sixguns as we both know failry hard slugs best and also to hpld rifling. Never checked twist in my 458 C & h will have to do so, the narrow lands sure did not spin slugs ans Beyholed allmover hell. 60 grains 4895 Dont think I will work ,uch more with lead in those two rifles just load jacktedand both are tackble with 510 soft nose. Cut c;over leaves

Think Nixon tryin to straighten out our rotten Govt and alrrady started on the Court which sure needs cleaning out all those commies etc.He has a terrible big job but maybe in four years we will have a better go t and all public sentiment now against t is gun law and is only a harsship on all real americans and wull do nothing to solve one single crime but will stop onr boys from learing to shoot beforethey have to go in the rmy and they wont get any training there as you know.Its communism trying to undermone and ruin America so they can take overand every man wo,an and youngster should be taught to shoot and the Govt had best put a lot of sapce money in rifle practice for our youngsters instead space and other sources of huge expenditures.

Thomsons are coming overthis wekk ahvent seen them for couple years and we will do some s ooting Rivr awful high but may get some rout at Williams lake the 31st when s eason opens. All the best to you your Dad andall the famóly. Notice my poor typeing is getting o better, so we both qualify as worlds worst   As Ever Elmer

WHEN GUNS ARE OUTLAWED ONLY OUTLAWS WILL HAVE GUNS

The real truth about firearms has been distorted to the point of being ridiculous. There is *no gun problem*, there is a *crime problem*. We need to fight crime by enforcing existing laws. Guns don't kill people, people kill people and people were killed before guns were invented.

False figures of murders by guns are given by the liberal news media of 18,000 when the FBI reported 772. A figure of 17,000 accidentally killed was printed although the National Safety Council reported 2,200.

Ramsey Clark, LBJ, HHH and other liberals (who were in office) confused the issue and made it difficult for the average person to know the truth. Also, this is not a race issue.

Gun ownership "fees" would surely be established. Like car, home, etc. it would become another tax but as bitter to pay as alimony.

As the protest against citizens owning guns grows — so will taxes on their firearms. Many Americans would be forced to turn in their guns rather than pay a high tax on them.

Protection is of great concern. "Who will protect the home when the police are in another section of the city fighting rioters?"

Everyone advocating registration of firearms is not a traitor. But the COMMUNISTS want Americans disarmed!

Register Communists — Not Loyal Americans

Add'l. copies: 100 for $1.00—500 for $3.25—1,000 for $5.00.
JOHN W. BIGGERT / 413 Wagner St., Memphis, Tenn. 38103

MAGAZINE • ELMER KEITH SHOOTING EDITOR | SALMON, IDAHO

June 12th-69

Dear Tishue:

I would put a plain 23/4 Redifle, 3X weaver or K-4 or 3X Leupold on that 375 with whatever reticle you prefer. I hate those damn tapered cross wires as they fadeput on all dom lights and he only fine wires that are worth a whopp are the dual post type with heavy wires to near center field and then fone ones across intersection This is a good reticlwas is also a flat top posy wih horizontal wire and for long range Thomsons two dot or my double horizontal wire Weavwr. I have a Leupold 3X on my finest 375 Champlin and Haskins with the dua; cross wire heavy to near center their 4 plex also a joke and much better to have the wires very heavy to near center so you can frame an animal between them in dim lights. Glad you receied the book as per P.S ON envelope.

Id put the 3X 9 on the long range 30 caliber rather than the 375 H & " which isbone of our best all around cartridges. The Cpne trol makes the snoothest of all mounts and very good. ave them on several rifles.I also dpnt like side mounts c t s ocks and receiver fukl of screw and pin hokes but was best we had 40 years ago.Never saw a Khuarsky mount so cannot comment.If ots the B & L form of my old Tuner mount which george urner and I developed then I dont like their present set up of springs and huge bases. We had a good mount, then Pike King took ut up and Turner let Ackley have the patent and he put out someterrible specimens also ot away with it and some $ 7000. of Turners money, Then Stith and B & L copied it and put out vnery nuch inferior jobs to those George Turner made. "eavy rifles often throw the scope offin recoil with all of these but Turners old original. It does allow use of scopes on several rifles, but mounts fairly high and I have quit it even though was a good mount when we first brought it out and patented it.Our patd long sice run out. Also saw many aluminum tjbq scopes dented when hit overthe V rests.Then of course point of impact changed and you nees steel tube weavers for this type of V mounts . We used to put steel clollar around aluminum ones where they bore in mounts.

our 285 O.K.H. was 30-06 necked down and the 280 similiar but .2845 instead of .2850 bore.Our 180 grain Duplex load flat base bullet printed just 5" high at 200 when soghted for 400 yds while the 300 mag 180 grain B.T. Western factory load printed 7½" high at 200 and on steel theb285 O.K.H. blew corks out of 5.8 ar or steel at 50 yards while the 180 grain 300 H & H magnum Wester load went half way through at 20 yards so figure it out.We used 26" bbls.55 grains 4350 180 grainDuplex tubed case powder compressed and tight chanbered guns

My wife has two 358 Winchesters, one light weight 60 other new model '99Savage and with 250 grain bullet only makes fine ladies rifles for everythikng and ood on elk and moose as well. Short barrels and magnum calibers for yhe birds dont burn the powder. Best

MAGAZINE • ELMER KEITH SHOOTING EDITOR | SALMON, IDAHO

June 22d-69

Mr. Jack R. ishue Jr.,
28 Vista Ave.,
Ferndale, Md. 21061

Dear ishue :

I would not have anything but a good 4 to 4½ pound double bitted axe. The Plumb axe is a good one. The pole axes are good for driving tent pegs butg not worthadam for anyserious hrd chppping as have no balance.

Have seen those fpam rubber chsion pads and they calim the re very good but also sterribly bulky and would covr one side of a pack horse so out far as I am concernted unless you travelled in camper or truck.

The Califprnios aboutcleaned outour mule deer here this last eaon and very few bucksleft so cannot rceommend it at all and think you wpuld do better for muleys in Wup now. That 25 dollar icense ruined our deer herd last falland they have it again this year but will be hll of a lot of unhappy hunters this fall as no deer lefy to slaughter and they left a great many lay wherekilled just too heads nd capes and others s ucked out littelfauns and left hide head and feet intact but no meat.

Land is very high here as so many want to ,ove in and only so m much lad available. Refused 40,000 for my little shoestirng ranch.
Yes mu old Hoffman Arms Co rifle No 1 a 400 whelen made by J V.Hov is oln the Spfld action and ut makes up into one of t bicest sporters of all.

Maynard Hollcomb is a good outfitter and has good elk and some mule deer alsoin his area over near ells Half axre in head of Selway. Best woshes,

Sincerely,

Keith.

GUNS & AMMO MAGAZINE • ELMER KEITH SHOOTING EDITOR | SALMON, IDAHO

Oct. 17th-69

Mr. Geo. B. Bredsten,
660 Fairbanks St. B-9
Fairbanks, A laska. 99701.

Dear Mr. Bredsten:

Just back from 6 weeks in Africa. Fowler and I had 30 days on ele and up aginst bulls every day of the 30. got 4 big ele and had good trip I also sjot 2 buffalo and a hipp/ with Petersen on the Kagera and my threeelephant all decked one shit from my 500 Boswell nitro double.

Have seen amny elk and moose rear up and turn over backawqrds also sheep after being h t through l ngs also deer and other game its quite common as lungs full with blood and chokes them.

The 41 and 44 mags will take anything on this cont9inent if placed right at close range.

Now for that Single shot ruger dont get it in 45-70 for the reason their damnncz cases are t o thinj near head for heavy loads we even had a new rem case rupture im front rim from fist shot im tight '86 winchester with 405 grain soft nose and 53 grains 3031.

Get that fine Ruger SS im caliber 458 Winchester, them you can use any load you wish from 45-70 standard up to 73 grains 3031 wi h 500 grain jack/ed and you will like the case much better thanthe old thinn 45-70 and it will do all the 45-70 will do and much more when meeded. Ruger has just shipped me a SS no 1 in 375 H & H caliber has not come in yet. That 458 S S Ruger can be loaded to nandle all american or africam game if ranges no/ too long.

Thanks for the excellent pix.

Sincerely,

Keith

GUNS & AMMO MAGAZINE • ELMER KEITH, SHOOTING EDITOR | SALMON, IDAHO

Oct 17th-69

Dear Tishue:

Just back from Africa and a hell of lot of mail to answer. H'd good luck killed two buff, three big bull ele and a hippo and a record lesser Kudu one shot each also a roan three shots at 300 yds with Peters rifle that was sighted 6" low at 100 and went under him one shot.

Barnes and Kynoch only ones making the big bullets for British cordite ctgs. That Churchill cant be regulated for the nitro 3½ 450 as it raies a heavier rifle and 70 grains cordite and 480 grain. Forget it.

333 Jeffery was and is .3330" and Taylor was wrong and also wrong on some of his other claibers as to diamter. Our 333 O.K.H. was just that and Winchesters 338 just rou old 333 O.K.H. short belted with slight shoulder change. You are wrong on 375 beating the 338, it may do so up to 200 yds but better sectional density of 338 275 and 300 grain outranges 375 at real long ranges I know as have four 338s and five 375s and killed a lot of game with all of them also two 340s and a 338-378 K.T.

That 450 Rigby Nitro if good shape is very cheap and best doubles now cost $ 4,000 up to over $ 5,000. Domt agree with you at all on the 06 being an elk rifle it is not and can never be. Will do the job if placed exactly right but damn few chances occur for such bullet placement. The 338-06 however with 275 to 300 grain O.K. You got to have 250 grains gs up for elk. Best,

Sincerely,

Keith.

Oct 27th-69

Mr. Ken Lomont,
4421 So. Wayne Ave.,
Fort Wayne, Ind. 46807

Dear Ken:

Had letter from Pittman and just answered it. Glad he is casting my 22/ grain 41 mag and 250 grain 44 mag slugs. I do not have H & G catalogue so did not know bullets by number I designed both . Also have two packages bullets here from that other outfit you recommended and wrote them up good work. Have to write and thank him or you do so for me.

HAd good african trip, shot only 8 head myself, a Roan on the Kagera ri er and two buff and a huge hippo, pne buff only 32" shot for lipn bait and Petersens m/vies, other a nice 41 incher I took for myself. Then to the Galana with fowler, e got a tr phy ele with 8'4" tusks and long 37 " nerves that still weighed 92 and 98 a beauty. I killed three first one 6' and 6' 10, long 40 inch nerves and only went 55 and 58 but pretty matched pair, Second one 7' $2 4" and long 34" nerves but weighed 76 and 78, my best pair, Third one ver old also as were the others and right tusk 7'6" and 80 pounds and left 6' 3" and 73 pounds not ma ched but a lot of ivory. I dropped the two buff the hippo and all three elephantvpne shot each from left barrel of the 500 Boswell. Then also got a record class 30" Lesser Kudu with Mikes 375 one shot 105 yards only head showing amd took him off handunder chin. Truman also got fine rhino, a leopard and a lesser Kudu, We had wonderful hunt, then I went fishing on lae while waiting for thru plane to NYA on Sat and the 3rd they started boat motor and threw me overboth seats and landed with right side on gunwale. Broke last tow ribs near spine and was sick as hell for five days and they brpught me ho e via four air lanes and four wheel chairs through customs etc, but now wearing elastic corset and getting ar.und, expect to ta e in Win seminar in N.J. the 10 h and Rem seminar down at San Antonio the 16th but dont look like will be able tol do any meat hunting here as all of Claifornia here again and dust never settles on any forest trail or road.

Tha is wonderful shoo ing you did with the 5" 44 mags. I just ot a 5" had ordered three yea s and is a peach. Makesnice all around gun n 44 mag S & W. Also Ruger fiannly sent me a bea ty of a No 1 single shot, engraved wi h grizzly on left siadeadmy name in gold right side and scroll borders and lever. caliber 375 H & H and think will do most of my hun ing here with it soon as get tu ned up properly.

Will look for you out next summer and maybe we will have a few jaks left at any rate. That AR16 be good for chasing running jacks but I cant ee as military rifle except for close range fighting. Have a raft of material to ge out so all for now. Best to you and your Dad,

As Ever, Elmer

Elmer

 MAGEZINE 5959 HOLLYWOOD BOULEVARD, LOS ANGELES 28, CALIFORNIA • HOLLYWOOD 6-2111

ELMER KEITH
SHOOTING EDITOR   Dac 1st-69

Jack R. Tishue,
28 Vista Ave, Ferndale , Md. 21061.
Dear Jack:

    Iver Henriksen, 1211 So. 2nd St, Missoula, Montana can make you a 33, O.K.H. for that is what it is pn the 06 case. and I would prefer it taking regular brass to Gobbs blown out shogt neckversion. With 250 grain bullets its abetter killr at long range than any of the 30 calibers.

    R.C.B.S. can furnish the dies and you have the breass and it will take 58 to 60 grains 4350 with 250 275 and 300 grain bullets. Its a da,n good cratirgde and you can get 2400 with 300 grain for the heavier game. used a 333 O.K.H. pn first trip to Africa and clobbered all mu plainsgame with it.

    Hof man Arms Co has been out of business since 1926. They mademost excellent barrels and I have threeof their rifles I have severl most excellent stainless stell barrels and Winchester made a lot of them that were excellent.

                                           Sincerely,
                                           Keith

MAGAZINE 5959 HOLLYWOOD BOULEVARD, LOS ANGELES 28, CALIFORNIA • HOLLYWOOD 6-2111

ELMER KEITH
SHOOTING EDITOR

Dec 19th-69

Daar Etter:

Havent seen Dec Gunsport so send over a copy. I notice these boys you mention who are soloud mouthed never want to put up any money pn a shoot out at long range with a sixgun. This special forces lad in Voet Na, knows the score. Down at Ogden Arsenal during the war P.O.Ackley and several of his gunsm.ths got very loud in thewproclamation that a 45 auto wasno good over 20 yards and no one could hnut a man at 60 yds. I called them the argument got hot and heavy and Col. Capron ordered us out to the rifle rangeone sunday. 200 yds to the butts and 50 yds beyond was a snow drift a foot high and about three feet long at 250 yds. I laid down on the ground on mu side cocked up the right knew rested head on lefthand and held my 45 auto in hollow of bended knee.First s ot way low held front sight much higher so could see lot of slide between sights and next shot over, then put other 5 on the snow drift, put in anothrr clip abd put the, all in the snow drift then asked Acklet to go lay down where snow was and let me shoot another clip and we would have no more argu,ents. Col. Capron said Amen.

Might try those wyo antelppe with you if get time next fall. Andy hagel brpught some 18" heads out of these someplace and Bob may know the district.

I used three rounds with Petersens 375 sighted for 70 yds in Africa on a big roan at 300 yds, first shot low withb holld top f withers broke front leg, next held over withers wet under chest then held level top horns and decked him. Then went on to kill two buffalo fist one 140 yds, second one 71 yards, a huge hippo 21Feet, the three big old elephant, first 30yds, second 55 yds andthird 65 yards, then a re ord lesser Kudu at k05 yards with Mike Hisseys 375, all one shot kills. Then down to Y-O ranch in Texas withV emington Seminar, a five point a side whitectail about 80 yds damn kittle 6M M Rem took top of heart off andwent 30 to 50 yds and piled up then two wild gobblers 17 poundes 12 bore No 4 shot oit of a bluncing scout at 30 milesa n hour head shots one raound each, so did not use up much ammo this fall.

Have had a lot of phone calls and letters on the long range sixgun shooting by men who have also done it and can still do it. E P.Sheldon of Norma-Precision etc. So think truth will win out over lies and arm chari expert criticism, but they are doing an injustice to the kids we arw trying to train. Returning t e letter from Viet, that boy knows the score. Best for the coming season.

Sincerely
Keith Elmer

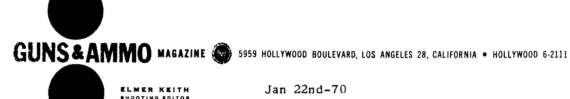

GUNS & AMMO MAGAZINE 5959 HOLLYWOOD BOULEVARD, LOS ANGELES 28, CALIFORNIA • HOLLYWOOD 6-2111

ELMER KEITH
SHOOTING EDITOR

Jan 22nd-70

Mr. John T. Stuart,
685 So Oak Paek Ct.,
Milwaukee, Wisc. 53214

Dear Mr. Stuart:
          Have never heard of anyone making any long range machine resttests witha sixgun. Also frankly I dont know how accurate they would be from a machine rest. f properly constructed and gun clamped firnly as part of the assembly might prove very interesting. Have seen many machin rests from th factories and they run good but not as good many times as hand holding from sand bagged rest and scope. Also remember that years ago when they were testikng the ibternational match rifles for our teams back in the 20s they found that ezpert match riflemen usually made smaller groups than the same rifles from machine rests from probe position with sling . I have no such equipment and maybe Jeff could scare some up down there in Calif.
     I have always been able to do better shooting with barrels up to 7½" maximum than longer barrels. The buntlines seem to whip up and away srom the hand more and you have go ride hell out of them or they tendto shoot to left for me at least. Also shorter barrels puts the two sights more in the samw focal plane and are more accurate for me at least. Was once shootong a 7½" 44 Spl S.A.COLt target sights and 18.5 grains 2400 andmy bullets against factory at 400 yards at a rpck, The heavy loads got there very fast and was an appreciable time lag with factory load with 246 grain bullet but the craziest fact w as t at both loads hit the rock with xactlt same hold up of front soght, due tol the fact the barrel recoiled higher with the slower barrel tome of the light loads an thus gave them the needed extra elevation. It wont work with the 44 mag however but did in that 44 Spl.
     would not advise any bullet heavierthan my 250 grain Ideal 454424 and in fact would advise no other bullet for the 45 Colt. If yours is a modern gun use 18.5 up to 20 grains Maximum witb bullets cast hard and sized to exact groove diamter asbest of all heavy loads. Unique in ten grain charges has not given me as good accuracy in my flat top 7½" target S?A. Iver seen about everything in Colts 45 from .450 to .456 so slug the barrel and size exactky same H-110 seems to habdle about same charges as 2400 and seems very accurate but start a grain or two lower. My loads should give1200 feet or maybe 1300 from that long barrel and I would not advise the heavier bullet. Cylinder walls too light for the pressures. One freind bl swtspfbeä Titoo24o04 Spl with 4227 and I have never used it being

Page two.

H-110 gives about exact same vel as 2400. I have used both regular and Mag Speer primers, the latter seem to develope slightly higher pressures and you can cut charges one grain but burn powder a litt;e better. Re ular primers have worked aboyt as well for me. 2400 has to be up to fair pressures before it will burn and unless very heavy pressures will not be complete combustion butvthis does no harm. I use Lyamn lub or any good lub and have no preferance but like a graphite impregnated or silicone conet lub as seems to shoot zleaner. Also used straight elk and deertallow for years when had nothing else and worked O.K?. Hope this helps some and I try to answer all letters as a service yo our readers, but they sure as hell pile the hn me at tkmes, even though Ackley and Cooper supposedto answe4 them, Got 33 letters yesterday.

                                          Sincerely

                                          Keith

MAGAZINE • ELMER KEITH SHOOTING EDITOR | SALMON, IDAHO

March 2nd-70

Dear Tishue:

The address pf the Kynoch outfit is as follows. Imperial Chemical Industries Ltd., Whitton, Birmingham 6. England and the home office address is Imperial Chemical House, Millbank, London SWI, England.

I dont think you will have any luck at all as they require huge orders even on their old British ammo line let alone a few hundred cases special. Best

Sincerely,
Keith

MAGAZINE • ELMER KEITH SHOOTING EDITOR | SALMON, IDAHO

March 30th-70

Mr. Jack R.Rushue,
28 Vista Ave.,
Ferndale, Md. 21061.

Dear Jack:
      Think J.O.C.s dope on Taylor about like he peddles about me but not to my face. I corresponded with John aylor for over 25 years and we were good freinds, nevermet him but had standing invitation to come and hunt with him but did not have the money.
      A few days before is death pne of his freinds in London sentme a big picture of john he had just taken beforehis death. John Taylorworte the best books on african rifles ever to come out and he knew wherof he spoke. A Dr. Whiye in missoula hasone of hosrifles and I shot it here a few weeks ago. This man in Londo held John Taylor in very high regard and also another autraliajn freind who hunted africa with John and wanted me to go with them holds him in same high respect and I dont thank O'connor for peddling dirt when he never met the man and knows nothing of him and nothing in all my correspondencever ondicated OConnors accusations.
      Think he left a rica because of health and went to London o write books on his experience as he got batteredup a bit in the Wolrd war two.
      450No 2 ocselete as to ammo but could be made from regular 47502 I think by necking downand inside neck reaming before loading same as can be done with 500-450 from 476 or 470 cases.
      I had a freind make a bullet of my design for 577 that is the mould and the Lyman minnie ball 58 caliber can be had with square plug for flat baseheavy bullet andsized down to 584 to fit the 577s .
      Those doubles very cheap if any good. Have to leave for New Orleans the 1st I guess and dony know how plane transportation will be looks dark now.Magazine has an article now on The Kagera end of my hunt and the G & A Annual has another on the killing of our best elephant TexxTrumangreat 8' 4" inch acthed pair that went 92 and 98. ave my three sets capped and hung on the wall here and look mighty nice. Best

                                              Sincerely,
                                              Keith.

GUNS & AMMO MAGAZINE • ELMER KEITH, SHOOTING EDITOR | SALMON, IDAHO

April 9th-70

Mr. George Bredsten,
660 Fairbanks St., B-9
Fairbanks, Alaska, 99701.

Dear Mr. Bredsten:

      Am shipping an autographed copy Safari to Mr. Alder today insured.
      Ha ent seen or had any chance to testv the new 44 auto magnum, but Tom Siatos said he had seen and tested and was a very good well made relibale auto ;isto; for the most powerful load ever put in an auto Should be good gun for those who like the autos bestand be bi enough to hunt with. Think it will require a big man with long fingers to reachthetrigger unless they shorten the case and then may not quite equal the full length load account powder space unless they got a hod dense powder instead of 2400 that I use in the 44 mags.
      Alders 458 American will do a lot better job pn moose than t e 308but he should have gotten the 458Wikn cartridge at least as he could haveloaded down to 45-70 velocity if desired and hadthe advantage of the big load for longer range when and if neexed. Thank for the book order.

                                        Sincerely,
                                        Keith.

JUST Back from the NRA Convention and fingers dont trachtoo well this morn.

MAGAZINE • ELMER KEITH SHOOTING EDITOR | SALMON, IDAHO

April 28th-70

Dear Jack:

    Jphn Bishop gave me a blank from a whole tree he cut of fiddle back walnut, very hard and dense and curly ful; length most 11 blanksfrom that tree. That was a good many years ago and Iver Henriksen made the stock, 1201 South 2nd St Missoula.

                                              Sincerely,
                                              Keith

GUNS & AMMO MAGAZINE • ELMER KEITH, SHOOTING EDITOR | SALMON, IDAHO

May 27th-70

Mr. Ji, Leatherwood,
Rt # 1, Box 111.
Stephenville, Texas 76401.

DearMr. Leatherwood:

The 3X 9 Realist and mounts now working out very well for long range pest shooting since we fitted new bases. It works well with either 75 or 80 grain bullets in the 243 and seems tp be well collimated for the various ranges and shoots very close tothe yardage on the drum or change band.

I have now sent in a wrote -up for my column on ut and belive for pest snpigg from a car pr where it doesnot have to be caried on a horse or lugged all day in steep country will wprk /ut very well particularly for long range pest or antelope shooting as well as military sniping.

I would much prefer the 1.5 X 4.5 variable however for any big game mountian huntong or timber shooting account both weight nd field of view. Let ,e know if you want this scope back pr not as if not will leave on this 243 est rifle.

About the onlu other file I have on handnpw that I could test the 1.5 X 4.5 is a mannlicher 30-06 new model Win 7Ø and could pull present scope from it and replace it is very accurate in fact the best shooting new modevl 70 have uet seen and could be claibreated for 180 or possib;y better 220 grain and used as a timber fifle and shooting under 300 yds or up to 400 and not more. Should be sighted at 200 however and then 300 and 400 graduations on the drum or on out to 500 for pests. Guess with rangetests would also work with 180 grain for long range by finding what range each bullet weight carried to, Might be best to caibrate for the 80 grain loads however as they would be used to longer range and then field test to find w at gradu taion to use for he 220 grain in closer timber shooting. Id have given a lot years ago for such an outfit when hunting coyotes for a living.Then used a target scope and when time permitted setthe scope for exact range near as I could judge it nd itvworked on a 14 pound bukl gun but was damn heavy to lug on my shoulder day after day on a horse but iy paid dividends in pelts.

Sincerely,
Keith.

GUNS & AMMO HOME OFFICE: 5959 HOLLYWOOD BLVD., LOS ANGELES 28, CALIF.

Feb 22nd-71

Mr. Jack R. Tishue Jr.
28 Vista Ave.,
Ferndale Md. 21061

Dear Jack:
    Autographed and returned your books last week and they should be there by now.
    Frank E. Hendricks engraved and inlaid my 338-378 C & H rifle and itsaround a $ 5,000.00 job. He is oneof themasters and his address isRt # 2 Box 189-J, San Antonio, Texas 78228. Of course this riflealso has avvery fancy stockof French as well.
    That 505 should make you one of best bolt guns for Africa.You can check groove duamter but you might be able to use the 570 grain steel jacket solid 500 Nirto Express bullets. Best

Sincerely,
Keith

GUNS & AMMO MAGAZINE • ELMER KEITH, SHOOTING EDITOR | SALMON, IDAHO

March 15th-71

Dear Jack:

OConnor copied andre-wroye my articles ect for several years before the magazine sent hikm all over the world. Just for the record i have seen more big game wounded and lost wit the damn 27 than Jack O onnor and his good wife ever shot with tghat capbberput together.Four ekk all shoulder shots lost one trip alone in 30 years guideing, failed on mountai n goast six well placed hits, one beat and two deer one trip for a lady I guided

Have made three african safaris and last trip killed but eight head, a nice roan. Two buffalo one 44 ", okne hippo a huge record three tonner, and three finelld bullelephant, the smallest carrying at least twice the ivory of O'Connors JanO'Life elephant hunt and a record Kudud one shot each rhe big six all wit left barrel of my 500 boswell and none of the two buff hippor or three ele ever mo ed a sikngle step. Ive shot wit bthat big Irishman and can beat him any day or night wit rifle shotgun or sixgun and never done him any har in my kife and he just must be jealous of my knowledge. He has been panning me for yeras but too many poeple have hunted wit ne and seen me shoot and he is only hurting himself. He is to be pitied I figure.

I grew up under a big stetson likked itband still see no reason to change head gear. I prsctice whatI preach and will take him on any day in any kind of shoot and I dont point an autp shotgun at him andpul; the breech backand let it go to battery on hin twice as he didto me atWinchester Seminar. I have no yse for the rotter and he dont measure up to my standards as a man or a gentleman.I know I have seen manyvtimes the big game killedthat e and his wife have together in spote of t eir many african s afaris.

Iverrad many letters from W.D.M.Bell giving me hell yo my freind Gerrit Forbes, but Fornes sadi if bell had usedmu 577 he would still be alive instead of dyeing of a heart ailment due to runnong after ele he had pinked with the damn 7 M M and Forbed made three trips across africa with bell butvused apair of 405s and a577 as back up. Iver forgotten more than the poor ladwill ever know but the publick likes to be fobled and he is an expert writer.

Sincerely
Keith

GUNS & AMMO MAGAZINE • ELMER KEITH SHOOTING EDITOR | SALMON, IDAHO

Aug 4th-71

    First I ordered your 44 mag direct from Doug Hellstrom, V.P. of Smith & Wesson and had a letter back from him it had been scheduled and was in prod cyion with the engraving you wanted on side plate. Intended sending you his letter but got mixe up with letters and answwrs I sent back to the magazine and so t went. Soo you best write to Dougg Hellstrom direct and give him you jobber and retailer so the gun can be shipped through regular channels and to your retialer when finished. This engraving means you have to wait your turn and takes some time.
    I justvordered ano her 4" 44 mag for ourpolice cheif Joe Sharp from Bill Gun the President amd he wrote back its bing sent out soo as possible and he shippes them for us here to Bob Brownell as Jobber at Montezuma Iowa, as jobber and then Bob ships tl Haveman Hwd. Cpl Salmon and they have been com ng through O.K. Bill Gum wrote me he now had another production line on the magnums in fu 11 blast and would be able to turn out ,ore mags than ever before but be sure and give Doug Hellstrom your jobber and retualer. guess Bob Brownell would do for you retialer to get gun through as they have to go through channels on fair trade agreement.
    Truman Fowler wrote me old 270 has a book o t the Hunting Rifle n in which he takes me and Fowler to task for most of a chapter, I have not seen he book and sure wou d not pay any $ 8.75 to read his reahas of some of my material as well as his own alarky. Anyway Truman wrote him a six page letter and quoted exact excerpts from the book which were copies of my work and reall took him apart at the seams.
    The Load willing we will hunt wimh Thomsons ap in this fall but pver on the other side of the Colo river. That Avalanche canyon full of cows but damn few bulls annd or calves showing lack of bulls and need of straight ow season there for a couple years.
    Fowler wamted me to call old 270 on that book chapter, but I prefer to ignore him as I have done for many years. DuComb told me he and JAc k put 17 280s and 30-06s in one black bear and heard it from Wes and called jack on it at Rem seminar when he got out of hand and he said a G.D. Lie so asked him if Dpc and Wes were G.D. liars and his face got red and he left the table/ . I was not there so dont know.
    Enjpyed your article and from my correspondence see that a lot of hunters have tuned to 338s and 375s after losing a lot of elk. Sent four hunters from Calif to Charlie Snook at Elk summitt, two of them shot three elk each and two two elk each and lost the whole works wounded they were using 150 grain bullets in 270 Winchester, They wante dto boo again with Charlie for next year and he told them nothing doing unlessthey co e to me and took my recommendations for elk rifles, They did so and I recommended four 375 H & H and 300 grain and Charlie booked them. That fall they came by and brought me four fifths whiske add reported four elk with them and all one shom kills. but the ten elk they wounded he year beloe no doubt deed.
270 JAck has done most to deplete our elk herds of any man. Best Elmer

MAGAZINE • ELMER KEITH SHOOTING EDITOR | SALMON, IDAHO

Oct 6th-71

Mr. George Bredsten,
Box 3208 Airport Annex,
Fairbanks, Alaska, 99701.

Dear George:
First I must return your check as all copies of Sixguns sold and go e that . could get my hands on andthe damnpublisher has he says turned it over to some publisher to bringput a big cheap edition of it to sell at around $ 4. so maybeyou will be able tol get a copy then. have returned some 200 checks and M.O. in last couple years. Theyreprinted a 1000 and they soon went out.

gree with yiu 100% on the 444 markin being a lot more elk and moose gun than the 7 Mags regardless of elocity. .t still takes bullet wight and caliber to anchor stew inmy humble opinion and killed my 50 elk last fall. The 444 is best with 265 Hornady and 48 to 50 grains 3031 and would been a much better gun if they

had cut with quicker twist to stabalize a 3 0 grain bullet at lower velocity. Thanksfor all the dope on moose, I have only killed fpur of thembut like elk they take some tkme to die at times even with hert shot out of them or lungs destroyed. Id rather have

my 44 mag sixgun on elk at close range than any 270 and the 444 Marlin is a better close range gun rhan even the 300 mags. I killed over 30 big hereford, angusand short horn bulls many going well over a ton with 6½ andalso 4" 44 mags and their nose hit the concrete at the slaughter house always before gun came down out of recoil. Tried all loads and the soft point jackted factory jobs ot to the

brain but stoped in the cavity while myv250 grain backed by 22 grs 2400 often wentback in the neck and many had two inches cartilage on front of skulls, One shot in back of head and his eyes popped out of their sockets.

I consider my load in the 44 mag better t an the 45 Colt with any permissable load. he 45 is good but wont penetrate with the44 and yougot tobhave lenetration when killing heavy stuff wiyh a sixgun. A man In Utah has made five shot 45 Colt cylibders and driving 300 grain at 1700 feet and 250 at 2000 but the spit lead tie up the gun and recoi; cutsskin on trigger finger from the front wbd of the trigger guard and theywould blow any standard cylinder up am sure so wont write them up and also not very accurate, there is a limit in a hand gun regardless of strong heat treated cylibders. You gain about 30 to 35 feet in vel for barrels over 4" with 2400 bu t they dont seem any ore accurate, Long tubes gove hogher vel but not b tter accuracy.   est,   Sincerely, Keith

GUNS & AMMO HOME OFFICE: 5959 HOLLYWOOD BLVD., LOS ANGELES 28, CALIF.

G&A MAGAZINE • **ELMER KEITH** SHOOTING EDITOR | SALMON, IDAHO

Oct 12th-71

Dear George:

Shipping copy of Safari today to Barry Haight as per your instructions. Just learned Stackpole a Pub Cp hadsold rights yo republishmy suxgun and shotgun bolks and will sell at much lesser price than from Stac pole so wil hol your check the Safari is $ 8.50

Postpaid and insured and will send you a copy of Sixguns soon asI get a supply in and also checkfor the difference asthey hinted it wpuld now be a $ 5. booo lus postage and ins. Sp wi;1 hpld you checkuntil I get books in and price etc when I come back from Colo elk hunt with Thomson.
      Theyhave to shoot so,e game with the smll calibers and then use a heavier claiber before anyone wil; realize the difference. Ive killed 5 elk now 4 ,oose all the big bear etc plus three safaris in Africa andstick to my coclusion nothing less than a33 caliber nor 250 grainspflead at anythin; from 1850 to 3000 feet vel and best more lead than more veloci y over 2500 feet except for extreme ranges. Best and will let you know cost of Sixguns when I get the newsupply and god knows what it wil; look like thpugh supposed to have all the ol text.

                                      Sincerely,

                                      Keith

Thanks for thedope on the moose kill it checks with many I have seen.

MAGAZINE • ELMER KEITH SHOOTING EDITOR | SALMON, IDAHO

Nov 5th

Dear George,

Got some saple copies pf lastedition pf Sixguns from
Out;etbook Co NYC who bought rights from Stackpole so the book
willnow stay inprint and retai; price of $ 3.95 so I will sell autpgraphed

copies at $ 5. tp take care of ;acking shipping and ins and time. s
enclosed my check for 4 6.50 to cover balance asyou sent $ 15. for
the Safari that I shipped to Barry Haight some tbree weeksago. best
and thabks for the dope on the moose killing bearsoutp my onw
experience and I dont hunt anything any more with less than a 338

Sincerely
Keith

Nov 7th-71

Mr Ken Lomont,
4421 South Wayne Ave,
Fort Wayne, Ind.

Dear Ken:
    I had george Hoenig pf Boise fit a syronyer recoil spring and a larger rear sight pin in my Gold cup and it handles hard ball perfect and wonderfully accurate and think freind Jeff Coppwr is sadly wrong when he says they wont syand up and your extended tests prove us right.
    Fpr me the S & W best of all D.As but can also shoot the Fibe olld Colts and Ruger S.A. I have but fact remains the old S & W best made of all but getting lots reports and saw severl S & W late ly that not up to standard and their inpection is slipping badly as is also Rugers and several more I could name.
    Ohaus scale out fit now making moulds for my bullets ut they inststed they must use roujnd grease groove which we know is no good and fact is they simply dont know how to cast bullets. Bestand most accurate 41 mag is my 220 grain H & G and they put sqmare grease groove as ordered, It can have a slight taper and wider at outside than inside and cast and drop out easy and no damn round grease groove asgood as dont hold as much grease and it falls out when loading etc you know the score. Also on many buklets both Ohaus and Lyman and Saeco as well they made the front ban too barrow when should been same as the front driving nadn and a taperedcrimp groove abd many dont put a taper on the crimp groove damn em.
    Like 2400 best of all and th ink more uniform velocities as Whites Chronog showed with loads Dr. and I sent them 22 grai s average around 24,000 psi and velocity around 1400 and variation lessthan 3,000 psi and onelt of Peters factory we sent shpwed variatoob of 11,600 I belive it was in teh rounds and wasup to nearly 50,000 in one shot fired. I just stick to ,y old 22 grain 2400 loadand to hell with allmothers as have given me best resukts for a long time and superb accuracy.
    Get a copy of the new Guns & Ammo Annual and see my article on the 338-74-Keith and also have an elephant article therin. Got back fromColo. with an elk and two bucks and have to go Win Seminar at houston then double back tol Luttle Rock Ark for Rem smeinar and ave to leave in few days so all for now see you next summer.

As Always, Elmer

Elmer

MAGAZINE • ELMER KEITH SHOOTING EDITOR | SALMON, IDAHO

Nov 26th-71

That was a very good answer you gave that lad on elk rifle calibers. However here is one for the record on twist of the 338 Mag. I have an olympia grade browning 338 and with that crazy 12" twist it will spin and stablize the 275 Speer nocely and very accurate wth 275 Speer and 74 grains 4831 and CCI 250 mag primer, but will not stabaliza the 300 grain winchester with any load I havetried. I also had a plain Browning for the same load andkilled a good many elk withbitwith above load but it let ,e down badly when yriedto hit a bull out at long range with 300 grain. idid clobber three at around 400 and one of them hit twice low throwugh chest went aquarter mile in belly deep nsow for the horse and i ga e he a big cow the last shell I had squareon shoulder broadside and she never even flinched and stood there for several minuted apparently missed lean thenreared and turned over and that 300 grainexpeimental Winchester silver tip had hit center and blew up in chest cavity. Been trying to get browning to go to ten inch rwist for ears for the 338 but no luck.

ten inchtwost is right for all the 333 and 338 calobers even our big 338-378-K.T. and is wonderfully accurate wih any heavy bullet 250 Noslyers up through the 275 Speer andthe 300 Winchester but a 12" twist simply will not handl the 300 grain and they tip even at 110 yards.

We had a darn good goose shoot and also some fun up at Littke Rock as well. Corssman promised me somepix andwill need them for ar icleson the seminars.If you have any extra shots send me a couple. Think the engraving is what has heldup you 44 mag at S & W as they get a lot of such orders and have to wait uour time but be well to write Bill on it anyway. Thanks for the invitatoin, but doubtvif we get out except to the NSGA and NRA shows this winter.Snowing here now and 20 above. best

That Win 94 NRA sporter 30-30 ideal for those little Texas white rail and a hell of a lot better than the 6 M Ms they had us use a cpuple years ago that went only half way through. Gritts Gresham abd I killd our with one heart shot each and also usedbut tow 12 gauge for our two 17 lb gobblers.

Ever, Elmer

Pge two,

I have killed sheep put to 600 yards with the 338s and 340s and they dont go anywhere and even on deer wi.thlung shots not asmuch meat damaged as with a high speed 30 or smaller caliber.

I guided 30 years and have hunted big game since I was 12 and will be 70 this next march and I never yet saw the man who could always hit his game right and anyone who has hunted much has lost game but damn few admit it. You know and I know the game seldom present the perfect shot out in the open and in the ti,ber almost never and you need a load that will put them down. The little 358 Winchester with 250 grain bullet to my notion is betŧer than any and all the 30 calibers for timber shooring even the 300 Wby and I have seen them all used enough to know

Leading in sixguns caused by roo soft bullets, half jacket pure lead bullets, oversize bullets or too hot and fast a powder melting bases. I never have any trouble and load 20 grains2400 with my Hensley & Gibbs Keith 220 grain bullet in the 41 mags and 22 grains 2400 and my 250 grain bullets in the 44 mags and cast slugs never softer than one to 16 ton and lead and soze .410" for the 41s and .429" for the 44s.

The sixgun which according to the Aaskins famdly is long obselete , and does have a jump fro ctg case to barrel throat, also has to upset to fill chamber throat, then swaige down to fit barrel. Many colts especially in 357 and 38 Spl have .360" cylinder throats and .354" groove daimter and these guns wkll lead unlessyouh size bullets down to groove diamter and also cast them hard as hell.

Proper bullets properly loaded and lubircated and sized to fit a good sixgun whose cy inder t roat is compatabile with the groove diamter do not lead at all. Of course the autos have no barrel and cylinder junction and gain a few feet in velocity but the old 45 auto is the omly one worth a tinkers damn for defense or game shooting except small game. Best

Sincerely,
Keith.

MAGAZINE • ELMER KEITH SHOOTING EDITOR | SALMON, IDAHO

Dec 17th-71

Mr. Jack R. Tishue,
28 Vista Ave.,
Glen Burnie, Md. 21061

Dear Jack:

enclosed is our price sheet and for two people with one w ate hunter would cost you $ 6840. and three weeks of course would be less but no object in taking four persons as that would necessitate two lorrys and two land rovers and two white hunter and cost about the same.
We can get you a good buff and elephant in 30 days but a lot of provinces will not sell ele and the major species licenses unless a 30 day hunt=
So dont see how you are going to make a good hunt for $ 4000. each, as licenses will cost uou a lot and Air fare will be at least 4 1500. I was out around 4000. on each of my trips andthe huntes were given to me by Bob Petersen, John Lawrence and Truman Fowler, that just for licenses and shipping back trpphies hotels etc. Also Peteren paid for my Tanzania licensebut bought them for kenya and Tamganyika in 57.
There are some outfits will take you for less but am not acquainted with them and dont know how good. ou might write to Glenn Cottar, Nairobi and get his charges or John NorthCote, Uganda Wildlife Safaris at Kampalla. That outfit quoted you far below our prices and I havenothing to do with setting them up. Enclosed is our old rate for 1970 and has increased. Best

Sincerely
Keith.

Jan 5th,973

Enclosed is a long epistle against our freind Etter from your ex-magazine. I think you and earl wise in quitting that publication. Listen to this vice presidents statement that 6.5 bullet is effective on edium sized game at 1500 yards when ou and I and e rl have seen far heavier loads fail miserably many times at 300 to 400 yards even when fairly well placed.

Also am sending you two khowledgeable ripes I got from my magazine. Evidentl the one lad on Sharps never did any a,bacore fishing and came up with only a head from a 30 pound albacore after the sharks finished him and neither does he klow that a woumded and bleeding shark has only seconds to live before the other sharps eat him and guess he never heard of the boy out swimming and yelling sharp and then when the recused him he said too late Too late the shark has got his genitals.You cant please them all and those with the least knowledge are he most vociferous.

Let me know if you got the Shotgun book I sent Xmas. and again many thanks for the ring have been wearingit sinceit arrived and like it very much. Think you will like to wrok for Jack Lewis a hell of a lot better, Best for the new year and keep in to ch. HAve to go back to Shelbyville to the Super-Vel shindig the last of the month, then the magazine phoned hey want to fly mom and I back to L.A. fo something or other and wanted me to bring an ebrgaved sixgun, told me nothing doing hanged if I will chance it under this new fedhj-Jack law.

As Always,
Elmer.

P.S. If you want to take a crack at these two letter, go ahead.

MAGAZINE • ELMER KEITH SHOOTING EDITOR | SALMON, IDAHO

Jan 11th-72

Dear Tishue:

Bonanza Books Inc. boughtStackpole rights to shotguns and Sixguns and now have them out at $ 1.95 shotguns and $ 3.95 Sixguns. Putlet Book o. of N.Y.C. sold me a batch of Sixguns and still ha e some copies shotguns at old high price. I carry them merely to fill orders of those who want autographed copies and have losy money doing so every year as I also have given away a hell of a lot of them to freknds and callers. I wi l furnish auto raphed co ies Sixguns at $ 5.50 postpaid as have tp pay fo-bits postage and insurance plus 15 cent cartro ns plus parce;s post from N:Y.C. here and then ave to brun gas to take ti P.O. a da hell of a lot of ti,e lost doing so and autographing so hope not too many want autographed copies and evenworse they send them to me with postage nd want auto raphed and then have to furnish re mailing catons and a lot of time repacking and taking to P. O. Only thing it does is place a copy in hands of about everyoje watjgg these books, Stackpole said they would get 10% roya tyb and spliy it with me and only think Iever made clear on books is the ruoyaty checks from the publisher.

If uou forgoe elephant you might make that trip cheap. Vant understand the air fare as cost me around 1500 plus first trip in %57 and about same for ticket round yrip in 69, so dont know but never heard of such cheap far to africa, maybe they are getting it down now.Africa going to hell fast at least East africa and rotten politics taking over and dont think I ever want any more of East africamyself, might be sfe yet in Rhodesia and surrounding small countries ᴛhe blcks are kicking out old land pwnders right an left and giving them nothing in return for big land holdings cattle and ranches and the situation gets worse monthly from all reports I get ifyou want to hunt africa better do it this year.

that 7 M M Rem mag will do nicely for antelope andbplaced shots on mule deer sheep and goat but last trip down river on a hunt I saw a black bear take a 270 raking shot at 300 yds and get away an saw an old Billy got take a 175 grain 7 M M Rem core lokt right through middle braodside, he rolled offthe ledge, fell over alciff then hobbledto another ledge and fell 50 feet and git up and went into timber and got away, next day those four Texans went after him as he was again peeched on his ledge and when he got up and turned around I could clearly see a big blood patch on each side about middle. they yried stalking him up hill which . yold then would not work nd long beforetheygot in range he g otbup and dissapeared in tumber Hope he lived. Ive long ago quit suing my 7 M M and 300 mags for anything but pests and prefer the 338 in various forms even for

long range ob mule deer as its certain the smaller ones are not.

MAGAZINE • ELMER KEITH SHOOTING EDITOR | SALMON, IDAHO

Jan 24th-72

Dear Tishue:

Have writgen eight bpoks and only three left in circulation so to speak. The Shotgun and Sixgun Books have been reprinted and a darn good job as good or better than Stackpoles last printing and guess they printed a hell of a lot of them. I have to pay freight on hem from N.Y.C. and then pay for mailing cartons or padded envelopes and then fo-bits postage and insurance nd on top of that time to autograph and pack and drive to the P.O. tobget tjem off so will sell the Sixgun book at $ 5.50 delivered and $ 5 here and the shotgun book at $ 3.50 and $ 4. I think, have some of the $ 8.50 shotgun booksleft will sell before I biy a stock of the /thers. Make no money in these I sell and autograph in fact go in the hole counting the ones donated and the time and expense incident to autographing and getting them off but di it for th few who want autographed copies.

Regardless of Jack OConnor and Warren Page I have seen more big game killed than oth of them and dont want any 7 M M for africa myself as have seen too many failures both here and in the north from the cartridge. See no reason to use it when bigger and better loads available.

Also dont like two bullet weights in one rifle except soft npse and solids, use one bullet weight and learn where it shoots or you /will never be worth a damn wi h either nor will you learn its trajectory curve. A long heavy bullet at 2500 to 2600 is all that is needed and to hell with the short light weight high speeds as o t at 40/ to 500 yards th heavy bullets have already caughy up with them and are flatter over longer ranges and have a lot mpre authorit at any range and dont blow up.

Yes fowler was going to use a 225 grain 338 and a 300 grain I belive and tolld him better go to 250 Nosler alone or 275 Speer alone but hear laste ussue speers not doing so well one shed its jac et at close range here and did not go through big bull elk braodside All I have used for years were superb as were thoseused by George Gelman in Africa on 22 head game ihcluding buffalo from the 338-378-K.T. Bikl Jordan sed 250 Noslers excelusively on several wounded buff and all game from his 338-378 K.T. with perfect success.

The 338 O.K?H. is darn good cartridge only beaten for veloc ty by he 338 Win mag which isbour old 33e O.K.H. belted for all practical purposes but a bullet .008" larger diameter and not asgood sectional density but available

I booked a party for Africa some tikme ago and they wanted roan Greater Kudu and Sable and have to go to Tanzania for them. dont know of any Sable or gretaer Kudud available in Kenya.Unless you want elephant which you dont think you might do better getting Jack Atcheson of Hancock St, Butte, Mont to boo you for Zambia asthey have a hell of a lot of sable and Kudu and buff down there and lower cpsts I think. also situation better politically for americans than Kenya or Tamzania asgetting pretty rough there now from what I hear.

Sincerely
Keith.

April 4th-72

Mr Ken Lomont,
4421 So.Wayne Ave.,
Fort Wayne, Ind.46807

Dear Ken:
Many thanks for the pix they are excellent, also for tghis 6 shot 100 yard gorup. That is wonderful accuracy and damn well proves what the 41 mag will shoot.I dont want any jackted through my guns if can get my 220 grain H & G buller loads as too hard on t hroat and also on top strap and same goes for gas checks and both raise pressures.
That auto-mag promisedto dend e agun for test and write up but never done so like H R and that Officers Spfld promised but never done so so to hell with writing up an thing on them if t ey cant keep their word. Not much intereted in the auto magmyself anyway as a good Ruger or Smith 44 mag far better suited to my needs.
Been having helln of a hout with Flu sinne being back there and seemedtol effect heart as well they hadme hospital three days made very onceivable test and phoned heart beat to Pottland a couple times came up finally nothing wrong except poor circulation and damn doc wantingvto fly me to Salt Lake to see if a heart surgeon there could get some excuse for a heart operation, hell with them and I am not going for any heart surgery at my age 73, might as well die in pone piece when t/t/me comes.
Have new Ruger 45 Colt 7½ front sight coked off to one side so cut to 4 5/8" and fitted sight straight, so will see what it wull do but sure is a rough job as compared with my new Frontier Colt 7¼ 45. That is best sixgun Colt ever turned out and have ine of thevolld original 1880 vintage flat top target 7½# 44 Spls target sighted. and its a peach abdnow worth lot to collectors.
I dont mind recoil of 44 at all shoot it same as 22 but lot of lillie fungers gents do almost cr when they shoit it. So that cimpensator might help them/ But like these knotheads who insist a 243 or 308 adequate for all big game and one just wrote he had killed 70 hread and neverlost any animal withn t hem. now dam well he is worlds bes shot or most monumental liar.
Come o t and we will, try bust some jacks this summer and hope o seeyou then. have to go NRA show and then to Ariz Tom told me to Thell eeds live ammo fast draw show the 6th and 7th May. All bhe best and keep your powder dry, put paragraph in column that you are back in business and hope they run it. Best yo your wife and Dad.

Sincerely,
Keith.

GUNS & AMMO MAGAZINE • ELMER KEITH, SHOOTING EDITOR | SALMON, IDAHO

4th-72.

     Been racking my brain trying to remember who bought tow books of me at the show and I gave them a check for change. Looked through cancelled checks and no luck figured sooner or later someone would give me hell or cash that change check so i would know who ordered the bokks and which ones, so a, damn glad you wrote and your books are on the way today insured P.P.

     I thought I had a note in bill fold but must have lost it and did noy remember whichone of uou ordered and paid for a cpuple books.

     I put your order in through Doug Hellstrpm vice president nd he answeredme but his letter got mixed up with some I sent the magazine as intended sending to you, so have written him agin on your order and hope t is brings results.

     I have asked Sierra several times and their engineer to get a 250 to 275 grain B.T. spitzer soft point oyt in 338 and he talked very favorably but bo luck yet also went after Nosler to again bring oyt the 300 grain 3 5 as was bet bullet in that caliber on game. Thwir 250 is a peach on most all of our game as well asthe 275 Speer.

     Going make up another 338-74 Keith Farquharson Have everything now but the wood and wonder of Keith ˘teegall of Gunnison has s me good french in thick shorgun and foreend bfanks with good fancy dark strsak figure.

     My old Golden lab did not get much work tghis fall but he did put some blue grouse, sage hens chukars, huns and xcpuple mallards in the back of the car for me. ᴮest and let me know if you get the books and that 44 mag,

As Ever Elmer

GUNS & AMMO MAGAZINE • ELMER KEITH SHOOTING EDITOR | SALMON, IDAHO

12th-72

You got me wrong from that book Introduction, Am no kin whatever with Quantrell. Had an uncle who fought in Civil war Southern side, Oleander J Berry, who married Dads oldest sister. He was with Quantrell start of war said he found he was just a damn outlaw and quit hi and went to General Price and fought under him and was put out of commission at the battle of lexignton when rolling a cotton bale up to the fort which they took , he reached up over the bale to ram another ball down his old big bore Kentucky rifle which he used for sniping and a federal minne ball took him through roght arm breaking it and he was done for the duration. I am owever a deirect decendent on grand mother Keiths side from Capt Wm Calrk of the Lewis & Clark xpedition. Also Bill Keith an ancestor gave Gen Washington and his staff a dinner and toast in Madera wine the night beforethey forded the Delware, so guess am as much an amerixan as any but the indians'

Iver Henriksen will make up my latest 338-74 Keith on this fine engraved Farquharson action.

I dont want anythong to do with any bullet light than 250 grains in the 338 340 338-74 K and the 338-378 K.T. as that is light enough an not sodamn sure but the 275 Speer may even beat the 250Nosler for trajectory over 400 yds. Thos two are my bullets and ha e beennin correspondence ith the head engineer of Sierra for a 250 or better a 275 B.T. match grade soft pount spitzer and they have invited me to see thm at the NRA convention and am also after Nosler to make a 300 grain 375 agaun.

My son had tough luck several years with 358 Norma as those 250 grain steel jacket went through both elk and mule bucks broadside with no expansion, one elk and one deer he lost but gpt other two elk and several deer but that steel jacket too stoff as I wrote Sheldon of Norma and Ted finally sold the rile and I gave him ny 340 Wby by Winslow which is a gol rifle as had another fine one from Wby with no free bore and premium Doug bbl and ten inch twist that shoots ingo one hole at 110 yds.

Haveing ell of a winter and not enpuhgh big game left for seed and the winter will get most of them and the damn Game Comm sold us down the river with cheap out of state licenses and O'Connor fro, his latest blurb is as ppular as a skunk at a wedding around here. Hope & W gets your gun out soon. Best for the new year and maybe see you at Port and if tghey send me there.

Ever, Elmer

ELMER KEITH -

(08) 756-3210

Sept 13th-72

Well am finally getting over the damn Hing Colg Flu, too seven million 200.000 units penicill9in in the butt via the long needle plus six days of eight penicillin pills per diem and shrunk from 170 odd to 150 and now feeling lot better as was the damn Flu eeffecting my heart am sure, as have had no chest pains and feeling better.

Well at lomg last Robert D. Haydem, Manager of Operations, Sierra Bullets 10532 s. Painter Ave., Santa Fee Springs, Calif/ 90670, just wrote me that according to my wishes as I talked with him at last NSGA show they have brought o t a 250 grain 338 spitzer as I wanted and asked for. HAs 6.5 caliber ogive and 11 degree boat tail .200 lomg. Should be what we have been wanting and is sending me samples for test. Suggest you and Etter both get some of him for this falls hunt and maybe one of the three of us will find some thing left to shoot at.

Really enjpyed your good article In Gun Sport you sent me and also Etters last one. See in last O Life Sept ot Oct dont remember but just came in he is panning me abouy tghe seven elk lost with shoulder shots from the 264-140 grain By Sid Hinkles parties uver at Selway Lodge and also my observance of the four elk lost one fall with 270-130 grain in Lochsa. Panning me as usual AND THEN GOES ON TO SAY THExxxxxxxxxxxxxxxxX Dam this hunt and peck machine goy in gear pn capitals. 338 and the 375 might kill quicker but says a high lubg shot wull kill as we all know even from a amn little 222 but his malarky needs calling again and at every opportunity you and Earl get.

Am tapeing my autobiography and about half through and working all I can stand a day trying to get it out so all for now. Bill Jordan wrote said he heard I was to be nominated for first Super Vel tropjy. I recommended Charlie Sskins myself. Jordan had good shoot in africa 32 head I believe used the 338-378 K.T. and a 25-06 on smaller stuff but saw no elephant worth shooting and did not get lion. Best and keep in touch

Ever Elmer

Jan 3rd-72

Mr. JAck R. Tishue Jr.,
28 Vista Ave.,
Ferndale, Md. 21061

Dear Jack:

Thanskf for you good letter on Africa. Glad you got ho e O.K. asA Africa is fast going to hellas far as I am concerned and dont think I'll ever go back, Certainly I never asked any man for anything in my life and wont start now even if O'C promotes many more trips, I am not built that way.

Sent avgood Texas party over to East Africa for a 45 day hunt the firts of Sept last and no word whatever from thm to date so wonder if something went wring or they got clobbered or what will writw Caulfeild and see if he can tell me what happenedas they wereput with a good man George DeBono.

I have my house and cabin so full of heads now no place for more so think will shoot meat only from now on and more shotgunning. Considering all handicaps think you and your wife did pretty well.

Malnarick phoned me a cpupl,e days ago said Jack O'C asked him for a free trip next fall.Guess he was never on anything but a guided hunt in jis life.

No dpubt some of finest Kudu and Sable down where you hunted but I got a cpuple nice ones greater and kxkgxx lesser so will do me as am not like some of them wanting to be at the top of everything.Hell with that as we will all crawlunder the rocks ere too long.

Sorry you did nit get a good buff and elephant butvthatvths some hutting i better cpuntry tjough they got a lot of buff down in Botswana and theyshould have put you one some. Ele down therego to 45 pound average for old buils. Best wishes and many thanks for trying to promote a free u hunt for me but I sure will not write anyone asking for such and dont know if would go anyway the way Africa is going at present. Best for the ew Yea

Sincerely,
Keith

Jan 3rd-73

Mr. Jerry L. Nelsen,
Ranchester Hotel,
Box 149,
Ranchester, Wyo. 82839

Dear Mr. Nelsen:

    Rifles for Large Game sol,d out years ago and will be no more to be had as far as I know.
    The 30-348 will make you a good deer rifle but I dont recommend 30s for elk or big stuff. My 338-74-Keith would be a lot better in a single shot if you can jeta supply 9.3X 74 cases to neck down.
    The 30-348 should give about same ve,ocit es asthe 300 Win mag but I would prefer it chambered for the regular 348 and hand laad as its a hell of a lot better cartridge with a 250 grain bullet than anything possible from a 30 and then too tyat case has a 50 caliber head and throws all thrust boack on breech block, so personally Id much prefer the 348 to any necked down version.
    I too tried a cattleman and they are junk. This one had two chambers way off the normal group and we had to do a lot of work and 5th shot frpn end the wholedarn extractor and housing flew over my shoulder and frame not case hardned but color blued etc.
    Best singl actions are the Rugers and Cilts and S & W in the D.A.Guns. Damn these imported spanish and italian revolvers have yet to see a very good one. tested a Garcia and it also was haywire would not group two chmbaers and could not lower fkmmx rear sight enough and still shot a foot high at 2' yards and pierced near:y all primers, so buy American is my advice. Agree with you on the 30-30 as elk rifle and also most all other 30s for that matter to my notion and after 30 years guideing. Best for the new Year

                                                                   Sincerely
                                                                   Keith

Feb 23rd-73

Dear Mr. Nelsen:

Glad you are getting some co yote shooting. The damn ecologists and bi ologists here have about all predators including eagles and cougar as well as the blue heronm fish duck and kinfisher as well as all hawks and owls with complete protection and wonder why our game is go ne. Idaho is compleye sh shot out as far as big game is concerned and very clo se on small game as well. The biologists run ou r mountain rams donw with H elicoters and put radio beacons on them and wonder why they die in three days, also o ne bilogist given permit to shoot 30 pregannt does to see how the Foe tus was doing. Another killed around 120 deer one winter here to see what they were eating. We ned a three year closed season all biy game in Idaho and an open season and a damn big bounty on Bio logi sts. The coyotes are getting co mplet ely out of co ntro p since they took away the cyanide guns and 1080 from our govt h unters. Mow killing calves and sheep broad daylight on the ranches.

I dont l iek a sixgun barrel over 7½" and that for horse ba ck or hunting use anf fact is have done some very fine game shooting the 4" S & W44 mag I pack all time. Do nt recall the pic tures you sent as I answer letters and send them with my carbons to the magazine so God knows where they may now be. Have over a 100 letters laying here now to be answered as havebeen damn sick with Flu and also back to Shelbyville Ind and then to L.A account the Handgunners award.

W e had Calif hu nters he by the thousand for several years account cheaperthan other state license and they cleaned us out.

Sincerely,
Keith

Feb 26th-73

Mr. Jack R. Tishue,
28 Vista Ave.,
Ferndale, Md. 21061

Dear Jack:

    Greatly appreciate your workingvto promote an african hunt for me but dont think I'll ever go over again as am get ting too darn old andalready have specimens of about all I wanted. Like wise my health. Been fighting the darn flu and still prety sick since getting back from theHandgu nners award at Shelbyville and then o n to L.A. and back. Blod pressure went up and have gotten it down again but surely have not been able to write since getting home and have aboyt a 100 lettrs piled up to ans and a lot of magazine work to get out for my column as well/

    Am glad you folks had a good trip over there and down around Rhodesia is about all that is left uncontaminated by negro and communist rule. Am enclosing the pictures and you surely got some nice heads, Too darn sick to writ e more,

                                                   Best,
                                                   Elmer

larch 5th-73

    Been too damn sick to write my freinds or keep up the magazine work and am way behind. They gave us the Hangunner award, then the magazine flew us to L.A. for some pix and then Salt Lake soked in and we were five days down there. Caught some form of the damn Flu again and been sick ever since not in bed but too ornery to write or accomplish anyt hi ng.

    Enjoyed both your good artic les and believe we are turn ing the corner on thi s amall bore versus big bore deal and mo re hu nt ers are finding out through dear experience that it taskes caliber and bullet weight to anchor heavy stew meat. Glad yoiu got a better assignment. Jack offered me one if I ever needed it but this has been my best and enjoy working with our fine crew.

    Betwixt high blood pressure whcih we have gotten down, an old hart and will be 74 the 8th, I have got to lick this darn Flu bug , Fi shed wit h S lim Pickens at a Winchester Seminar down off tip baya Calif Cabo Lucas. Caught a 155 marlin but sli m did not get h is hooked his one bits, great guy t o be with. All for now as too dan sick to try to write,

                                                    As Ever,
                                                    ELMER

March 8th-73

Mr. Jack Tish u e;
28 Vista Ave.,
Ferndale, Md. 21061

Dear Jack:
First dont think will ever be able to physically handl e
ano ther Safari as D oc has about grounded me. Blood Pressure
skyrocketed to 182 over 120, have it down now to 150 over 80 and
think I am l icking th is combination of London Flu and heart
deficiency, but a hunt in Africa I think will be out as am 74 today.
Hvae a loo or more letters piled up here now to ans so wlnt
write your friend Grobler, but you can send him my letter. He is
not entirely wrong either as I shot coyotes forten years with 150
frain 30-06 service bullets and never lost a coyote as they tjmbled
to beat Hell. Then the winter of 1925 I l ost 15 coyotes sho t through
lungs with the 173 grain B.T. 30-06 that did not tumble, so you see
Grobler is also right on his count.
For American Bison, African Buff, elephant , rhino and
hippo I would use nothing but vsilids from mybown experience but o f
course is not a drop in the sea to that of many African hunters.
Dont send any check for a book th at wont be out until
fall. Rhe damn publishers right now have not filled my last order
for Sixguns sent before Xmas and have a stadck o f checks and mon
orders for it and guess the failed to anticipate size of Xmas sales.
Now the Over unders, For many years I have recommended
the Browning as tops, but since have found many good ones the
the new R emington 3200, while it looks like hell with pen space
between barrels is probably best engineered of them all. Co st field
grade $ 450.Not a single screw head appears on whole action or foreend
iron and two screws in grip cap and two in butt plate. The Winchester
101 has proven a very fine gun for me and have shot and thoroughly
tested several of them.The Aya in high g rade is another good one
as is the Perazzi . Personally I prefer side by sides to any and
all over unders, swing faster, open less wide for reloading and look
like a gun instead a club.Hve not seen the Shadow nor about ten o
other new over unders on the market. Th ink Id as soon stick to
Browni ng Winchester or Remi ngton as the foreign.Re tu rning y our
pix and thanks for all the dope. Best

Sincerely
Keith

GUNS & AMMO MAGAZINE • ELMER KEITH SHOOTING EDITOR | SALMON, IDAHO 83467

P.O. Box 1072

April 24th-73

Dear George:

        Rifle

Just a note to say the <u>rival</u> arrived safely, front siht bent o ver and ru ined and butt pad perished, so am having front sight made and new Pachmayr installed and then will test with both 270 and 300 and see if she will shoot, If it does may keep it myself and send you ch eck and if not to suit will sure sell for you anyway as did the 285 To Jack Avery.

        Feeling btter dailiy but have hig h blood pressure, goes up and down one week 144 over 80 and last time 188 over 100 and taking damn lot of pills, dont k n ow if would help may try scotch next.

        Quite dry h ere now rains for three month s or much snow sure hope we get some moisture as stays cloudy all time and a bit of wind as well. Worried about Don as he has been in hospital in Missoula near a week now. Phoned Iver and he was going to see him but has not phoned me back yet, will keep you posted, damn cancer flared up I think or else treatment s caused a blockage. All the best,

                                        Ever, Elmer

GUNS & AMMO HOME OFFICE: 5959 HOLLYWOOD BLVD., LOS ANGELES 28, CALIF.

GUNS & AMMO MAGAZINE • ELMER KEITH SHOOTING EDITOR | SALMON, IDAHO

May 2nd-73

Dear George:

Had a new frontvsight made for t he double rifle and also a present ation Pachmayr pad fitted properly and took it out for test, It is absolutely hopeless as a rifle, Fou nd the top rib loose at rear end and for a foot up right side of ri b. After five shot s left side started to oepn up betwen ri b and barrel also. At just 20 yards from bench rest it shot three inches wide with both 270 and 300 grai n factory loads. If both barrels fired had to break it over the knee as cases swell and very hard to ext ract

Dont tghink would ever work right except hand loaded with a ten grain reduction in powder charge and then would possibly not group both barrles together.

So am going try and sell the stock foreend and engraved acti on for replacing of barrels to a fine mag 20 bore shotgun as belive can be done and at not o ver 150 to 200 buck cost as this is a fine French walnit stock and well engraved action and all of actio n seems O,K. as well as ejectors, but as a rile is done am afraid. Think I can get uiyr $ 225. o ut of it sooner or lat er for making over into a 20 bore shotgun.

DonMartin back from Missoula and feeling alittle better and look ing bett er but is very thin. All the best and will sell this gun sooner or later,

As Always Elmer

GUNS & AMMO HOME OFFICE: 5959 HOLLYWOOD BLVD., LOS ANGELES 28, CALIF.

GUNS & AMMO MAGAZINE • ELMER KEITH, SHOOTING EDITOR | SALMON, IDAHO

July 3rd-73

    Broke my darn ridgepole the 9th June car accident, Refused hospital though fith lombar showed crack in X ray, toughed it out at home, hurt like hell first two weeks and stillaches a lot but been up and around every day and feel will heal quicker that way and if had went to hospital as Doc wanted my hide would look like a de-quilled porcupine fromHypo shots. Going lick it onmy tw0 feet alright. Getting better and less ache every day. Be sure come by here when you get around and will be able to shoot sixguns I guess though dontvwant to shoot any of my heavy rifles until this busted vertebrae knits solid again.

    Sure sorry to learn of your dad's death. I lost my mother in 40 and Dad in 43, and as you say sure makes you look at your whole card.

    Havent been down to Hagels in several years, think he sort of high tûnes me now even though I bought his first artócle when gun ed for Outdoorsman and also rer-wrote and helped him getstarted in the game also used him as aguide one trip and he spent a good part of the time getting my party to go with him next year and even had the temerity to ask me to guide for him as he got Doc DuComb the next yr but dont think they hadmuch luck. He has gone small bore on us as Etter writes so let him go along with 270 Jack, Page and Bowman far as I am concerned.Glad you got out of that gunsport mag as that is all it will ever be under present 2300 yard woodchuck shooting experts.

    I had Don Milhaljevic test my Patriot and sent in write-up and targets today will shoot into inch and quarter 20 yards with 40 grains black best load we found and to exact elvbtion and point of aim, shot high with 30 and little lower with 35 and with 45 grains too much powd and groups enlarged and lower out of bull, faster bbl time.

    Have to change positions quite often to ease this old ridgepole but getting better all time, See you when you get into this neck of the woods.

    Fowler was here and spent a couple days and he shot a couple of the big doubles and we had darn good visit. I took another poke at thos crazy 1000 yard deer shooting of hoyers and any sane hunter with a thimble full of experience would never countenance such waste of game as they are bound to lose most of them hit at any such range. They cant kid me and Fowler took one jerk named Harry Kieser apart at the seams, you will enjoy his letter or get Etter to send you a copy. No plans yet for fall and want to do some shooting and have invite from Remington for deer hunt down on Apache reservation new Mexico in Dec and havent heard from Win yet. Expect to make the smeinars God willing at least. Best and be seeing you,

                                  Ever, Elmer

Aug 31st-73

      Glad to get your good letter and agree with you 100% on these small bore advocates and their teaching the youngeters to buse inadequate calibers simply because a lot of magazine editors know no better and think the public likes to be fooled. Jobson Oconnor, Page , Bowman and others havebeen taking cracks at me for years on this score but among all the old guides, here, in Canada and Alaska and the white hunters that are still left in Africa, they agree with my logic on calibers 100%. So I just go on reporting what I have seen and experienced and let the fiction writers go their way.
      Sent the magazine my last elephant hunt article for their Annual but now see it announced in their new Hunting magazine and of all things old 270 jack who retired, I think forcibly from O'Life is now editorial director. Sure wish they had not run my article in any magazine under his editing.Since he turned a damn auto loading shotgun on me and pulled operating handle back and let go to battery on live round at Nilo and when I jumpe d to one siad and yelled at him he followed me with muzzle and pulled the breech block back and let her go again at my middle, trying for an accident. The boys with us and Cotton the dog Handler were very mad and I snapped my safety off as had not unloaded and would if enough life left in me have given him thebworks if he has shot me and I have seen too damn many gjns go off when they go to battery. First time I ever shot with him at Nilo at Winchesters first seminar he lew my hat over my eyes whehn the pheasant was on my side and my bird and he did same thing to little Bev Man when guns wer supposedto be unloaded and both Bev and I told all Remington and Winchester ofrficials we would never shoot with him again and he has not been at last three seminars at either place. Wish him luck but dont wantcto be an oconnor accident. At Nilo I was just getting over bad coronary and they would not let me slug the mud first day but made me shoot trap. Next day Cotton the dog handler said Elmer get in dog truck with me and you canstrdoll along the road, as could only go twenty yards then and had to rest. and sho9ot what birds come up and cross the road. I did so and downed about a dozen pheasants, then we cam to another strip of corn and old 270 got in the barrow pit bwtween me and the group of shooters working the strip. Cotton called to him three times to let Elmer have those birds crossingvthebroad but he pretended not to hear. I knew he was just going try show me up, so when three different pheasants exploded from the barrow pit, I blew each all to hell and he shot in tghe feathers, then he put his gun in the truck and got a camera out and when Cotton told us to all unload he pulled that accident stijnt on me. That is the truth asGod is my wiyness so you can see whay I have no use for the big Irishamn. He rewrote my articlesand book chapers for several years aftertaking the o'Life job and people would send me tear sheets and tell mewhat stuff of mine he had used.

Page two

Gene I wonder howlong the shooting public will fall for that stuff with you, Etter and I and a few others trying to get all hunters to use adequate calibers. The whole substance is the fact these small bore addics cannot stand the slight recoil of an adequate rifle and cartridge.

Last fall my son put a 250 grain 340 Wby into an elk across acanyon and two old african hunters were close enough to the bull to hear theplunk of the slug going home, but as elk was tipped up going up steep mountain across canyone feel sure Ted hit him in the panuch and as you know they will go for miles with such a hit as that 300 pound water and grass filled paunch will stop any high velocty rifle and only the 1ld 45 Sharps, 500 grain 45-40, 400 Jeffert and 400 Whelen will have any chance getting throughb it and sometomes they also fail.

I have a couple 7 M M mags and a couple 300 mags and the boy also but we dont use em any more even for mule deer as the 338s and 340s and my new ctg 338-74 and the 338-378 K.T. kill so much bter at long range with far less damage to the meat.

. Likewise several of thesehunters including 270 dontvwork on elephant and buffalo, but prefer inofensive plains game and maybe alion and leopard or two, but you notice tyhey dont hunt ele and buff steady, as Fowler and I did to the exclusion of all lesser gaem.

The 350 Rem mag with 250 grain is a good killer and when used in the 700 so you can seat bullet out and use more powder is very close if not quite as good asthe 35 Whelen thatI used for years on everything. The lityle 358 Winchester si a peach and the only small cartridge I will ecommend for elk and the big stuff. Mom has two of them a 99 Savage and a light weight model 70 and everything she has hoit with them has went down and stayed down. No so with the damn small bore even 06.In 30 years guideing I saw so much game take a gun full of 270s and 06 and go for a long ways that I soured on all the small calibers. These boys who claim all good luck are not telling the truth. Wild BillWatson had old 270 and that texas oil man out here and they both missed a big bull standing broadside at 150 yards/ Sure an elk can be killed with a 22 L.R. if hit just right at butt of ear. Wild bill once plugged a cow atsome twenty five feet back of ear and killed her with colt woodsman and the bull came out of the brush and chased Bill around a tree and finally he shot him at butt of ear and killed him also and he did not want the oldstinker in the rut.but for any years I have refused toi recommend any bullet of less than 33 caliber and les than 250 grain weight and know from many years e experience am right so will stick to it,

Reaction around the old guides here of 270 heading the new magazine is far from good, Like to see Pete and Tom make a popular magazine out of it, but time will tell.

Damn sorry to learn of your family trouble, Menapause?? maybe, women go off their rocker at times from it and sure hope your good lady sees things traight and moves back home and soon.

I am not a writer thnak God just a reporter of facts and when I see many of these writers turning to fiction to try and impresstheir readers, makes me sick, I dont even want to try to count all the game I have killed as shot for two or three famlies during the depression, but all meat was used and badly needed do lknow I have killed 50 elk on my onw and god willing will try and get another this year if plans go through. They ptomised to come get mom and I and bring us back, Best, Ever Elmer

Oct 16th-73

Thanks for your good letter and also the Swiggett article and to think I prevalied on S & W to build him a 44 magnum. He is knocking both you and I and also Bill Jordan and Earl Etter and all of us who are trying to get people tonuse adequate rifles for the game hunted.

The 358 Winchester and the 350 Rem mag best small cartridges we have and only ones I will recommend on elk and then only with 250 grain bullets. The 350 Rem in the model 700 become areal rifle where you can hand load and seat bullets out for a decent load and you simply must have a 250 grain slug to anchor game reliable of the elk moose and bear class.

Myabe you think I am crazy but I used 300 mags from 1926 on for years and had Hoffman built their last rifle for me in that caliber back in 1926 and god knows the game I shot with it including two grizzly, but from here on out I wont use any 7 M M mag nor anh 300 mag on our big game veen deer and have had so many more clean long range kills withbthe various 338s that i will never agin shot the 30s on game except for pest shooting.

I saw agoat take a 175 Gr. 7 M M mag right through the middle fall off his cliff 30 feet get up and hobble to next ledge and fall off it for 20 feet, get up and go away in the timber. Next day he was back on his original perch and when he got up and turned around had a blood patch size of my hand through scope of 20 X on each side. the four Texans who had wounded him said they would goit up and get him. Told them only chance of doing so was to drop out of sight in a gulch and go up it to top and come down on each side of the ledge. We were ahalf mile away but i knew the goat has already seen us. They would not gake my word and approached uphill and the goat got up and left when they were 600 yards away Put seven of eleven 220 grain 300 H & H in a grizzle 400 yds first shot thenallmrest running shoiting at 400 yds down to last two at 150 yards. then he went in the alders and then charged the guide and a couple 44mag finished the bear. That was enough 30s for me and have used 338s or 375s ever since foraboyt all our game

Coyotes and eagles got most of our good faun antelope crop this year only few fauns left and they have killed especially the damn eagles some 80 to 90% of our sheep and goat lambs every year as long as I can remember and seen eagles kill full grown mule deer, elk calves and one 15" antelope buck and this on deer on many occassions. Coyotes gaining in number and some sheep menm quitting and some on acct of eagles as well getting the lambs. They say an eagle cant pack a lamb but it dont take him lo ng to cut one in two.nYears ago Capt Guleke and I picked up Mountain sheep lamb legs under one eagle nest and had nine lambs and three legs left over. Wrote 19 page article on Predators or Game for G &A and Tom said would run it but never appeared and

also disaaperared when keesee was editor, Our game is gone.

Elmer

GUNS & AMMO MAGAZINE • ELMER KEITH SHOOTING EDITOR | SALMON, IDAHO

Dec 1st-73

Mr. George Bredsten, 4069 Birch Lane,
Fairbanks, Alaska, 99701.
Dear Mr. Bredsten:
Glad to have your report on your african trip.
I have only killed three cape buff but consider them the
toughest animal on the face of the earth to stop or bring down
and usually only spine or brain hits will do it with one shot
and the best killing shot i know of on broadside shots is to go up
the shoulder in line with the spine and try to break both spine
and shoulder at same time. Killed my last two one shot each with
500 Nitro express double left barrel, first one a spine shot
behind shoulder next one frontal neck shot and broke neck
My first one back in 1957 shot through heart with 476-520
grain solid and he just barged into hard run and secknd barrel
hit square in shoulder and boke both shoulder and spine and
killed isntantly.
The 375 is neither and elephant nor a buff gun to my notion
but the 458 should have done better and wish you had used factory
Win or Rem steel jacket solids. Hornady did have a fine
nickel silver solid but went back to something ese at present
and am not getting good reports from it at all,. as have anotyher
letter and 30 hits in a grand old elephantg before they got him
down, 8 475-2s, four 404s and a bunch of 458s, mnany well placed.
Your 405 grains oft point 45-70s were no doubt doing more damage
tahn the 500 sooids from the 458 as they were expanding. My load
of 53 grains 3031 would have been even better I believe. There
is no substitute for caliber, bullet weight and penetration on
buff or elephant eit/her for that matter and high velocity is
not the answer. You can bet the 45-70 405 grain soft point with
53 grains 3031 will beat any 375 load at any range up to 150 yards
for actual killing in my opinion. Have used it a lot of deer and
elk.
You can see why I do not recommend 30 calibers or smaller
for elk moose and big bear nothing less than a 250 grain slug an
33 caliber for me at least on this game. O.Connor, Jobson, Bowman
et all to the contrary. They are doing a great dis service to
young hunters by recomending t-he pop gun 30 calibers for the
heavy game and have caused loss of morebig game than anything else
except predators. I also found all white hunters over there,
Nicky Blunt, John Lawrence, John Northcote, Mike Hissey whom
I hunted with all of them had no use whatever for anything
under a 375 even for plains game. and hated the thoughtvof the300
Wbys. Also george DeBono and another hunter whose name I dont
now recall showed me two clinets 300 wbys just before the took
off with Two Italians and one was going take is 577 and
DeBono said he would take both his 500 doubles as they knew what
to expect from the300s on the African game. Have heard nothing on
the proposed 45-120-550 Ruger but hope he brings it out I used it
in Sharps for years and is a good killer busted my first Amr.

buffalo with one, Yes your 20 grain 2400 and my 454424 wil beat any 41
mag for killing. Best, Sincerely, Keith

GUNS & AMMO MAGAZINE • ELMER KEITH SHOOTING EDITOR | SALMON, IDAHO

Dec 4th-73

Dear Gene:

    We now have a new dditor for C &A and I belive a damn good man isntead of red haired Martin. Tom promised to straighten things out down there as I was ready to send Pete my resignation. A grea t'many shorts I sent in for my column later appreared as full length articles by Cillins, James and the staff. Also theye ven told French the new deitor they had to run questions and ans in my dept account no material on hand when the articlesnadshorts sent in wojld have filled my column for next two years. Roomed with French at Shelter Island at Winchester Seminar off Long island N.Y- had damn good circle shoot on pheasants and mallars. I downed 14 mallardsand four pheasants and missed afew more that morn also quail and pheasant shoot with Askins Kozicky and Warner. Not much new from Winchester a beautiful $ 650 engraved model 101 trap gun with fine Frenchw alnut etc, a new auto shotgun tgyhat dont load as fast or easy as the o-ld 1400 and looks and balances like the Model 12 and a new auto loading clip loded 22 that was it.

    Hope you will be at Remington Seminar at Ro swell New Mex the 12 so we can renure acquaintance so to speak. Never fired a rifle shot ghis fall either here o Colo. went out three days here and hunters from allmover U.S. by the thousands, Bugled one and got two elk hunters so enough of that. Maybe will get a shot at a buck down on t-he mexcalero apache range where Rem takes us.

    The magazine took my good elephant article I wrote for the annual and cut in half and used front half in the Jack O'Connor Huntkng mag. I finally got hgold of Siatos and he promisedto straighten things oyt down there or would have quit and went fishing. I got a damn rotten deal for some tkme and had enough. Getting lot of kicks on the new Hunting mag already so belive enough readers will write in to show them the error of putting 270 on top in the new mag as belive he was fired from O!Life in spite of his saying retired if retired what the hell is he doing now in tghis magazine.//

    Enjoyed your pecarry and sheep hunts in GunWorld I belive. have killed nine old rams myself and guided for 25 more but all native wild sheep from mexico to Alaska.

    Hope your new assignment pans oyt well and sure should as Lewis a hell of a lot different from that 1000 yd deer shooting editor of the other magazine. Just finished getting caught up on answering letters and also sent some more material to the editor for my column and wrote up the Win seminar and now am free man for day or so I hope. Someone got away with a hell of a lot of material and even long articles I sent in and ruined my elephant article also so am not happy with former ed even though pretended to bemy freind. Coloins also out of it, maybe fired and he re wrote and messed up a lot of my stuff and even thought elephantbpix captioned they changedthem toread elephant and Lesser Kudu on the Kagera when that shootinbg was on the Galana. Hell of a kote Had good report on45-70 on cape buff, but another bog elephant took 30 rounds and still on his feet from

Best Ever Elmer

Elmer

ELMER KEITH • *SHOOTING EDITOR*
BOX 1072 • SALMON, IDAHO 83467 • PHONE: (208) 756-3210

Jan 15th-74

Glad you like the book. Winchester Press say they will b
bring oit my auto-biography in the spring and expect
galleys in Feb.
Wont beat NRA but intend making the NSGA show
and the sne annual handgunner award as on the committe for
selecting the next recipient.
Missed you at both seminars and they wre very good
flew right over your twontwice in a Cessna 130 going and
coming from Ruidoso. busted a three year old mulie down there
on the apache reservayion and nice fat meat but that damn igh
speed 150 grain 7 Mag they madeus use ruined the near rib cage
by blowing back particles of jacket and trachea contents etc. Hear
dissapeared all except a 1½ inc section of the very tip and poure
it and lungs out. damn aface blow up bullet on meat., Could not get
a head shot acct limbs and only 100 yds could have done t-he job
with my sixgun easy but acceded to the Remington wishes and they
gave us the rifles.
Told Siatos I did not want my name kn the Hunting
mag as longs 270 in it and he said would oblige me and give me
my wishes. they to0k my good elephant article that I wrote for
the Annual and took fro nt half and run i nHunting and kept the p
pictures that I wanted returned also changed my captions on them
and had me hunting elephant and lesser Kudu on the Kagera and
since have had three long distance calls from old elephant hunters
wanting to know where in hell i found elephant and kudu on the
Kagera. Thank allah our old editor is now moved to the Hunting
Mag and we have a new editor Howard French whom I have every
confidence in. The-old regime got away with some six months
material I had for my column and have been busy ever since
getting a new supply to mr. french. Hope you have good luck with
them and that the magazine prospers but I want no part of it
as above. Weh a man tried to deliberately kill you by a so called
accident as he did I want nothing to do wth him/
aHad two weeks damn cold weather 15 to 30 below and
has no thawed out and raining and slick as a greased onion everywher
you cn hardly stand up let alone travel and will be lot of car wrecks
today I am sure.
Get a 338 O.K.H.instead the 333 O.K.H. account no bulets
the 3330" and plenty for the 338. and Iver Henriksen, 1211 So. 2n d
St, Missoula, Montana best man to do all the metal work and uses
cold rust blueing and has been making a lot of the 333 O.K.H.
rifles and knows the score.Id then use the 300 grain Winchester
for timber shooting and youbcan go up to 60 grains 4350
behind the 300 grain bullet, fine accuracy great penetration
and wont blow up all the meat. Crook an elbow for me. Best for
the new year,

Ever, Elmer

ELMER KEITH • *SHOOTING EDITOR*
BOX 1072 • SALMON, IDAHO 83467 • PHONE: (208) 756-3210

March 13th-74

Dear Allen:

    I have autographed three pix I think is Stan Holland and his wife. Met so darn many people cant remember names. You should not have gone to trouble of sending all these pix out here but I have marked a few five I believe wouldlike when you have time.

They sure came out good add would not mind one of Joes trophy room Have been very busy trying to catch up with magazine work since getting back havent even had time to go fishing and the darn Game Dept closes steelhead season in few days and now have got to get reservations and go to Atlanta to the NRA show and will double back by the Y-O ranch as they offdred me a free Oudad Barbary sheep ad try and get him for a head and also some sheep meat. Sure hope you can all make it out next summer though our rabbits and game is gone here thanks tothe damn game dept protectiing everything in the predator line cougar, black bear and grizz, all hawks owls and blue cranes fish ducks and kingfishers and now they even have protected all crows ravens and magpies. We need an open season on these bird brianed biologists and a $ 1000. bounty on them as well.

    Many many thanks for lettigg us see all the fine shots you took of the hangunner award and also Joes place. Give my best to Ken and his wife also. Never did hear from that lad thht Jurras said was sending me a 44 auto-mag, not that I need another gun but would have tested and found out what i could of it. Been referring quite a few to Ken for bullets, mostly want my sixgun slugs.

Best to all,

returning album
re-insured
E.K.

Ever, Elmer

GUNS & AMMO

ELMER KEITH, EXECUTIVE EDITOR • SALMON, IDAHO 83467

May 25th-74

Dear George:

     Don is getting very low, confined to bed now and damn cancer getting allmover him I think. mind clear and sahrp and I go to see him and take him magazines every few days. Its a hell of a way for a good man and your best freind to have to go.

     Write him when you can will help. Come up and make me a visit as I have a brown jug of No. Carolina white lighting, double distilled corn and about 180 proof would make Irish coffe maybe if you used enough coffee with it. Some carolina hujnters brought it in last fall. Took don a small jar and he said made him several drinks but now can only drink wine, cant eat hardly at all as sets up gas in stomache so lives on wine principally.

     Had bad weathrlast fall 15 to 30 below and river gorded 25 miles and over flowed and flooded but then fell ofto a mild winter lots of deep wet snow in hills and only few light showers here-in Salmon for last few months, Need rain badly in the lower country but have lots of snow for summer irrigation.

     Magazine has kept me very busy, had to go to long Island N.Y. for Winchester seminar and some good duck and pheasant quail and chucker shooting, then to Ruidoso, new Mex for Remington Seminar hunting with the Paches and gave us each a mule deer and some got white tails. Then to NSGA show in Chicago and the 2nd annual Handgunner award, They gave it to Askins, Want to see Bill Ruger get next one and then Bill Jordan, they gave' me the first one.

     Then to Atlanta for the NRA show, smallest NRA convention I have yet attended and about all my old freinds gone and only new faces I did not know and magazine kept me busy autographing books pix etc. Then home via Y-O ranhc as they gave me an Ibex hu-nt and' got a nice head but a small black on beard nearly foot long. Told the taxidermist I had shot the Mormon Bishop and would hemount the head and front quarters for me.??? Made 7Ø pounds damn good Salami out of the meat.

     Magazine made me executive ed and raised salary to $ 1200.00 a month so cant kick. We both hadthe damn Flu and little Mom is down with it yet and hard to break up they get different kinds of flu bug s and now Penicillin dont seem to work on this varietymay have to get something elseto get her over it.

     Not much else new, would like to crook an elbow with you if you ever get up this way. All the best to all of you,

                                          Sincerely,
                                          Elmer

Home Office: 8490 Sunset Blvd., Los Angeles, Calif. 90069 • (213) 657-5100

GUNS & AMMO

ELMER KEITH, EXECUTIVE EDITOR • SALMON, IDAHO 83467

Oct 15th-74

Dear George:
Glad to hear from you and I also wrote a piece for my column and sent it in on Don'death. should come out in two or three months. Part of time he was out of his head and part of timme doped up untidl he did not know what was going on and suffered in the dram hospital over a year.
Some two years ago when he got back from Missoula he told me," Dont know what I will do with my guns as Doc says I T is aterminal cancer. I told him I would be glad to buy his old colts and add to my collection. No he says they are yours and you cant buy them but want you to have them and better take them now I refused to touch anything as long as he was alive. Then before he went to the Hospital he called Lorraine and I over to his house and told us to take anything we wanted and aslo the old Colts including Bill Howell's old ivory stocked 45 S.A.Colt.I refused to tough anything. He had two rifles and some six or seven Ruger pistols I had Bill Ruger give him also three fine S & W guns , there cap and ball colts and couple more imitations.
Marie gathered up all of them she could find but the Neighbors Schallers had already stolen the bill Howell Colt ad they had a key, and also I think Bill howeels 45-70 86 Winchester that I had gotten Don the last nickel steel barrel from Winchester and Iver Henriksen rebarrelled it.
Don had a great many meals with us after Isabelle died as had him over at every opportunity and also for breakfast and to help me for three days when I made a big mulligan in winter.He told us then he had willed everything to Marie and she had Willeverything to him and Snook was lawyer. At any rate after Don went to hospital the Schallers, Adams another neighbor must have gotten Don drunk or when he was full of dope and had Snook make out a new will and Schallers got all his guns and car and Adams his whole library, and even gave Snooks secty $ 250. and Shcallers and Adams and another woman all $ 1000 each. They had gotten numbers of guns I think and had someone call Iver and tell a big lie to get number of a little Ruger 22 Don had given her that Iver had target sighted. Then some three months ago Don had a nurse call us and wanted us to come over to hospital Nurse said he wanted togive us some books, but whenw e arrived Don said I am in my right mind today Elmer and want you to have all my hand guns as you willtake care of and use them and the Schallers will simply -trade them for beer.He said you better go overto Marie and get them now. I went and told Marie but she said she wanted himnto sign a realease on the guns and next day when she went over he was out of his head and didnot even remember our being there. So I guess they got everything unless some monies went to Marie and are nowbtrying to getDons home as well. Sorry mess.Lawyer Snook called on Marie and she tured all the gu-ns over to him, so no chance you or I everhaving any of his guns.
Book supposedto be out next month, They lost a lot of copy and just shipped them my copy yesterday, Hell of a note should have them in Nov. They say price will be ten bucks. Our best to you all and keep in touch.
                                         Ever, Elmer

Home Office: 8490 Sunset Blvd., Los Angeles, Calif. 90069 • (213) 657-5100

GUNS & AMMO

ELMER KEITH, EXECUTIVE EDITOR • SALMON, IDAHO 83467

Feb 3rd-75

Dear George:

Just got home last week from Houston NSGA show and handgunner award. they gave the trophy to Bill Ruger and hope Bill Jordan gets the next one. Havent seen Marie since getting home snowed under with work for column and have to write up the show and award as well as raft of letters. Marie sidd she had one of Don's guns for you and gave me his old 1917 S & W that I once killed 16 hopping jacks with without a miss in Hooper lane obove may. the jacks were coking oyt from a haystack thatbthey finally ate under until it fell over in a steady streal and not running fast but just hopping along across the road some 40 yards in front of my car. I then gave thebol,d gun to Don and he killed several more before he missed one. Sure am glad to have that old gun to remember him by. Sont know what she has for you,s she hi-graded them from the big box before the crooked attonery and Schallers got them but will see you get it whatever it is if she will let me" Think just sealed up and have Haveman twd ship to your dealerwill be dafest way.

They got a lot of loading tools of mine and a melting electirc furnace also I ha doaned Don but ill gotten gains will rpofit no man so let me have them.Don had a lot of ammo somehwere think in cellar and she gave me some odds and ends but only trifle of whant he must have had on hand and guess they got all the rest. was a half box reloads wthmy bullets for the 45 1917.I know he had some of my moulds also. also a bullet sizeing and lubricating machine and other tools,. he is only one I loadned tools to and did not bother him to get th-em when he was sick, he gave me all his handguns but I did not have sense enough to have it written up and notorized so they got them all but the old 1917 I guess.

Winchester press changed my text in severla places an all captions as well and tried to give them a braggadiocio effect which is not my style at all. I am throughly disgusted with them and their use of the wealth of materila sent 330 pictures and should have been run fullpage many of them an all t-hrough th e book and alos books shouldnhbave been 8¼ X 11½ at least and a good slick color jacket. They took six down to the NSGA show and sold fie in first hour or two and refused to sell the sixth as they wanted to take orders from it but someone stole it nekt hour, so yhou can see how far ahead of their nose they can see.Maybe it will sell quien sabe senor, but it surely is not hwta I wanted and would never recommend them to anyone. I shouldmhave had it porinted on my own by Caxton Press of Caldwell but I do ot have the marketing arrangements they have so maybe will sell but sure is not what it could have been. Dont think anyone will, notice the discrepansy on y-our writeup but but they added stuff here and therethat I nbver wrote and this may well be just a small part of it. They cut out a hell of a lot should have beenbrun all about Fly epidemic and my brother's death and I lost a rib from empysema operation and six months in hospital etc. Best

Ever, Elmer

Home Office: 8490 Sunset Blvd., Los Angeles, Calif. 90069 • (213) 657-5100

GUNS & AMMO

ELMER KEITH, EXECUTIVE EDITOR • SALMON, IDAHO 83467

Feb 28th-75

Dear Mr. Bredsten:

        Am shipping you two copies of my autobiography today autograped as you wished. Have to charge $ 11.00 each now account havi ng to pay shippage from New York, wrapping postage insurance and gas to deliver to P.O. So you can send me the other two bucks at your leisure.

        I dont knwo what revolver mr. Heter of Speers tested my 454424 bullet with 20 grains 2400 in as I shoit it regularly with 20 grains 2400 in my new Colt Vlat top target and also in three Ruger supers with no heavy pressure whatever . However for the Rugers and also the new Colt I cast them faily hard and size them down to .451" which is groove diamter of the new Rugers and late Colts S.A. and I'll bet me Heter used some 454" bullet and probably soft ones at that otherwise he never could have gotten any heavy pressures out of my recommended load of 20 grains 2400. One man over the divide in Darby Mont has killed for black bear with his 4½" Ruger and uses 24 grains 2400 in his gun with no undue pressures and easy case extraction and said my slug went clean through shoulders on all four and two of them pretty good sized blacks. Another man back east uses 24 grain 2400 behind my bullet also but again sizes to .451" and no extra pressure,. Personally I only recommend 20 grains so will be safe in all the late -Co-lts guns if they size bullet down to .451" and cast them hard as they should be for pebetration, for expansion my 235 grain Hollow poi nt in either 45 Colt or 44 mag or 44 Spl cast one to 16 tin and lead works fine for expansion, and for the 44 Spl use 17 grains 2400 in the ew solid head cases or 18.5 in the old ballon head and for the 44 mag use 22 grains 2400 with either bullet same as the charges for either bullet in tghe 44 Spl and the 45 Colt 235 grain hollow point with 20 grains, then if some nut pust them inaColt they will work and even thoughbthe Ruger with its thicker cylinder willbstand more I do-nt recommand it as some may get heavy loads in a Colt and bulge cylinder stops or crack rear end barrel.Have had many accounts of gunfight wehre super vel 357 has failed and taken six shots an some good officers killed.

        In the 41 magnumuse my 220 grain bullet by Hensley & Gibbs, Box 10 Murphy Oregon, the only one making moulds to my true desighn anymore. And I use 20 grains 2400 behind it sized .410" with perfect success in both S & W and one Ruger black hawk. Killed 5 calibou in the arctic with the pair of S & W guns when up there with ken Oldham and git my big polar bear several years back. Gav the caribou to the eskimos who damn well neded the meat. Best

                                              Sincerely
                                              Keith

Home Office: 8490 Sunset Blvd., Los Angeles, Calif. 90069 · (213) 657-5100

ELMER KEITH, EXECUTIVE EDITOR • SALMON, IDAHO 83467

March 6th-75

Mr. George Bredsten
Box 561,
Wrangell, Alaska, 99929

Dear George:

    Shipped the book to Barry Haight yesterday. Glad to have your report on my sixgun bullets and loads up there on the heavy game. It coincides exactly with my experience. I killed over 30 hige range bulls at the slaughter house with 41 and 44 magnums and found my 250 grain bullet in the 44 mag backed by 22 grains 2400 often went through the entriee skull and brain pan and ibnto the neck while all factory loads stayed in the skull. I killed elk, caribou and a good many deer with the load as well and never did fond a bullet in a deer always went through and one man killed four black bear with the load from a 7½ " ruger and had complete pentration on btoadside shoulder shots. I killed five caribou for the Eskimos with the 41 mags and Remington factory loads when up in the arctic foom close ramge ouyt to 400 yards the longest shot and required eleven shot s before I saw where the tenth one landed and made correction and killed him. Snow blowing and colder than hell.
    Lyman ruined my bulolets by cutting down diameter of front band and also its width and only hensley & Gibbs, Box 10 Murphy oregon make my true bullet designs and I designed a 220 grain copy of my 44s for them. It does best for me with 20 grain 2400 also and beats factory and dont wear the barrel or lead.
    You must have penetration on anything from deer up for certain results all angles presented and I favor the hard solid Keith bullet that will penetrate better than about all high velocity rifle loads on game except the Nosler and possibly the 275 heavy Jacket Speer and Bitterroot in 338 caliber.
    I dropped the 45 Colt back in the early twenties when I fiund I could hand load the 44 spl to amuch more powerful ad higher velocity load with same bullet weight and my old load of 18.5 grains 2400 and my 250 grain in baldoon head cases is not so very far behind the 44 mag or 17 grains with the new solid head cases. The 44 mag is tops and the 41 mag with 20 grains 2400 and my 220 grain H & G bullet very good and like my loads better than any factory jacketed soft core bullets for big game. My experience bears out your findings 100% on all counts, Best wishes,

Sincerely

Keith

Home Office: 8490 Sunset Blvd., Los Angeles, Calif. 90069 • (213) 657-5100

GUNS & AMMO

ELMER KEITH, EXECUTIVE EDITOR • SALMON, IDAHO 83467

March 9th-75

Dear George:

Well passed the 76th milestoe yesterday. Had snow squall this morn but thing spring is on the rails as snow about gone from the yard.

Gave Marie the address to shop that gun to and she said it was the little Serial No 52 original single six Ruger 22 L.R. that iver Henriksen fitted target sights to and Don gave it to here but she told Lorraine last week she wanted to keep it awhile, Quien Sabe Senor. Judge told me Schaller got $ 1500.00 Dons guns were appraised at. Aslo his car and a $ 1000. cash etc. I had some mould blocks and an electric melting furniach and and bullet sizeing and lub machine over there had loaned Don and would not bother him when he was sick so guess Shcaller got all them also. Hope Marie decided to send that gun on to you and offered to help in any way, but up to her as Don gave it to her. She did give me his old 45 1917 that i once killed 16 rabbits straight without a miss as they crossed the road just hoppingf along, all moving butg not running all out coming out of George Santee's Field where they were feeding on his hay stack and it finally fell over after the undercut it enough. Glad to have one of his guns anyway though he gave me all his sixguns but Shcallers had already gotten away with the Bill Howell ivory stocked 7½" 45 s.a. amnd also Bill howells 45-70 model '86 carbine that I had procured last nickel steel barrel from Winchester and Henriksen rebarreled it for Don, as they were not in Box when Marie collected them and Don told me they were when he left home. He died thinking I had his sixguns and I would not tell him otherwise as would have upset him and I went overto Marie and told her Don had given them to me and askedme to go to her and collect them but she wanted to have him sggn a chit to that effect as the scallers had already had him change his will and wen she went next day he was out of his head bad and stayed that way. Hope she send you that littel Ruger as its a good one and Iver did a nice job on it but nothing I can do about it.

Got a lot of letters to get out and more testing guns to do and more write ups for the magazine. Lorraine and I fig urging on being down to Oroville, Calif the 14th for Fred Huntingtons open house the 14th and 15th, then on to San Diego the 16th for the NRA show and also to help pick the next ten nominees for the hand gunner award, Hope we can give next one to Bill Jordan. Autobiography selling preety weell from al, the phone calls and letters been getting in spate of the lousiest job of publishing Iever had when I sent them 585 pages text and 330 pictures and they sure did not make use of the material sent. Hell of a note as it could have been a good book and plenty full pages pix instead the tiny things they jumbled together and then picked out the poorest of all sent and also tried to give it a braggadocio slant and changed about all photo captions as well. Best to you and the ladies, As Ever Elmer

Home Office: 8490 Sunset Blvd., Los Angeles, Calif. 90069 · (213) 657-5100

GUNS & AMMO

ELMER KEITH, EXECUTIVE EDITOR • SALMON, IDAHO 83467

March 9th-75

Dear Lawrence:

      The holster arrived and I had to move the strap that goes around my chest back about 2½" and also sewed it to the shoulder loop there, then removed the bucke from then adjustable chest strap and got the leather just right and sewed it to hold the snap. Now the rig rides just right and is very comfortable and prefectly fits my 1917 pair of guns and also will hadle my 5" 44 mag perfectly as well. Its a darn good outfit, light in weight and comfortable and the gun hangs just right now. Have been recommending your no 7 for a lot more years than I care to remember and will continue so to do. Many thanksfor this good gun rig, It will be used,

      Hope you got Jerry Haskins fixed up for all his slings. havent heard from him since the show and he never writes but does call once ina while. Having a snow storm here this morn but think spring is breaking. All thebbest,

                                    Sincerely,
                                      Keith

Elmer

GUNS & AMMO

ELMER KEITH, EXECUTIVE EDITOR • SALMON, IDAHO 83467

April 10th-75

Dear George:

Shipping the book to mr,.Goosen in africa this morn an d hope it arrives safely but cannot insure to africa or Canada.Thanks.

I tried back in 1953 to get Remington to load my heavy 44 Spl load 18.5 grains 2400 and 250 grain keith bukletwhen I spent a week with them at the factory but they were afraid of thebold T. lockck so i suggested the 44mag and that was the start of it.

I would like to see S & W agai n bring out their 1950 Targetv44 Spl and 45 Colt but doubt if they can see through the fog . Also wonder about the K Frame, troubłe is the frame is small and the cylinder would have to be five shot and the rear end of barrel would be very thin and subject to cracking. It might be possible for the 41 mag but i doubt it and certainly would be too thin rear end of barrel for heavyv44 spl loads.

Have long urged Bill Ruger to bring out a larger version of his Security six in 41 and 44 mag but dont know what he will do about it. San Antonio, Rex, Amarillo, San francisco, The Nevada state partol and several other cities have now went to my 41 mag for arming their police depts and a great many sheriffs outfits a s well. They are gadually learing after having some 850 odd officers killed in gun fights a year ago when armed with 38s and 357s and as you say the 41 or the 44 would be much better but I doubt if we get either on the K frame S & W though might be possible in the 41 mag but doubt it for longevity.

The mag-na -oort outfit offere d me a freejob but did not want any holes in my sixgun barrelsm However they did cut the vents in a 44 auto=mag just received and as you say greatly cuts down both recoil and uplift of the gun and for those who wantcto do fast D.A. works would be a considerable assett.

Hope you get the American Big Game handgunners asso together and this 44 auto-mag would be great for those who prefer an auto loader but for me would much preferthe Ruger or S & W 44 mag as is big clumsy heavy gun and slow to get in action and dependednt on ammo to function and costs $ 500. and the ammo $ 19.50 a box and throws empties where are often hard to find and cases must be exactas t o length to make certain functioning of the arm. Cant see it for myself in comparison with a good Ruger or S & W sixgun but a lot of hunters will want and no doubt prefer. It.

See Mr. Wood in his gunsmithing ciluymn got off on the worng foot and wrote of solthing he knew little about caliming my 22 grains 2400 and 250 grain bullet would in tikme loosen up any sixgun. Ken Lomont puty 80m000 rounds through one rug er with my load and still going strong and developes only 34,000 PSI and only less than 3,000 psi variation when one ten rounds of Peters factory 44 mag varied 11,600 PSI in ten rounds and one wontht up to nearly 49,000 psi on Whites lab tests. Best, Sincerely

Keith

Home Office: 8490 Sunset Blvd., Los Angeles, Calif. 90069 · (213) 657-5100

GUNS & AMMO

ELMER KEITH, EXECUTIVE EDITOR • SALMON, IDAHO 83467

April 28th-75

Mr. George Bredsen,
Box 561,
Wrangell, Alaska. 99929.

Dear George "

      First Hope you can get the American hand gunners association going, not only for its sake and the great many gunners but also as another strong force against these crazy communists who would outlaw hand gu-ns and hunting. Will do what I can when necessary,

      Now as to taking a lion with a hand gun. Can be done nicely if a standing shot is obtained at reasonably close range and a hit made in brain or spine, otherwise will result in a wounded lion and a damn lot of trouble for someone. I killed as big a lion as they ever get in 1957 with John Lawrence and have no room for another lion rug now and would not put out the $ 2200 .00 American dollars plus another $ 1600 in air fair to kill another one and cant afford such trips myself. Likewise am past 76 years young now and not as active as I used to be though I can still shoot. I woujld preferto use one of my 500 doubles or at least my 404 on a lion by preference but am also sure I could turn the trick if a 50 yard shot could be obtained anda s standing shot as well so one could place my 250 grain slug in brain or spine. The 44 mag with my load woujldpenetrate best and if factory loads then the steel jacket Norma is best and the auto mag could laso be used but I would be charry of trusting any auto on such game.

      My freind and employer Bob Petersen I belibe would be the man to do tqhis stunt with Tom Siatos backing him up and if Pete dont want to tackle it then perhaps Lee Jurras and Georbye Monte backing hik up coujld do the job. Steve Herrit als o migmt want to tackle it but he damn well better use something in the 44 mag line rather than any pip squeak light bullet 30 Herritt.

      I will send your letter on to Pete in case he would want to make the trip and he can afford it whoich I cannot. I coached him when he killed one of his forst mule deer with fhis 6½" 44 mag S & W and he later went to Alaska and took as large a o polar bear as they come and also a big brownie and also a fine moose all with the 44 mag and Norma ammo. So think he is the beas man for the job as he is a damn good pistol and rifle as well as shotgun shot. All the best and thanks for the fine offer. If I did not already have a fine lion my be tempted but now rather see someone else get a tomcat. Best

Sincerely
Keith.

GUNS & AMMO

ELMER KEITH, EXECUTIVE EDITOR • SALMON, IDAHO 83467

June 3rd-75

Dear George:

    Sent your letter to petersen but learned he was now in Japan but may be home by now. If he and Tom Siatos dont take up the african lion sixgun hu-nt suggest t/hat you/- cobtact lee Juras, Box 163, Shelbyville, Ind. 46176 as he and Nonte might take on that trip. Can ill aford either time or money myself.

    Have one of the automags here now and some 180 grain Juras loads. Very accurate but also very creepy lousy trigqr pull and they cut mag-na-port slots in barrels and throws muzzle blast back in your ears. Big heavy cumbersome gun have to carry in shoulder holster, for my own use woujld not trade a good S & W or Ruger 44 mag for several of them.

    Have recently sent in write up on sixgu-ns for big game and my recommendations and guess it will come out in my clumn in tikme. have no use whatever for light bullets in sixguns useful only for squib load ten yard indoor shooting . like heavy bullets and my 44 mag load suits me best of all 22 grains 2400 and Hensely & Gibbs moulds of my 250 grain hard cast slugs. You got to have penetration and my loads beats all factory badly for that-Also covered the fact this load beats most expanding bullet high power rifle loads badly for penetration. Penetration mandatory for sixgun work omn big game. Have not seen any factory 44 mag loads that penetrated as well as my load on game except the Norma with steel jacket, rest dont go deep enough. the 357 and 41 auto mags cannot be near as good as their 44 mag and Juras said would load me some 265 grain Hornady and that should be best ofall for this auto-mag. Personaily the only auto pistol I care much about is the 45 Colt National Match, accurized or Gold cup and 230 grain hard ball and that for use on man not game but it beat all the Lugers and super 38s years ago for me on everything from jacks to mule deer. Nop comparison of it with the 41 or 44 mag for game gun however.

    Afraid Mr. Wood has a lot to learn/ø Lomont put over 80,000 my loads through a Dragoon Ruger no ill effects and many rounds also through the S & W 29s but said they required some tightening up after many thousand rounds. The 41 and 44 mag will beat anything out of the auto-mag to my notion or that crazy 30 Herritt as it is not even equal to a 30-30 and my hand load 44 mag beats the 30-30 badly on game up to at least 150 yards.

    We have a raft of young gun writers who do not know and never will as there is not now t-he game for them to larn on but they can write rings around me or most of the yimers, but also use plenty fiction which I do not. I have seen all those small calibers fail too many times in 30 years guideing and No hunt even mule deer with 338 Win. 340 Wby, my 338-74 Keith or the big 338-378 K.T. in preferance to any and all 7 Mags and 300 Mags. The 256 was and is a failure in a revolver as is any bottle neck ctg. It has no compariosn in kiolling power withbthe 41 amg as you state so shows Mr. milek does not know hwerof he writes. Earl Etter tested 30-30s with much heavy loads and bullets than the 30 Herrit and found t-he later wanting.Super vel 4 125 grain 357 through one crook did not prev his killing both officers. Have no use for less than 250 grain llets in 333 Best, Keith

Home Office: 8490 Sunset Blvd., Los Angeles, Calif. 90069 • (213) 657-5100

GUNS & AMMO

ELMER KEITH, EXECUTIVE EDITOR • SALMON, IDAHO 83467

June 10th-75

A freind of Bob Thomsons phoned me wanting me tocome down to Grand Junction for t-heir two day gun show. However would be an expensive trip for me as hard to get in and out of here would meant at least four days. Aslo they charge $ 90. each way to fly one out and in or else rattle around on a stage half a day and get hom way late on return, so unless they senta plane in for me and bring me back cant see where my ugly mug would do much good to the show. He said Jean thomson would be there and he wanted to meet me so told him to drive Jean over after the show and she could spend a week with us.

Now this high blood pressure, I have been fighting it for years and think that and the fact Bob got so fat was what killed him. Get some aldomet and water pills and take one each night and morn and while tghey will run you to t-heyused beer dispensary every ten minutes for a while they will also reduce you and fast. I tried cutting down to one each a day and pressure jmped back up to 170 over 90 so went back on them and now went down to 154 over 90 which they say is not bad for my age past 76.

Hope you can get a bear with that new 250 grain Sierra we have all worked so long for and please let me have details if you do. your boy will have no trouble with the 250 Nosler in the 340 Wby with 83 grains 4831 and CCI mag or 250 Federal primers. Killed my 47th elk with it at 450 yds before a bunch of Bob Thomsons hunters . Ted my son lost an elk the next year with the 340 Wby Winslow shooting across canyon as elt going up other side steep. Two old african hunters heard his slug strike the elk but got away as guide with ted said he missed, think bullet went down into paunch and gave song the devile for not going overand trailing him a couple miles to be sure. However he clobbered abig buck with the load.

Our game De;t just as dumb now protect all predatory birds even to the magpie and croww in Idaho all cougars and black bear except special license when the bear are eating up good part of our elk calves and the damn cougar which is very plentiful here take an awful toll of both elk and deer. Ray Torrey jumped a big tom off a six point elk he had just killed and treed him butvthouggt he had a paying party coming next day so did not shoot him. However he back trailed the cat and found he had killed a cow elk three days before. Had good antelope crop last spring but coyotes and eagles got most of the fauns. Nancolas and his Govt hellicopter pilot have killed 88 coyotes here last I talked to him and the govt Pilot said he had now flown for over 800 coyotes this winter and spring, that should help some. Damn these ecloogists who think predators eat only crippled,. Man destroyed the balance of nature a great many years ago. I have trailed cougar right past three legged deer and they never even tried to catch them. Coyotes wont touch an old ewe that has lain down to die, They know got meat as well as we. Best
Ever, Elmer

GUNS & AMMO

ELMER KEITH, EXECUTIVE EDITOR • SALMON, IDAHO 83467

June 19yh-75

Dear Mr. Harris:

      All our hand gun manufacturers are so hard pressed to keep upo with deman that tghey have slipped baldy on both inspection and proof firing and i - tghe cas e of many rugers fitting of parts and stock straps as well. So you are in luck that you have a very accurate gun which some I have tested were not.

      All the side swing 44 Spl S & W guns will take a normal and also considerably heavier loads thanthe factory load but none of the older ones including the T locks have the strength of the modern magagnums in either construction or steel. The magnums also have gar less protrusion of barrel back through frame than the ol,der models but you can safely use a charge of 7½ to 8 grains Unique with my 250 grain bullet sized .429 and cast failry hard or a charge of16,5 grains 2400 and I shot up to 18.5 grains 2400 in the olld balloon head cases in my 44 Spls for years both colts and Triple locks but teh new solid head cases will not-handle as much powder and charges should be cut to 17 grains for the modern gus like the 1950 Target and the older ones even lower to 16 to 16.5 grains 2400.

      Only the factory who knows the steels used could properly evaluate the strength of the early models and I have a considerable number of requesteds for a 44 specila like the 1950 target and the Rugers in this caliber. However the factories cannot keep up with orders so see little chance of them again brining oyt- the 1950 Target in 45 Colt and 44 Spl, hence these alterations to that calibre. Thanks for your kind invitation buytvgod knows if I wille ver be back up t-herebut have been through Juneau many times in the past-

                                Sincerely
                                Keith

Home Office: 8490 Sunset Blvd., Los Angeles, Calif. 90069 • (213) 657-5100

GUNS & AMMO

ELMER KEITH, EXECUTIVE EDITOR • SALMON, IDAHO 83467

June 30th-75

Dear George:

I dont know how to thank youvgentelmen for all the honor you have accorded me in the A.B.G.Ga Association.Think the are others more deserving. I also want to t-hank you for the life member ship.

The magazine keeps me far too busy to act as an official measurer of game trophies, what with all the phone calls and the house full of people a lot of the time and the gun inquiries besidestesting and writikng new stuff, keeps little Willie's nose to the grind stone. Havent been fishing in over a year, and now the salmon and steelhead fiishing prohibited. and got in very little hunting last fall as well. We are pretty well shot out here as far as big game is considered. some deer and elk in places far away from any road, but not one deer left now where we did have a thounsand a few years ago and elk going same way.

Want to thank you for keeping me abreast of developements in the associatioon and hope it grows steadily as we need desperately all the organized Americans to fight this crazy anti gun idiocy and the 1968 gun law. I will send copies of this material down to the magazine in case they wish to give the association any publicity.

Thanks for the dope on the black bear kill. Like you I want a clean wound channel t-hrough an animal broadside and want bothand entrace and exit hole the more blood let out and the more ari let in an animal hastens quick kills and a blood trail to follow. I have no use whatever for light high velocity bullets that explode on entrace and ruin a damn lot of meat and if not properly placed leave no blood trial and the game is lost. Likewise such loads ruin a quarter to half an animal. I like them and they are usefu, for just one purpose and that is destroying msall pests. Buit on all big game and especially meat animals want a clean wondhd channel through on broadside and deep penetration on raking shots, that will anchor an animal and not ruin his meat in tghe process. High velocity fine for long range where needed but even then long heavy bullets at moderate velocity far outrange the livht high speed stuff. Like you have taken a lot-of game elk and deer mostly with the old 45-70 especially in my old 1886 Winchester with 53 grains 3031 and 405 grain soft point and many head with the old black powder Sharps rfiles before that. All best wishes and many tnanks for you more than kind treatment and let me know anytime I can help.

Sincerely

Keith

Home Office: 8490 Sunset Blvd., Los Angeles, Calif. 90069 · (213) 657-5100

GUNS & AMMO

ELMER KEITH, EXECUTIVE EDITOR • SALMON, IDAHO 83467

July 14th-75

Dear Mr. Marshall:

    I hate to pour cold water on any new project, but must do so in your case. I have tested the 454 Casul and also the 45-70 revolvers made by wilson of Wisconsin and both are for the birds, inaccurate and in the case of the 45-70 and your proposed 444 far too heavy to carry except on a sling and even then you would be far better off with most any good carbine both for accuracy, killing power and getting into action quickly. Further cost of such a project would be astoonomical, and even the 44 Auto-Mag still has many breakage problems, but it and the 44 magnum Rugers and S & Ws in same caliber are the largest heaviest and most practical big game hand guns extant.

                                                  Sincerely
                                                  Keith

GUNS & AMMO

ELMER KEITH, EXECUTIVE EDITOR • SALMON, IDAHO 83467

August 10-75

Dear Mr. Noble:

      I am sneding your letter and check on down to L.A. to Mr. French our editor and he can turn over to circulation fØor for your subscription.
      The 38 S & W uses a 147grain bullet around .360" diameter and was loaded with 2.9 to 3 grains Bullseye and that is still a good load for it. However in the later solid frame S & W guns like the militray model heavier loads can be used up to 3.5 grain Bullseye or 4.5 grain unique. However itctakes a larger bjllet than the 38 Spl and 357 mag and the British used it with 200 grain slugs. Its largely obsolete now.
      For the 38 Spl depends on gunbused a s aligbt frame gun wont handle as much pressure as a heaVy one. For your good Ruger in 357 you can load my Keith 173 grain solid or hollow point with 14 grains 2400 for best load 358429 and this load also good in the heavy frame S & W guns and in 38 Splncases use 13.5 grains 2400 in heavy 45 frame S & W guns or Rugers. But in light weigyt small frame guns and even the Colt Officwrs model I dont like to go over 12 grains 2400 or 5.5 grains Ubique. 2400 is the best powder for heavy loads and Unique a medium velocity powder and Bullseye best in shot barrel guns. I have no data on a 190 grain but am sure you can use it in the Ruger if it is sized down to.357" and shoyld take around12 grains 2400 i n that gun.

                                      Sincerely
                                        Keith

GUNS & AMMO

ELMER KEITH, EXECUTIVE EDITOR • SALMON, IDAHO 83467

Aug 10th-75

Dear George:

    Thanks for the membership card and hope membership continues to grow.

    Two freinds and I have been after Sieera for a 250 to 275 grain 338 for years and the first ones they made no dman good were wonderfully accurate but blew up on everything and for two safaris in Africa as well as on elk here. Gene West knocked a cow elk down six times with 338 and this first bullet and lost her. The new one has 30 percent thicker jacket over ogive and 50 percent less lead exposure and no damn cannnellure to bust the jacket. These bullets form tghe 338-378 K.T. shoot under an inch at 100 yards and out at 500 yards printed 8½ inches higher than the 250 Nosler with same 100 grain load of 4831 and also shot four inhes closerto the wind than the Nosler and the 250 Nosler has always beena a whale of av good 338 bullet in all the various cases both here and in africa. Let me know how the new ones perform up there as they are flattest shooting of all and hope thse wilkstand up on heavy game.

    That 300 grain Winchester is best of all for reasonabl range or timber hunting and has given mesmallest groups of all of them in several rifles and cases from 338 Win, 340 Wbyv, 338-78 K.T. and my 338-74 Keith it also stands up on any heavy game with good penetration. Best wishes,

                                        Sincerely
                                        Keith

Home Office: 8490 Sunset Blvd., Los Angeles, Calif. 90069 • (213) 657-5100

GUNS & AMMO

ELMER KEITH, EXECUTIVE EDITOR • SALMON, IDAHO 83467

Oct 27th-75

Dear George:

Yes I read that hogwash by a Mr.-Cowgill in the Oct Rifleman and also had some 40 phone calls and letters from a similiar pamphelt put out by the F.B.I. some time previous recommending high speed 38s and 357s over 44s and 45s. I have in my books and many articles stressed the fact that there is no substitute for caliber and bullet weight to anchor either stew or man and not much use going over it again although the kids will believe it and the experenced old gunmen will scoff at it as you and I for we know better.

Long years ago I tested every damn 38 Spl and 357 mag and 9 M M and Super 38 loads availabel on everything from jacks and ghu cks to deer and in all cases found tghe old 45 auto hard ball superior in killing and stopping power. Why the F.B.I put ot that crazy bulletin from the tests of some laboratory in texas is beyond me as it is all a fallacy. Many old peace officers phoned me and some wrote as well about it. Looks lioke Govt, would not only lie to disarm us but also make our peace officers be targets for the criminals and under gunned as well. I think it is just some more of the Communist anti-gun kovement and shows how deeply it is now imbedded in our Government. Any damn fool that has shot game at all with- the various guns knows the difference ad God know the hundreds of gun battles that have been brought to my attention during last 50 years wherin the 38 sps the 357 mags and the Super 38 and 9 M Ms have failed miserably and many fine officers killed after making repeated hits on the criminals. Looks like the Commies want to kill off our officers as well as disarm the rest of us.

Agree with you on the Mag-na-port holds gun down in line and my freind Bill Jordan likes it as he says he is deaf or nearly so, For my part dont like it because it about deafens me and even others behind me and while wonderful in D.A.shooting is wrong for the S.A. guns as I want them to turn up in my hand so thumb will cobtact hammer in recoil, and come down cocked out of recoil. Harlon CArter and Bill Ruger both making good fight against gun control in congress and we all have to fight with them.

I pack a 4" 44 Mag S & W model 29 with 22 grains 2400 and my 250 grain hard cast solid all the tkme and that is my load. Have killed a lot of game with it caribou. elk, mule deer bear cougar and god knowsthe smaller stuff. I want penetration more than my old hollow point will give. On the sea this load gave kills on sharks under water out to 60 yards regularly but the factory soft nose hollow points expanded on water hit the damn sharks and richocheted off their hides and skipped across the sea. I want penetration first in a sixgun but on man targets you load with my hollow point 235 grain 44 is no doubt even better but one of my loads between the pelvis and the top of the head of any criminal will prevent any return fire. General Hathher was so far ahead of these new kid brain storms they will never ctach up as he had experience which they will never get and arm chiar theory is refuted in every gun fight.

Bestm Ever

GUNS & AMMO

ELMER KEITH, EXECUTIVE EDITOR • SALMON, IDAHO 83467

Dec 9th-75

Dear Mr. Bredsten:

Havenot seen Nonte's new book, but have seen a lot of his articles and his recommendation of 9 M M and 38 and 357 calibers for defense which I cannot buy at all. Likewise dontg thhink he has shot much of anything larger than antelope or maybe deer witbn those small bore hand guns and I cannot subscribe to Steve herritts 30 Herrit for big game at all even deer and antelope and to say the 30-30 is better than the 44 mag shows grows ignorance of the two guns on game The 44 mag goes through an elk lungs and the 30-30 seldom gets through in fact I have found them imbedded on off side of elk tghat actually got well from 30-30 13ng shots probably long range and bullet did not open too well and a string of scar tissue right thorugh lungs. Eben had a coyote I shot through lungs with a 250-3000 get caught in one of my traps two years later and he had a baeplace on each side the left higher than the exit asI shot down hill at him and a rib with big bulge each side and scar tissue string through lungs and he was then in good condition so recovered from the tikme I rolled him with that darn 250 Savage.

Nonte has done lot of work on cartridges and loads and is veruknowledgeable on ghat subject but I cannot buy his small bor epistols on either man or game nor his statement as you say that theb30-30 beats the 44 mag. It damn sure does not and we know it. Likewise I cannot agree with jeff cooper on the 30-30 vs the 44 mag a d God knows have seen both used on game enough. I have yet to get one -f my 250 grain bullets back after shooting a mule deer with 22 grains 2400 and even the first gas check really part jacket Rem 44 mags went through t-hat- buck I kileld at 600 yards or over with Paul kriley.

A man down in Texas and a freind were experimenting on bulletbpenetration with farious high power rifles. They had an open top water tank some ten feet long. One end blocked with some sort of one inch plastic fowm and the far end with two layers of this plastic. The various high power and magnum rifles stopped their bullets along the nnine feet of wate as they expanded and of course threw water all overthe place. then t-hey tried my 22grainbs 2400 and 250 grai n bullet from 44 mag sixgun and it went through the first baffle of one inch the nine feet of water and the two inch rear baffle and then dented the back end of the tank. there you have pentration of the 44 mag at its 1400 feet velocity against a hell of a lot of high power rifles with expanding bullets in that ni ne feet fo water and I remember killingsalmon several times under four feet of water with a 44 Spl and 18.5 grains 2400 and my buloet and also kiloing a lot of sharks with my 44 mag load and the Winchester hollow soft point merely richocheted off their tough hides after expanding on t-he water. Killed 12 one trip out of Calif coast withb my load and many shots out at 50 to 60 yds and bullet must have went through several feet of water as held a foot low and a foot forward of t-heir dorsal fins and got reults every tikm efrom a 4" SC& W,   Best, Sincerely Keith

GUNS & AMMO

ELMER KEITH, EXECUTIVE EDITOR • SALMON, IDAHO 83467

Jan 7th-76.

Dear Mr. Powell:

For your Marlin 45=70. I have for years used 53 grains 3031 behind the 405 grain soft point in my 1886 Winchesters and believe the 1895 new marlin just a sstrongbut anything from 50 to 53 grains makes agood load the latter going 1850 and under 30,000 PSI. I have also seen warnings but wonder what diameter and weight bullets used.

I have a 455 rechambered to 45 Colt in Triple Lock 6½ fixed disghted S & W and shoot factory or other loads up to 9800 feet in it. Cy liner walls are thin and with modern 45 Colt cases being thicker and less air space than old Balloon head case might be best to use 17½ grains 2400 tops. These guns usuallyu bored 457 however and the 454" old style bullet upsets to fill and the fine wide lands have considerable displacement Min e is very accurate. With late Colts and Ruger in 45 Colt you must size bullet down to .451". However as long as six fired empties extrace free and easy simultaneously then you are not getttingv t oo high pressures and that 457" groove diamter greately relieves pressures.

Sincerely
Keith

Shipped you book several days ago.

To
Bill Powell
with all best wishes of the author.
Elmer Keith
Salmon Idaho
Jan 6th 1976

GUNS & AMMO

ELMER KEITH, EXECUTIVE EDITOR • SALMON, IDAHO 83467

Feb 19th-76

Dear Bredsten:

        Well I also voted for Bill Jordan and he won the award this year and has damn well earned it. Skeeter is also a prime candidate in my book, but he had been in a bad auti accident and unable to attend. We had a good meeting and I sent them another Charter member as well. Dont think I'll go to Indianapolis

as so darn hardto getvin and out of here in winter or even spring at times. Had great NSGA show, but they kobbed me so did not get to see half of our advertisers or people in the aindustry I wished to see and some one ven put my name up on two big bulletin boards as a VIP and that done it as far as getting anywhere around the show.
        I fail to see how you canever equal the 300 G & H with any load you can getin the old Krag case. It will make you a fine rfle but still think you would have been better off with it chambered for abigger cartridge even the 375,I gave Bill one lf my 338-74 Keith rounds and t-hat long 4" slim cartridge I think best of all for our game in the single shots and it willbgroup in one hole at 100 yds. The lld Krag is a fine cartridge with 200 Nosler and I killedmy first elk witha Krag carbine and 220 army amy with tip filled and lifted off apoor procedure but it worked and thatwas damn long time agao.

        Have a 375 and a 458 in Rger single shots and the 458 will ct clover leaves at 100 yds bench rest and the 375 with hand loads of 250 Nosler or Sierra B.T. but not with factory 375s now days. Best of all single shot rifles to my notion. Have seven Farquharsons to prove it as they are tops but Ruger is best in all modern one sand lot neater slimmer action than the big Farquharsons

        Try for spine hit with the 44 mag on brownie or side base of ear shot and if you have tovtake broadside at too great range for brain then break shoulder and pour em in in that area in line with spine and the 44 mag wil, do it. Petersen got his with 44 mag also huge polar and his alaskan moose. I coached him on his first mule deer with that 6½ S & W and he did fine job. Let me know how you make out. Best,and think we should have all our organizations somehow brought together to fight these commy anti gun fanatics in Wash.
        Sincerely
        Keith.

Home Office: 8490 Sunset Blvd., Los Angeles, Calif. 90069 · (213) 657-5100

GUNS & AMMO

ELMER KEITH, EXECUTIVE EDITOR • SALMON, IDAHO 83467

Feb 29th-76

Dear George"

       Hope you can getthehandgun big game records going and believe you can.Bill jordan has his gu-ns magneported and as he cant hear it thunder he says likes the system that keeps barrel down in line. I have the magnapprt on a 44 auto mag and it knocks your ears off and even standing tne feet behind the shooter you get it so dont like it myself, but am sure hekps a damn lot for recoil sensitive people or those who wear ear muffs in the summer time which I dont.It makes gun reclil back in line and not lift but with single action I want the damn gun to lift so can hook thumb over hammer spur in recoil, but is faster for D.A.guns but not for little willie as dont like the muzzle blast back in my ears,

       my old 45-70 load of 53 grains 3031 with 405 grain worked out amny years ago by Gus Peret and I gave 1850 feet and under 30,000 psi and save in 86 Winchesters. a freind here GrantVHaveman has a ruger single shot and uses 60 grains 3031 by seating one cannellure of 405 grain bullet outvof case and gets at least 2000 ft. That load might also be safe enough in the browning, Dont know PSI on it but must be around 45,000 at least 40,000.

       Trying to get caugyt up with writing since being back to Handgunner Award and NSGA show, Best and keep up the good work,

                                          Sincerely
                                          Keith

Home Office: 8490 Sunset Blvd., Los Angeles, Calif. 90069 · (213) 65

GUNS & AMMO

ELMER KEITH, EXECUTIVE EDITOR • SALMON, IDAHO 83467

March 6th-76

Dear George:

    Been intending writing you but been snowed under withletters and phone calls. Mom and I attended the 4th Annual Outstanding American Hand gunners Award at Chicago the 4th Feb and then spent three days on the floor of the McCormick bldg at the NSGA show for the magazine and a hell of a piled of letters when I got home and the magazine between long distance phone calls and inquiries for every conceivable gu-n question keep little willie busy.

    Cant figure who that barrel maker was, but am sure you can sell all gu-ns easy by placing an add in t-he Shotgun News, published at Hastings nebr and at very low cost so write them for copy and price think is only ten cents a wrod and come out twice a month. Quite a lot more demand lately for 220 Swift since Ruger chambered a few model77s for it and it will sell. also hell of a demand for any and all good sixguns now.

    I get a hell of a lot of these gimme letters also and file most of them in file 13. Country going to hell as well as Africa and the whole damn world. Wish we cou-ld elect Reagan as believe he is best on the ticket since Ford endorsed that Saturaday night specila bill.

    Our Govt now so damn many political bureaus interested only in maintaining office and getting all their freinds on Govt payroll also that it will come to sad end ere long if Ford or Reagan dont cut out about 70 percent of the damn bureaus , Going down the road exactly as Russia wants to my notion. Should have had govt by up surplus grain and starve the damn commies into submission or else make their people over-throw them. Too much poliyics in Govt and right here in state Govt also. The damn game Dept has sold us clean out of game and fish as well by turing seasons over to the damn biologists who have four years colledge and then know all about it, now protect all predatory birds and most of the animals even the cougar and black bear and the blue heron fish duck and kinb fisher and expect to raise fish. Salmon rive mow closed to all fishi-ng and people getting mad and they plan a couple hjndred starting steelhead fishing theb20th in spite of the damn laws. Mom Ted and I went wyo last fall and killed threenice buck antelope and will go- agaimn for both mule deer and antelope this fall God willing.

    Saw Marie the other day and she said she wanted to keep that pistol a while so that is that. Schaller aNd the no good sheriff got all Dons guns I guess and he gave me all Pistols but never got them as lawyer went to Marie and demanded them and they got away with all she collected besides some they stole before Don died. All his book collection went yo a neighbor and Doc Leach bought it all for $ 150. Marie has all my books I gave Don, dont knwo what she will do with them as all but two now out of print and bringi-ng high prices. Our best to you all,

                                     As Always, Elmer

Home Office: 8490 Sunset Blvd., Los Angeles, Calif. 90069 · (213) 657-5100

GUNS & AMMO

ELMER KEITH, EXECUTIVE EDITOR • SALMON, IDAHO 83467

May 12th-76

Dear Bill Powell,

   Want to thank you for the finest and most beautiful jack knife Iever owned. Sure appreciate it as is very hardto get a goodbjack knife any mor e and this is not only a fine piece of steel but a most beautiful example of fine knife craftigg. I have some godold heavy sheath knives for heavy skinning but this is all t-hat is needed for deer and antelopebwhich I hope to hunt this fall and wilksure use it. Also for dressing soem fish I hoe to catch.

   It is an art work in itself and found it would shave and when a new knife will do that uou know you have a fine piece of high carbon steel. Expect to go back to Glenrock Wyo for another antekope hunt with my oldmpolar bear hunting partner Charlie Shedd and willusethis knife when we connect.

   I used 18.5 grains 2400 for many years in 44 Spls in the old balloon head cases, but cut the load to 17 grains n the smaller capacityh solid head cases and its still a swell load and second only to the 44mag or a heavy 22 grains 2400 load with my 250 grain bullet in Ruger S.A. 1r 20 grains in the modern Ciot S.A.guns, both have .451" grooves in 45 Colt caliber.

   Will mentionthis fien knife inmy next batch of arms notes but never know what they will run so dont countvon seeing it as so much materila I send in is never used account space for adds etc. I will be carrying this knife from here on out and my son Ted gets it when I craw under the rocks. Thanks again. and all best wishes,

                Sincerely,
                Keith

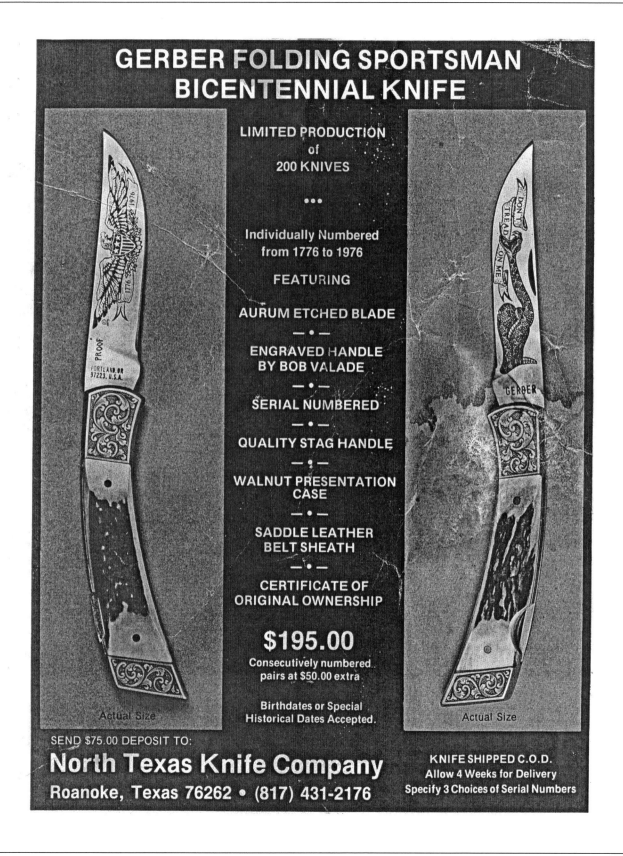

GUNS & AMMO

ELMER KEITH, EXECUTIVE EDITOR • SALMON, IDAHO 83467

June 9th-76

Dear Bill:

Glad you picked up a good 44 model 1950 Target as they are a wonderful gun and better finished and fitted than many new model S & W guns. Next to the old Triple Lock they are finest fitted of all except early models 29s but current production often shows lack of inspection proof firing etc.

I would not use over 17 grains 2400 behind my 250 grain bullet in that remodelled 45 Colt S & W withn the new solid head cases. Iused to shoot 18.5 all around but in the 1ld ballon head cases which had more powder space, but think you will like a lod of 16.5 to 17 grains 2400. in the 44 and size the bullets down to .429"

I have had several more letters on such remodelling of the 357s to 45 Colt by reboreing and rechambering and also as you have changed the 1955target barrel fitted to one being changed over and see no reason whyc it should not work out perfectly so long as the rechambering and fitting properly done. For my 250 grain bullet in these guns rechmabered and rebarrellled guns size my 250 grain bullet down to .451 an cast them very hard as the 1955 and 1o17 barrels have only shallow lands for jackted bullets and you must have a hard bullet to ho,d their shallow rifling. Use in45 Colt 8 grains Unique for a moderate load or arojnd 18 grains 2400 for a good stiff load.

I have four tripp-e locls three 44 Spl targets and a 45 Colt fixed sighted rechamberedform 455 Eley. Dont see wht such an article would not sell so you might try our good editor Howard French on it if you have some good photos etc.

Doug Wesson then a Major wrote me in the thirties he had just filled the last order for Triple locks that they wouldever made and shipped to a man in South America at a cost of $ 75. each. Drop in if you get up here this fall. Be home most of time except for the Rem and Win seminars and some huntibgf on my own. Got to dress something with this fine knife.

Sincerely

Keith

GUNS & AMMO

ELMER KEITH, EXECUTIVE EDITOR • SALMON, IDAHO 83467

July 8th-76

Dear George:

Mom and I had a good 50th anniversary celebration down at my son Teds place in Boise, Over 55 people attended and we even had a congratulatory letter from presédent and Bettey Ford.

Glad you had such a good shoot on the hogs back east, This country is fast coming to private ranch hunts as game gets ever scarcer.

I also had the same letter from Juras and agree with you 100% on changes that shoild be made, Just had a man here, Ron Crowe of chicago who says he is going for the $ 500.00 membership. Wróte it up for my magazine but dont believe been piublished, had so many callers havent even had time to read all articles in the magazine. I too thought the full page coverage should have been far more specific.

If first shot does not hit an animal right then succeedng shots have no shock effect and you have to hit spine or brain or bleed them out and the latter sometimes takes time. Reason I always strive my utmost to place that first one just right, as witness in Africa with peter and tom and later with Ted fowler I shot to cape buffalo, one huge hippo, and three good bull elephant, one shot each from left barrel of my 500 Boswell and none ever took a step after that left barrel fired. also a record calss lesser Kudud with mike Hisseys 375 model 70 off hand in had wind at 100 yds and only head and neck showing .

Agree with you the 45 Colt Ruger with my hard cast 250 grain slug and 22 grains 2400 is more effective under 50 yeards than the 44 mag. Over 50 yards am inclined to think the longer better sectional density 250 grain 44 is superior and I known damn well it is at long range. One man recently wrote was using 24 grains 2400 and no high pressure in a Rgger Super. Also some Rugers vary in groove diameter and tat may account for easy pressures with 24 grain 2400 load. I recommend only 20 grains for all late Colts and ruger to general publick but 22 grains also permissable in the Ru gers withbtheir larger cylinders. The printers devil of some wise boy down at L.A. has been making me out a fool in the last two issues June and July. I sig ht rifles 3" high and a half inch left at 100 yds for long range rifles and they changed it to 3" left at 100 yds and Placed Chicago at Lake Erie in the June issue. Never know what you write will turn out to be in print.

The larger caliber 451" over the smaller .429" is the reason for bettr killing at close range for the 45. GLad OBGHA is holding its own at least and am sure will increase in membership as time goes on. We have a hell of a fight on our hands and sure Hope for teh best, Best to you and the family,

As Ever, Elmer

Elmer

GUNS & AMMO

ELMER KEITH, EXECUTIVE EDITOR • SALMON, IDAHO 83467

Sept 9th-76

Dear Bredsten:

Be glad to autograph that book for you. That book now bringing $ 100. I am told at least two men stopped in here with them for me to autigraph and claimed they paid that sum each for them. So be sure and insure it.Damn postal Dept also gone crazy now costs 40 cents minimum for insurance and $1.00 to ship a book countingf 85 cent ostage and ins and then have to but the padded envelope.

Just tested and wroteup a single shot Merrill pistol that i lkke much better than the Fontender and does not fly up and hut my hat in recoilas the contender does. this oneifn44 mag but they makeem in everything from 22 L.R. to- 30-30. Most simple break top action ever saw and accurate and also have scope mt and should be tops in a single shot pistoAl . Address The Merril Co. Inc Box 187 Rockwell City, Iowa 50579

Alsojust testd a 45-70 sixgun this one a good one and a far cry from those Wilson Michigan 45-70 of years ago. This one to sell at $ 348.00 made by Earl Keller, 910 Keck St, Evansville, Ill 47711. Frame high tensile strentyh bronze 103,500 tensile strnegth cylinder 4140 steel and barrel of goodsteel. Hammer trigger and frame and straps all bronze. Adj rear sight. We found it shot very accurate at 20 yds with a hrd cast 405 grain slug and 24 grain 2400 but no good with 350 jackted and 30 grains 2400 and not as good with factory Remington 405 soft point but shot like the devil with the 405 cast and 22 to 24 4graibs 3400. No recoil to speak off. Had 8" bbl and a cross bolt safety so safe with six rounds in the cylinder, rebounding firing pin. Sq back guard a hell of a sixgun 5 3/4 pounds.

Gas checks will work fine in any single shot or rfile but cant see any advantage in revolvers and raised pressured 3000, psi in 44 mag at Whotes Lab. This gun takes factory or any 405 grain load cylinder tooshort fortheold 500 grain Infantry load.

If you get a heavy enough load a gas check myght hep in that contender but never designed that bullet with gaw check in mind.Best to you and the family.,

Sincerely

Keith

Home Office: 8490 Sunset Blvd., Los Angeles, Calif. 90069 • (213) 657-5100

GUNS & AMMO

ELMER KEITH, EXECUTIVE EDITOR • SALMON, IDAHO 83467

Sept 16th-76

DearGeorge:

Your copy Rifles for Large Game came in yesterday and I autographed and started it on its way back to Alaska and insured it for $ 100.00, You owe me $ 1.65 postage and ins. and an envelope. Let me know if it arrives. One man got a copy for $ 50.,at agun show and several have brought copies here they paid $ 100. each as only 2000 cppies printed.

Not much new except tried out a Merril single shot 44 mag pistol and also a good working and accurate 45-70 sixgun which will write up for the column.

Mom Son Ted and I going Wyo for antelope around 10th as we each got both doe and buck permits, will have to be our winters meat I guess as Idaho damn well shot out. Best to you and the family and help elect Ford as our remaining best bet.

Sincerely
Keith

GUNS & AMMO

ELMER KEITH, EXECUTIVE EDITOR • SALMON, IDAHO 83467

Oct 5th-76

Dear Bredsten:

Think you sent me too much money and I insured Rifles for Large Game of $100 so enclosing some money, Cant find my insurance recipt as sent book to P.O. by a freind but glad you got it back as tyhey are now damn scarce books and bringing crazy prices. Had two more sent in and they paid $100. each. Also had four of my books sent in and box corner gone, no letter no money and have had them two months and dont know who the hell they belong to. Hope the lad writes some of these days so can autograph and return his books.

Test and wrote up a 45-70 revolver by Earl Keller of Evansville, Ind. and it shot wonderfully well with 2 to 24 grains 2400 and a 405 graisn cast copy of my sixgun bullet, in fact three shot groups under a quarter restinbg frame on san dbags, 5 3/4 pounds a hell of a big gun Now his former pargner also going mae one and send for test he says . He is E.F.Phelps. 700 West franklin, Evansville, Ind 47710. Guess they were in parner ship and split the blanket they bought out the old Wilson 45-70 sixgun. Need to have a back pack to carry it, but would be good bear gun for a guide in a back pack with buut up over shoulder and extra ammo in pack.

44 mag Contender worst kicking 44 mag i sver shot barrel flew up and hit my hat each shot, but was dead accurate. Dont know why. this 45-70 with factory 405 grain loads not bad recoil at all in fact barrel raied up onl- normal and any kid could handle it as far as recoil is concerned

Think you fellows should have stuck with the 45-70 case and loaded it down with 2400 powder. If you get 2000 feet which may well be then look for the barrel of that T/C contender to knock you hat off each shot. Leaving for eastern Wyo for antelope last of this week. best to you and the family

Sincerely
Keith

Home Office: 8490 Sunset Blvd., Los Angeles, Calif. 90069 · (213) 657-5100

GUNS & AMMO

ELMER KEITH, EXECUTIVE EDITOR • SALMON, IDAHO 83467

Oct 23rd-76

Dear George:
        Had good antelope hunt and mom Ted and I got our buck and doe each and have them boned pachaged and inthe freezer so we have some fine met for the winter. Game shot out here terrible, not enough left for seed.
        I think if you will write Hensley & Gibbs they might make up a copy of my bullet but with a wider set of the three bands or else wider basebadd and in .458 caliber to nweig ht 300 grains for your proposed short 450 or 45-70/
        Have preached for many years that a big sixgun properly loaded is far superior to the 30-80-170 and in fact the pounds feet formulae give it the edge over the 30-30 and is far better killer and my doad will penetrate far better than most all expanding bullet high velocity loads including the 375 H & H. They wont believe it until they see it. Erv Malarich has over the years guideing killed a hell of a lot of elk with my load in his 29 S & W and his Ruger 44 mag and bullet usually goes hrough and out broadside shots behind shoulder. One man at Darby has shot four black bear through shoulders with 7½" ruger all clean kills and has not recovered a bullet complete pentratio na nd one shot kills. Two knotheads even tool 44 mags to africa a 6½ S & W and a 7½" Ruger and my load and each ,illed an elephant one with heart shot that evidently missedthe ribs and the ogher down the ear hole for a brain shot and they say they have the mpovies to prove it so it goes. Seeing is believing biut you cannot tell the bright boys like O.Connor.Page, Bowmen and other small bore enthusiasts as they simply wont believe, Same on Sharps killed 12 comingvin from one fishing trip in Pacific with 4" 44 mag ad my load. Another trip killed six and ran out of amm, got to shooting at flying fish and finally got enough lead to kill a couple, just a spray over water when you hit them but tghey go likke hell need twice the lead of a duck. Anyway switched to Winchester jackted 240 grain 44 mag soft hollow point. Hit several sharks but bullet expanded on water thnehit shark richocheted out and across the oily sea. Some lads down Texas way shooting into take baffle board of plastic and nine feet water to ctahc bullet for police use, High power rifles all stopped and everything but my 22 grain 2400 and Keith 250 grain hars slug. That went through baffle, nine feet water and dentedbottom tank so they hadto quit using it as bullet battered when hit other end tank.
        You are well qualified to write that articl so go ahead with it. Hope we can elect Ford, Wanted Reagan but that is out and God help us if ghat peanut cracker gets in. Best,

                                  As Always,
                                  Elmer

Home Office: 8490 Sunset Blvd., Los Angeles, Calif. 90069 · (213) 657-5100

GUNS & AMMO

ELMER KEITH, EXECUTIVE EDITOR • SALMON, IDAHO 83467

Feb 16th-77

Dear George:

Ross Seyfried and I worked up a load of 73 grains 4350 with the very hot 172 primer in a double 465 H &H and it hs 3¼" case. Think this malarky of only a jot fast po der like 3031 will do in straigyt cases is just hog wash.

Never used anything but black in my two 45-120-550 rfles and three more have had in that caliber but all side hammer Sharps andsmokeles damn dangerous in tghem as will blow back trough firing in even will blow the dovetail back plate off in back of firing pin had letter from many gotbhis bheek cut last week.

However the No 1 Ruger will stand anything eve n to mel ting head of case. Si I would use magnu-m primers and try around 80 grains to 90 grains 4350 and see how it goes. Think no reason you cannot work up a darn good load equal to 450 Nitro in that rifle.

I shoot 75 grains 4831 with mag primers in my two Farquharsons 338-74 Keith rifles with 250 to 275 grain slug s amd wonderfully acurate three in one hole so tight cant measure. 100 yds bench sand bagged rest. The slower powders bulk up better also and you can run a hard heavy wad down on powder tight and if you shoot patch bullets then you need a quarter inch lub under bullet, caribou or moose tallow will do as I used to use elk and deer atllow and if you have' beeswax then add half and half and stir makes good lub but any good lubrication wad with or without graphite will work and easy to stir in some powdered graphite. My 338-74 round is 4" overall lenhtyhnand 4831 works swell in it Hodgdon powder and see no reason 4831 might not work as well in the Sharps case with long heavy bullets. You have the safest of all actions to work up with so no danger to either man or gun.

I worked up a lod of 114 grains 4895 Hodgdon in my 577 farquharson with old No 4 berdam cap that shot wonderfully well with heavy wad on top powder. Dont anticipate your having any troubel at all geting a good load of smokeles for that rifle but will need a heavy oversize slightoy card wad over powder and gas checks would slso help. With paper patch only the wad and lub wad necessary.

Bob ward worked out a load for a transition period 450 Nitro for the modified load of 50 grains 3031 and 405 grain jackted that shot well in a Churchill double rifle. No wad but better to wad powder so uniform ignition in up and down hill shooting . Hope this helps some and wish you would send some of you warm weather and pussy willows down here. Dry as a last years birdnest and reservoirs empty and front down 5 to 6 feet and having water pipe trouble all over town. Best,

Sincerely
Keith

Home Office: 8490 Sunset Blvd., Los Angeles, Calif. 90069 · (213) 657-5100

GUNS&AMMO

ELMER KEITH, EXECUTIVE EDITOR • SALMON, IDAHO 83467

Jan 5th-78

Dear George:

I also read J.D.Jones article on buffalo killing and find his experience exactly opposite to all I havehad with all factory soft points as compared with- my 250 grain hard cast and 22 grains 2400.

Guess will have to class him along with many other fiction writers we have ghese days. I shot over 30 damn big bulls at the salughter house with the first 44 mag ever produced the tool room job Carl Hellstrom gave me. All soft point factpry ammo hollow point and plain soft point stopped in brain cavity. Did not then have any Norma which from all reports penetrates far better than any other soft point account lead enclosed to extreme tip.

On sharks killed 12 one trip my 4" 44 mag Mod 29 next trip killeda af dozen and ran out of my hand loads and Winchester soft point 240 grain would penetrate the water to shark with would be several feet then richochet off his hide and skip across thesea. Expanded on water, Sharps out 40 to 60 yards and held a foot below fine and a foot forward and never failed tohbring them up dead or rolling in blood with my load, but did not kill a single one with Win Factory, Neither did Weatherby's man with his 300 Wby magnum and 180 grain expanding, just a big spout kf water and shark fin ddd not even go down, no penetration blew up on water and soft point 44 mags also expanded before ever hitying shark.

One man at Darby Mont now has killed seven black bear one shot kills my 44 mag load from 7½" Rug er and has yet to retrieve a single bullet shot through shoulders he sayd and thik on garbage dump where he can pick and place his shots.

Bob Petersen used Norma and killed his Alaskan Moose, Brown bear and Polar bear but the Norma penetrates more like my bullet but no expanding soft point will ever penetrate as good as shown by the nine foot water penetration by Texas Police Dept

I am going to vote for Bob Petersen next election for the award, he has killed about everything this continent with that nidkel plated 6½" mo del 29 and also is responsible in no small way for the manyarticlesby Carter and other on gun control and showedthe damncoyote up in true light in Huntikng and I think he is a deserving recipient and hope he wins. We have far too many typewriter authorities who never had the experience and often do not know wherof they speak. Best,

Sincerely
Keith

Home Office: 8490 Sunset Blvd., Los Angeles, Calif. 90069 • (213) 657-5100

GUNS & AMMO

ELMER KEITH, EXECUTIVE EDITOR • SALMON, IDAHO 83467

Feb 4th-78

Dear George:

      I really dont know how best to set up such an award prograsm but you are at liberty to use my name on it and I think Bob petersen of Petersen Pub Co would and should be a recipient as he killednot only our game down here I coached him on his first big mule buck but also went alaska and killed his moose, t-hen broan bear and finally a record polar all with his 6½" nickel plated model 29 and Norma factory loads.

      Thanks for the Musk Ox pix killed with a model 29 44 mag and he would have had even better penetration if he had used my 250 grain cast hard and same powder charge. One friend of mine Erv Malnarich has killed countless elk with that load and gun also some ifth Ruger 7½" and same load. Most folks cant understandit but a big sixgun 44 mag and my load penetrnates far better than most big expanding rifle bullets and factory loads. Folks are fininding it out slowly but lot of them called me a crazy liar beforethey found out the hard way.

      Far as I am concerned hand gujns will stay available if we keep fighting and when they get mine they will be hot and empty and a big job for the ujndertaker, Damn it th is is a free country and I for one will never sureender to abunch of cmmie sob sisters,Wehave to keep fighting and now we have a real man to head NRA and a damn good one for the ILA as well so think things will shift for the better. Crater can never be elected again in my opinion and dontvthi nk hsi coming anti gun bill will get to first base as altogther too many congressmen up for next election. The next NRA concention at Salk Lake may change public opinion even more in our favor. THis give away of the Canal at Panama just another ruse to help Russia not America and hope it is defeated in Senate, Lot of N.Y.C. Money in Panama and they figure they will get some ofniut back from Panamanian handling of canal Best wishes to you and the family and keep plugging , Thank s for th pix that now makes about all American gqme killed with 44 mag so guess my ideas not so bad after all.

                                                 As Ever,
                                                     Elmer

Home Office: 8490 Sunset Blvd., Los Angeles, Calif. 90069 · (213) 657-5100

GUNS&AMMO

ELMER KEITH, EXECUTIVE EDITOR • SALMON, IDAHO 83467

July 7th-78

Dear Officer Decker:

My old load of 13.5 grains 2400 and my 173 grain solid cast hard and sized 357 is still the top 38 Spl load as well as best for all the early short cylinder 357 S & W guns. More accurate and better penetration ghan even the 357 factory soft points.

Am sorry but cannot tell you what became of the old Audley holster Co. They were quite common when I was a boy and I heard of one autghentic case where and officer git himself well ventilated and died trying to get a gun out of one that had fouled up with I heard some brush under the finger button or dirt.

Sugg est you write Bill Jordan.626 Ashbourne Drive, Shreveport , Lousiana,71106 about pix from the Border partol on the machine guns as he would know if availbbleand to whom to write for them. THis magazine might also have prints of those guns in their fieles. There are some training pictures in my Sixgun book and belive Bill Toney gave me them for it but wrote it in '55 so dont remember. Best wishes from a broher officer.

Sincerely
Keith

GUNS & AMMO

TH, EXECUTIVE EDITOR • SALMON, IDAHO 83467

April 24th-79

Glad you are still with us. Lost a lot of freinds last year. Bob Modisette, Vernon Speer, George Nonte, to name a few and we nearly croked with a year long dose of some kind of Flu. Thank allah getting over it finally and we hope to go to the San ton NRA and Handgunner award.

Had a hell of a winter here lost about all our sparrows and small song birds foze to death, got to 40 and 45 below and some snow but not enough moisture on tghe whole.

Mom, S -n Ted nad I and Ralph graham hunted antelope with Charley Shedd in wyo and got our two a piece and Ralph and I also got a couple mule deer in this shot out state after eight days hujnting all with myb338-74 Keith siggle shot rifles. Its a hell of a cartridge and will handle a few grains more powder than the 338 mag and wonderfully accurate often puts three in one hole 100 yds. 75 grains H 4831 with 250 Nosler or Sierra B.T. and 74 grains with Speer 275 for heavier stuff.

Idaho damnwell shotout so went Wyo,. Mule deer there in profusion but hadno permits in Wyo so had a hard time finding even two points here.

HOPE YOU do get to writing again need some factual articles in the magazine instead some of the malarky some of those kid writers are now turning out for us and I getkicks on the crap they recommend mostly foreign hand gun junck.

Got screwed down at Vermejo, Les Bowman am sure was the cause raised elevation on scope a full turn and I shot over fine cow elk only chances I had last day of Rem Semin-ar. Winchester press screwed me good on autobiography but now thank Allah Petersen is bring it out right in its entriety but had a hell fo a fight to keep a new guy Slim randless form adding his malarkey and drawings to it should be out in June. Winchester press now sold out and good think as crooked very writer I cohtacted and also me at the Outdoorsman of the year. Gave it toFrant wooner who invented red vests for wyo antelope hunting and only Woolner, Carmichael on t-he list of nominees. S o will be soft peddling on the darn Win outfit from now on. Keep you health and your powder dry and hope to see you eee too long

Sincerely
Keith

Executive Offices: 8490 Sunset Blvd., Los Angeles, Calif. 90069 • (213) 657-5100
Publishers of: HOT ROD, MOTOR TREND, CAR CRAFT, MOTORCYCLIST, GUNS & AMMO, SKIN DIVER, TEEN, PHOTOGRAPHIC, PETERSEN'S HUNTING, 4-WHEEL & OFF-ROAD, VANS & PICKUPS, and a variety of SPECIALTY PUBLICATIONS
Offices in: New York, Detroit, Chicago, Los Angeles, Cleveland, Atlanta, Boston

GUNS&AMMO

ELMER KEITH, EXECUTIVE EDITOR • SALMON, IDAHO 83467

Nov 11th-78

Dear Mr. Helwig:

For the 44 Spl the best load and one I have used for 40 years or more is my 250 grain bullet cast hard one to ten tin and lead or typemetal or any mixture you ca barely mark with your thumbnail. Hensley & Gibbs, Box 10 Murphy oregon make my true moulds but only in expensive gan style but R.C.B.S. is tarting to me the and have my true mold for the 45 Colt but only that abortion they bought upnin the 44 caliber. Lyman also ruined the design with round corner grease groove and narrower and sa smaller front band. R.C.B.S shows picture of my true bulletvon the box and Fred Huntington said would get on my true design soon as they wore out the O'Haus stuff they bought.

In old ballo ne head cases I used 18.5 grains 2400 with this bullet sized .429 and in modern solid head cases 17 to 17.5 grains 2400 with standard not magnum primers and a good stiff crimp. Nothing else has ever shot so well for me and use this Keith bullet with 22 grains 2400 all time in my 44 magnums and have found nothikng else as good pfor accuracy or penetration on game or sea water and sharks. Remington cases always served me best in 44 Spl.

Sincerely
Keith

July 25th-79

Mr. Ed Doherty,
Charlton Publications,
Charlton Bldg,
Derby, Conn. 06418

Dear Mr. Doherty:

     I am under contract with petersen to write exclusively for this magazine. Likewise so many daily callers, long distance phone calls and lettersto anser from gun cranck daily percludes the possibility of wirti-ng for any ither publication were I not on contract.

     Suggest you contact Mr,Jerry Nelsen, Ranchester Wyoming for articles as he is a gun crank, big game guide an ddputy sheriff formerly and can give you some good articles on most any phase of the shooting game.

     Thanks for the invitation to write for you.

                                 Sincerely
                                 Keith

GUNS & AMMO

ELMER KEITH, EXECUTIVE EDITOR • SALMON, IDAHO 83467

Aug 8th-79

Dear Mr. Werbe:

        This is the first copy of my book I have seen. Am supposed to have 200 copies coming but not here yet.

        Notice that Slim Randles who was in charge of producion of ghe book or some primnters devil surely changed all the photo titles and had 15 inch antelppe as 17½ inch and the big 17½ inch as a 15 incher and my smallest ivory labenned 76 & 78 and the real 76 and 78 tusks labelled 55 and 58. Aside from their damn fool change of aboyt all captions it is readable.

        I would personally for get both the 35 Whelen as the 338 O.K.H. beats it badly for range and sectional density and has a very wide range of bullets while the 35 is limited to Speer, hornady and Barnes, and Rem. The 338 O.K.H. willmputrange the 35 whelen and withsame weight bjlolets. The 358 Norma li mited to Norma ammo or reloads and the Norma steel jacket bullets did not expand worth a whoop for my son and I on elk a=d mule deer. You have a good 375 H & H which I like better than the bl own out wby version which gives too much vel and blows bullets and the 338 Mag and I cannot see where the 35 calibers would be as good or any improvement on either.

        Noslers are good but front end blows off at high vel, and the partition buloet the best. Sierras buck wind best and most accurate of all in their B.T. design. but Speeer hot core has so far provane most reliable of all ijn its action and dont separate., Have killed everything from deer and antelope to o polar bear with the 275 Speer 338 bullet. Best   p

                                                Sincerely

                                                Keith

Executive Offices: 8490 Sunset Blvd., Los Angeles, Calif. 90069 • (213) 657-5100
Publishers of: HOT ROD, MOTOR TREND, CAR CRAFT, MOTORCYCLIST, GUNS & AMMO, SKIN DIVER, 'TEEN, PHOTOGRAPHIC, PETERSEN'S HUNTING, 4-WHEEL & OFF-ROAD, VANS & PICKUPS, and a variety of SPECIALTY PUBLICATIONS
Offices in: New York, Detroit, Chicago, Los Angeles, Cleveland, Atlanta, Boston

GUNS & AMMO

ELMER KEITH, EXECUTIVE EDITOR • SALMON, IDAHO 83467

Dec 15th-79

Dear Jerry:

The box with my original manuscript and also the galleys of same for my book Rifles For Large Game arrived safely, also the copy of thes book I have autographed to you and the copy of the Little Brown BIG GAMR HUNTING for ralph has now been autographed to him and will give it to him when he comes over today. I have packed the Rifles For Large game mss and galleys and your book in a sturdy box but thought best to wait a few days before shipping Rlaph phoned he wanted to picknit up and ship so will turn over to hikm today.

It is authentic and no doubt about it. Where the devil did you get it. I sold that buok on contract to Herman P.Dean Standard Publishing Co. and he promised to keep it in print for 20 years when he solicited it butinever kept his word. Printed 2,000 copies and I heard sold out to Stackpole.Only Petersen and Little Brown Kept q-eir word with me also all the rest crooked me one way or other and their word not worth a damn.Samworth still owes me $ 500. for those two manuals. and Stackpole printed some five editions of Sixguns tthen sold out to Bonanza for a ten percent royalty to beat meout of their paying 15% andI now get 5% of the 10% that Bonanza pays Stackpole so be warned in writing a book that they dont crook you as they have me,Glad you like the holster, best I have seen high priced as hell $ 65 for ones I gave you and ralp and around 75 for the extra long guns, Best for the Holidays to you and all the family

Elmer

GUNS & AMMO

ELMER KEITH, EXECUTIVE EDITOR • SALMON, IDAHO 83467

Dec 28th-79

Dear Jerry & Family·

Been busier than a cat ona tin roof, so many callers and long distance phone and letters and book selling like hotcakes.
Enclosed a letter from a nut who has killed some six elk and panning me for not advocating 270s for elk. Maybe you can gettime to answer the nut and set him straight . Saw a damn 270 fail on a goat, a black bear and two mule deer one trip down the river and that went on until I refuded to guide anyone with a damn 270 that hs lost wounded more elk thane ver died from a hard winter.

Ralph and I showed his day some jack rabbits and one gilly. Saw no antelope nor sage hens, the gillys have eaten the young and chased everything ovt of the sage flats to the cover of the timbered hilsI guess.

Sill no snow here in town but rather cold and damp, sure need some moisture butrain will do here and wet snow up topside where it wil, freeze and last through the chinook winds in sring.

Thihk I woe you two letters but been too busy to answer my freinds. See Winchester now has Carmichael, Amber and I one their new list for the Oytdoofsman of the Year award, so crooked I dont think will attend at all.Carmi chael never did anything except for himself but Amber is a wroth man from his long editorial work in gun digest but dont know a dman ythink he ever did for the shooters or new equipment or for the game. Hope you ca n come' ver before the eqles eat all the rabbits, never saw so many of the great birds and they are going take over all our small game and antelope fauns and some old animals as well, and will again be working on t-hebdkmestic sheep lambs soon asthey are hatched

Too damn cold to write machine is lughist and my fingers worse but maybe you can readthis note . Glad you like the Holster best I have seen in shoulder harness. You dad Had me send a sheriff there two books hope he is not oenthat gave you the dtrouble.

As Always
Elmer

P.S be glad to write foreword for book also-you can photo my 17 double rifles including Corbett teger rifle.

Elmer

Executive Offices: 8490 Sunset Blvd, Los Angeles, Calif. 90069 • (213) 657-5100
Publishers of: HOT ROD, MOTOR TREND, CAR CRAFT, MOTORCYCLIST, GUNS & AMMO, SKIN DIVER, TEEN, PHOTOGRAPHIC, PETERSEN'S HUNTING, 4-WHEEL & OFF-ROAD, VANS & PICKUPS, and a variety of SPECIALTY PUBLICATIONS
Offices in: New York, Detroit, Chicago, Los Angeles, Cleveland, Atlanta, Boston

GUNS & AMMO

ELMER KEITH, EXECUTIVE EDITOR • SALMON, IDAHO 83467

Jan 17th-80

Dear Mr. Knox:

I have several 44 and 45 Colt sixgun we fitted up with S & W rear and special front sights back some 50 years ago and still going strong. Thanks for the pictures of yours. You will find pix of mine in my CSixgun book and I wrote extensively on them m-any years ago in tghe Rifleman O'Life and other magazines.

Load 18.5 grains 2400 with normal primers and my 250 grain bullet sized .451 and cast hard for your good peacemakers and think you will like the load. Idaho is fast settling up and our game at a very low ebb and the damn eagles which are portected along with all hawks owls and thecøugar as well as black bear part of year have about eaten us out of game.

Drop in if you get o ut this way. We still have some miles of sage bush they have not built condiminniums on to date. Glad you like the books.

Sincerely
Keith

GUNS & AMMO

ELMER KEITH, EXECUTIVE EDITOR • SALMON, IDAHO 83467

Feb 4-81

Dear Mr. Carriere:

      I do notrecommend smokeles in theSharps rifles of hammer persuasion a have seen even the dovetailpiece of steel in back of firing pin blown out with an overload tha pierced or blew the primer. The action will stand anything but if you want to shoot smokelesshwy the devikl get anold side hammer sharps at a very high price when for a thirdthe money you can get a No 1A Ruger sinble sho-t that beats thebest of the Saharps badly.

      The Shiloh as to barrel wood and action i s tghe equal of the originals first sights were not up to Standard butthey are imporving them also now and also going to put the safety notch to just clear the firingoin where t belongs. But if you want to shoot smokeles then gt the Ruger for a thirdthe price. If you must havethe old 45-120thebest ofttheSharps then useblack powder and paper patched bulets for best results. See an article of mine on Sharps to come out in march issue of G & A.

                                                     Sincerely
                                                     Keith

Executive Offices: 8490 Sunset Blvd., Los Angeles, Calif. 90069 • (213) 657-5100
Publishers of: HOT ROD, MOTOR TREND, CAR CRAFT, MOTORCYCLIST, GUNS & AMMO, SKIN DIVER, TEEN, PHOTOGRAPHIC, PETERSEN'S HUNTING, 4-WHEEL & OFF-ROAD, VANS & PICKUPS, and a variety of SPECIALTY PUBLICATIONS
Offices in: New York, Detroit, Chicago, Los Angeles, Cleveland, Atlanta, Boston

GUNS & AMMO

ELMER KEITH, EXECUTIVE EDITOR • SALMON, IDAHO 83467

MArch 20-81

Dear Mr. Werbe:

The book goes out to your friend Catherine Chandler Werbe to or mOnday. HAve tobcharge $ 25 for them now and you can send the other $ 3.00

I much prefer the 375 tothe highervelocity 378 Wby. because it gies the bullets all the velocity needed without extreme expansionand blow upand penetrates betteron big stuff

I have four 375s and a couple 458s as well. and for closer range shootingon dagerous gameor even elk and moose the 458 beatsthe 375. But for Gods sake shootthe300rgrain in the 375.

I donotbown a 378 Wby andnever have but do havde a 338-378 K.Thakdx that Thomson andbI designed .We shortened the 378 case a quarter inch and shouved the shoulder back a quarterinch and necked itdown to 338 and the inside reamednck and it probably the flattest shooting of allmlong rangerffles. and with 300 grain bullets Baqrnes or nosler is superior to the 378 in its trajectory curve.

For grizzly and brownies in the alders or elk andmoose in the timber wold prefer the375 H &H with300 grain but the 338-378 with 275 heavy old Speer bullets the 338-378 does a splendid job out to600 yds but no expansion at 600 I found but welplacedit killed. MAdethe ongest shot at a mule buck in my life withita full600or bitover twohits out of thre shots,no expansion. Also kiledone buck at same range with first44 magever made. If youhave a 375 H & Hor a 338 Win mag or a 340 Wby bot h the latter ourbo-ld 3330.K.H.ctgs then you dont need a378 Wby but getthe458 for dangerous game at reasonable t o close range. Best

Sincerely

Keith

Executive Offices: 8490 Sunset Blvd., Los Angeles, Calif. 90069 • (213) 657-5100
Publishers of: HOT ROD, MOTOR TREND, CAR CRAFT, MOTORCYCLIST, GUNS & AMMO, SKIN DIVER, 'TEEN, PHOTOGRAPHIC, PETERSEN'S HUNTING, 4-WHEEL & OFF-ROAD, VANS & PICKUPS, and a variety of SPECIALTY PUBLICATIONS
Offices in: New York, Detroit, Chicago, Los Angeles, Cleveland, Atlanta, Boston

GUNS & AMMO

ELMER KEITH, EXECUTIVE EDITOR • SALMON, IDAHO 83467

April 15-81

Dear Mr. Conley:

After Fitz and someoyer officials of Colt died I have had no known freinds among the personell. Dont have any therenow asfaras I know. They missedthe boat badly in not keeping their 4 3/4" targetsingle action in 44 Spl and 45 C and missedit even morein not bringing that good gun out in 41 magnum, No question thatboth Colt and S & W new managers out for the dirty dollar firstlast and al thetime tothe exclusion of carefuly engineered and inspected quality. Sorry thing but nothing I can do. I too lkketheold S.A.Colt andinpar icuiar theoneswe flat topped and traget sighted and their newfrontier target and they saved my life several times. Best,

Sincerely
Keith

GUNS & AMMO

ELMER KEITH, EXECUTIVE EDITOR • SALMON, IDAHO 83467

Oct 18-81

Dear Mr. Mullin:

I wanttothank your for one of teh best books I ahve seen on the subject and will try write it up for my next batch of arms notes.You covered a lot of ground-in that book and all to the good as far as advice is concerned.
Each month I receve factual accounts of gun fights fromall over the country from occiders. Now they are trying to go to,ittle 9 M Ms when ghey and the 38 S;ls and even the 357a have proven knadequate in so many gun batteles, guess thisnew generation will haveto learnthe hard wayas we did and as the Army di in the phillipine figghting when they triedto s top Moros with 38 long Colts and often let their heads in the process the bolo knife.

We stepped down when we dropped the30-06 as amiitary rifle ctg and firther when we went down to tghe500 yard 308 and now down to the 223 and if we ever get into open counytry figghting which is now buolding in t-eh e-areast we will get hell licked out of us withsucha short rangedinadequate ctg and the same reasoning seems to be going on in the heads of the military with regard tothe army hand gun.Never was a better army side arm than ghe 45 ACP Colt. Bestwishe and thanksfor ghis fine book.

Sincerely
Keith

Executive Offices: 8490 Sunset Blvd., Los Angeles, Calif. 90069 • (213) 657-5100
Publishers of: HOT ROD, MOTOR TREND, CAR CRAFT, MOTORCYCLIST, GUNS & AMMO, SKIN DIVER, TEEN, PHOTOGRAPHIC, PETERSEN'S HUNTING, 4-WHEEL & OFF-ROAD, VANS & PICKUPS, and a variety of SPECIALTY PUBLICATIONS
Offices in: New York, Detroit, Chicago, Los Angeles, Cleveland, Atlanta, Boston

THE RECORDER-HERALD

Official Newspaper of Lemhi County and the City of Salmon

Salmon, Lemhi County, Idaho, Thursday, February 23, 1984   Number 19

Elmer M. Keith, 84, dies

Elmer Merrifield Keith, 84, Salmon, died Tuesday, Feb. 14, 1984, in the Capital Care Nursing Home in Boise of natural causes.

Mr. Keith was born March 8, 1899, in Hardin, (Ray County), Mo., the son of Linnie N. and Forest E. Keith.

He grew up in Montana and ran a cattle ranch from boyhood until 1929 when he made his way to Idaho.

In 1926, he married Lorraine K. Randall in Weiser.

While in Idaho he became occupied with guiding, hunting, and eventually writing. He saw the old West depart and the new West take its place and played a part in both.

Mr. Keith is a legend to gun enthusiasts and possibly the most widely known small-arms authority in the world today.

Over the years he had written for "Outdoor Life," "Sports A Field," "Field and Stream," "American Rifleman," "Guns and Ammo" magazines.

He is listed in the current issue of the latter magazine as the executive editor.

Throughout his life he wrote and published 10 books on the subject of hunting, shooting and his life experiences. His best known books are "Sixguns" and "Hell I was There."

His hunting trips covered the whole North American continent, including Alaska and the Arctic. In addition, he made two trips to Africa, the last one in 1971.

He conducted extensive research into bullets, powders and gun designs and was a magnum man from his 10-gallon hat to the calibers he preferred. He helped to pioneer several wildcat cartridges for rifles and was most well-known for development of the .41 magnum and .44 magnum handgun calibers.

He personified an attitude for dogged independence, a love for justice and a respect for grit. In 1973, he received the first Outstanding Handgunner Award and in 1980, the first President's Award from Boise State University.

He was a 50-year mason of Lemhi Lodge 11, Salmon.

As a youth, he was badly burned in 1912 in a rooming house fire in Helena, Mont., and was not expected to live past the age of 21.

He served on a national survey crew in the Ovando, Mont., area in the 1920s.

He was a member of the national rifle team with the Montana National Guard in 1924. The team defeated the U.S. Marine team that year.

He then served on a national rifle team from the Idaho National Guard in 1925. He was a member of a civilian team that went to the national matches at Camp Perry, Ohio, in 1940. He and his wife were both high point scorers from Idaho.

From 1941 through 1944, he served as a civilian employee at the Ogden Arsenal, in charge of the final inspection and proof-firing for all small arms going to the Pacific theater of war.

Mr. Keith served 25 years with "Guns & Ammo" magazine.

The Keiths lost two daughters, one at birth and one 17 years of age, following an accident and illness.

They moved to Salmon in 1948 from North Fork and most of his writing success had been since that time.

The Keiths celebrated their golden wedding anniversary in 1976.

He is survived by his widow, Lorraine K. Keith of Salmon; a son and daughter-in-law, Ted F. and Betty L. Keith; three granddaughters, Heather E. Keith, Heidi M. Keith and Holly A. Keith, and a grandson, Gregory W. Keith, all of Boise, and a brother, Silas Keith of Baker, Ore.

Funeral services were conducted at 2 p.m. at the Salmon United Methodist Church with Ole Natwick officiating.

Burial was in the Masonic section of Salmon Cemetery under direction of the Jones & Casey Funeral Home.

Pallbearers were Frank Randall, John Randall, Wesley Randall, Clinton Randall, Joe Randall and Roy Randall.

Honorary pallbearers were Milt Havemann, Sherm Furey, Gordon Crupper, Bob Nielsen, Jim Sellick and Jim Herndon.

Services at the Salmon Cemetery were conducted by Lemhi Lodge 11, Ancient Free & Accepted Masons, with Harry Urell, worshipful master.

Performing a salute with .44 Magnum pistols was a firing squad directed by Ralph Graham, consisting of Russel Hyde, Jerry Nelson, Gene Autry, Don Mihaljevic, Joe Grefer, Berry Patton and Buster Blundell.

Ron Lopez, playing the bagpipe, piped the procession out of the church at the conclusion of the services, and led the firing squad into position at the cemetery.

A FIRING SQUAD, using .44 Magnum pistols, fired salute at the Salmon Cemetery during burial services conducted for Elmer Keith, Salmon. Ron Lopez, at far right, played the bagpipe to lead the squad into position.

Elmer Keith

MEMBERS OF LEMHI Lodge 11, Ancient Free & Accepted Masons, with Harry Urell, worshipful master, conducted masonic service for Elmer Keith at Salmon Cemetery.

Photographs

Elmer Keith in his study discussing "gunology" with visitors, 1975. Note the holstered Smith & Wesson 4-inch .44 Magnum on his right hip.

Keith in typical attire on a nice Idaho summer day, 1980.

Keith in his study with Alan Lomont (left) and Kent Lomont, 1975.

Keith in the study of his Salmon, Idaho, home in 1978 in typical garb with a holstered .44 Magnum Smith & Wesson.

Keith with .45/70 sixgun and bolt-action rifle chambered for .50 BMG, 1978.

Keith and a very young-looking John Ross, author of *Unintended Consequences*, in 1978 looking at a .50 BMG bolt-action rifle.

Keith receiving the Outstanding American Handgunner Award by Lee Jurras in 1974. Keith was asked to speak briefly, but as his comments extended to 30 minutes, the bronze must have gotten pretty heavy for Jurras to hold.

Lorraine and Elmer Keith at the 1974 Outstanding American Handgunner Award ceremony. Elmer Keith was the first recipient of this prestigious award.

A rare photo of Keith laughing in 1966 as he and Kent Lomont test a heavy single-shot rifle from the bench.

Keith in his study in 1966 hard at work answering letters on his manual typewriter.

Keith shows Kent Lomont (left) the first Smith & Wesson .44 Magnum sent to him by the factory and his famous pair of M57 .41 Magnums tested in the Arctic in the case by Lomont's feet (1966). Note the famed Improved No. 5 in Keith's hand, as well as various other well-known revolvers at Keith's feet.

Keith with Kent Lomont in 1966 looking as some of Keith's big-bore African rifles.

In the attic of Keith's home, which was also his gunroom, Keith shows Kent Lomont the first .44 Magnum that Smith & Wesson sent to him (1963).

Also in 1963, Keith and Kent look over some of Keith's fine rifles.

Keith's .44 Ruger Dragoons, 1966. The top one is engraved and restocked.

The two M57 .41 Magnums sent to Keith by the factory and used on his polar bear hunt in the Arctic to kill caribou for villagers, 1966. Note the restocked grips

Right- and left-side views of the famous Improved No. 5 .44 Special, one of the most famous revolvers of our day, 1963.

Grip-strap view of Keith's .44 Colt Revolver, formerly the property of Theodore Roosevelt and a gift from him to his western friend. Photo taken in 1963.

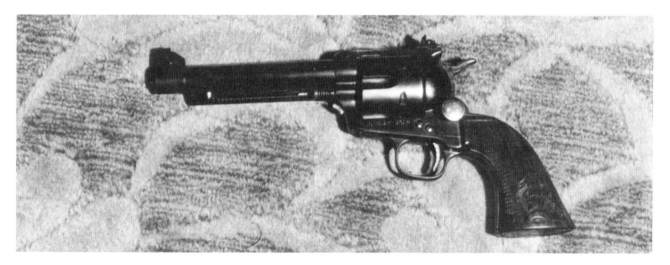

A Keith-modified Colt 5A with long-range sights and fast-draw swivel stud installed.

Right-side view of Smith & Wesson .44 Magnum sent to Keith by factory when firearm first came out. Photo taken in 1963.

Two engraved .44 Magnum Smith & Wesson Magnums sent to Keith by the factory when they first came out (1963).

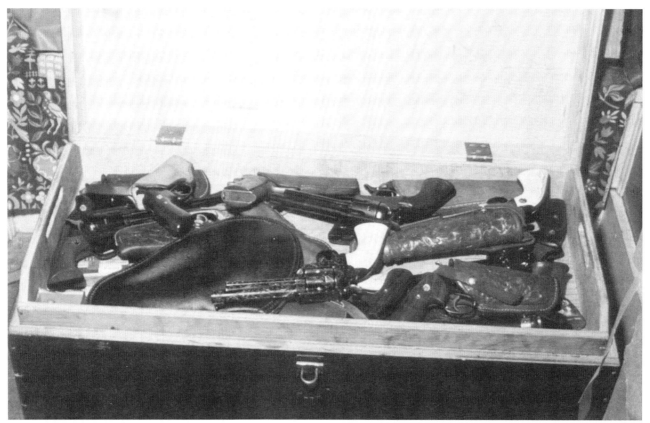

The trunk of Keith's revolvers in his attic gunroom in Salmon, Idaho (1963). A lone Government Model, as well as some excellent Lawrence & Gaylord leather, is also shown here.

An engraved .44 Magnum Smith & Wesson in Keith's hand (left) and a modified Colt .44 Special in Kent Lomont's hands (1963).

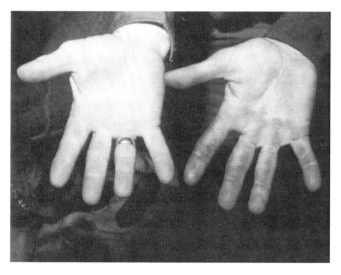

A comparison of the size of Keith's hand (left) with Lomont's dirty hand on the right (1963). (The fact that Lomont's hand is dirty should come as no surprise to anyone—no real machine gunner's hands are clean for long!)

Keith's original homestead outside Durkee, Oregon, where he lived in the 1920s. Photo taken on May 23, 2003.

Keith and Lorraine showing the results of antelope hunting with a .338-74 single-shot rifle.

Keith sent this photo to T.J. Mullin after Mullin sent him a copy of his book *Training the Gunfighter*, which Keith called "one of the ten best books" he had ever read (1981). That was high praise indeed.

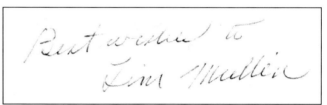

Inscription on the back of photo above.

A photo Keith gave to Jerry Nelson dated February 18, 1979.

Keith poses with noted local lawman Jerry Nelsen at Charley Shedds' ranch in Glenrock, Wyoming, October 1980.

Keith with Iver Hendricken in Missoula, Montana, at the latter's gun shop, where he built Keith many fine rifles (December 1979).

Keith testing an over-under shotgun with an ivory-stocked single action on his hip.

Keith at home with a revolver on his hip in what looks like a Spark's holster holding two ivory-stocked N-frame 4-inch revolvers.

Keith testing the newly released Ruger .44 Magnum double-action revolver.

Keith testing the newly released Ruger over-under shotgun on birds.

PHOTOGRAPHS 209

Keith and Lorraine at home in Salmon, Idaho.

Keith in his trophy room.

Keith with his Boswell Double 500 rifle.

Keith with Boswell Double 500 rifle with tusks from elephants shot by him at his back.

Keith showing E.E. Nelsen a couple of his books at his home.

Keith with Ralph Graham and E.E. Nelsen, July 10, 1980.

E.E. Nelsen with Keith displaying their Smith & Wesson revolvers on July 10, 1980.

Keith shooting Jerry Nelsen's M29 .44 Magnum revolver. Note the weapon breaking from his weak hand.

Keith with an M29 4-inch in full recoil (July 1980). Note the weapon breaking completely free of his left hand.

An extremely rare photograph of Keith with a 2-inch .38 Special Colt Detective belonging to E.E. Nelsen.

Various shots of Keith in Africa with the Cape buffalo he shot.

Keith pointing out bullet strikes on a Cape buffalo shot with his double rifle

Fleshing out the hide, the old expert watches carefully while the African hunter cleans the hide.

Other African hunting scenes of animals that fell to Keith's rifle.

Back home in Salmon, Idaho, Keith views his wonderful African trophies.

Keith with friends on a snowy day displaying the results of that day's hunt.

Conclusion

I HOPE YOU HAVE ENJOYED ALL THE LETTERS AND photos herein. The letters have spanned the years from 1924 to within six weeks of Keith's stroke in 1981. I would have liked more from the 1920 and 1930 period, but, alas, they could not be located.

What I think quite interesting here is that we see a consistent position throughout the letters of open-mindedness about loads and weapons as well as willingness to help others. Keith made his decisions not based on some prejudice about a topic but rather on acute observations about how things worked in the real world. It is clear that not only was he a careful observer but also that he had a photographic memory as letters retelling the same incidents over a period of years carried the same exact details. It is obvious that Keith's values were those of the late 19th-century western America. He was free, I think, from racial or ethnic prejudice and expected all men to be judged by their abilities and actions, nothing more. To some, this may seem to be a harsh standard, but to others who embrace the same value system, it seems to be the only fair way to evaluate people.

Keith's life was not by any measure an easy one, yet it was not a bad or tragic one, either. While he no doubt had bitter disappointments in his life—being badly burned in a hotel fire that left scars over much of his body, suffering the death of a child at an early age, failing to get his Army commission during World War II because he couldn't support himself while waiting for administrative steps to occur, and enduring many a cold, hard working day chasing cows or gut-shot elk improperly shot by dude hunters—still his life must have been very satisfying in many aspects. He appears to have had a good relationship with Lorraine, his wife of more than 50 years; he was clearly the best-known and most-beloved of gun writers in the period from 1960 to1981; and his death left a hole in the field that has not yet been filled as I write this—and that hole seems unlikely to ever be filled.

Keith is largely responsible for developing the .44 Magnum, of course, but also the .41 Magnum and the various Ruger single-action revolvers and single-shot rifles. His advice about cartridges, no doubt, caused a lot of men to take successful trophies in the field that would have escaped otherwise and, more importantly, saved men's lives in police and defense shooting incidents also. He designed excellent knives, saddles, boots, and holsters, as well as bullets and loads.

Elmer Keith was a remarkable man, and he cast a long shadow with his abilities and accomplishments. We are not likely to see another like him in our lives.

Author's note: If readers have letters from Elmer Keith they would like to add to the collection, please contact the author in care of the publisher (Paladin Press, Gunbarrel Tech Center, 7077 Winchester Circle, Boulder, CO 80301).